Issues in African Literature

Issues in African Literature

Professor Charles E. Nnolim
Former Dean, Faculty of Humanities
University of Port Harcourt,
Port Harcourt, Nigeria.

malthouse 𝒨𝒫

Malthouse Press Limited
Lagos, Benin, Ibadan, Jos, Port-Harcourt, Zaria

Malthouse Press Limited
43 Onitana Street, Off Stadium Hotel Road,
Surulere, Lagos, Lagos State
E-mail: malthouse_press@yahoo.com
malthouselagos@yahoo.co.uk
Tel: +234 (0)802 600 3203

All rights reserved. No part of this publication may be reproduced, transmitted, transcribed, stored in a retrieval system or translated into any language or computer language, in any form or by any means, electronic, mechanical, magnetic, chemical, thermal, manual or otherwise, without the prior consent in writing of Malthouse Press Limited, Lagos, Nigeria.

This book is sold subject to the condition that it shall not by way of trade, or otherwise, be lent, re-sold, hired out, or otherwise circulated without the publisher's prior consent in writing, in any form of binding or cover other than in which it is published and without a similar condition, including this condition, being imposed on the subsequent purchaser.

© C.E. Nnolim 2010
First Published 2009
ISBN 978-978-8422-36-5

Distributors:

African Books Collective Ltd
Email: abc@africanbookscollective.com
Website: http://www.africanbookscollective.com

Dedication

To my Children:

Emeka
Mrs. Chinyere Babajide
Amaeze
Mrs. Azuka Gratias

who, while complaining about how long Daddy stayed in his study became adults, and began, like Daddy, to face the serious side of life. You are all, in true Nigerian parlance, "the sugar in my tea."

Acknowledgements

I am very grateful to the "permanent secretary" of the Department of English Studies, University of Port Harcourt, for painstakingly typing the manuscript of this book. Who else is he but J. D. Williams.

Journals in which these essays first appeared are gratefully acknowledged at the beginning of each study. The epilogue is forthcoming in *African Literature Today* number 25.

Contents

Dedication
Acknowledgements
Introduction
CHAPTERS
1. A source for Arrow of God 1
2. Trends in the criticism of African literature 31
3. Utopian literature and the African world view 45
4. Politics in the West African novel 61
5. The Nigerian tradition in the novel 69
6. Prolegomena to a definition of the African aesthetic in literature 85
7. A house divided: feminism in African literature 113
8. Achebe's tragic heroes 127
9. Achebe's masked spirits: culture's hum and buzz of social implications 137
10. The critic of African literature: the challenge of the 1980s 149
11. Moral values in the Nigerian novel 159
12. The unhappy woman in Nigerian fiction: a mythic interpretation of the archetypes 169
13. The "Sons of Achebe": example of John Munonye 181
14. African feminism: the scandalous path 195
15. Contemporary Nigerian fiction 205
16. The writer as patriot 219
Epilogue 231
Index 243

Introduction

Contemporary African literature disparaged by colonial criticism, polarized by a multiplicity of critical approaches, divided on the problem of its language of expression, sundered by ideological camps, and driven by a divided audience is a boiling cauldron of unresolved issues. These issues are multifarious and keep rearing up their heads in conferences, symposia, and seminars on African literature. The first issue centres around the definition of African literature. What is African literature? Shall we accept without debate the definition proffered by the maverick troika:

> Works done for African audiences, by Africans, and in African languages, whether these works are oral or written, constitute the historically indisputable core of African literature.[1]

Or shall we rather have it clarified and ventilated by Achebe's dictum that we "cannot cram African literature into a small, neat definition" because African literature is not one unit but "a group of associated units—in fact the sum total of all the national and ethnic literatures of Africa."[2] The above might have settled the issue with a qualifier by Ernest Emenyonu that the literature of a people must be "an imaginative recreation of a people's account of their social, cultural, political and economic perspectives at a given time and place,[3] had the "language-of expression" issue not come to befuzz the finer edges of the debate.

In what language should the African writer express himself in his creative works? What is the status of that debate now?

---

[1] Chinweizu, *et al. Toward the Decolonization of African Literature* (Enugu: Fourth Dimension Publishers, 1980), pp.11-12.

[2] Chinua Achebe, "The African Writer and the English Language," in *Morning Yet on Creation Day* (London: Heinemann, 1975), p.56.

[3] Ernest Emenyonu, "African Literature and the Ethnic Imperative," *Afa: Journal of Creative Writing* (1982), p.22.

Between Obi Wali's "to be truly African, African literature must be written in African languages" supported by Ngugi wa Thiong'o's: "a foreign language cannot correctly reflect the historical consciousness of a people,"[4] and Achebe's "there is certainly a great advantage to writing in a world language,"[5] the audience of African literature steers a harassed course, as Senghor's dictum seems to confirm Achebe's position:

> French has enabled us to send to the world, to our brother men, the wonder message that we alone could send them. It has enabled us to contribute to this universal civilization something without which it would not have been universal, without which it would have lacked that inner warmth that is man's true hallmark.[6]

If it is true, as Ngugi wa Thiong'o argues that literature written in European languages cannot be African literature since it "reflects the historical consciousness of foreigners", where does African literature written in one of the tribal tongues leave us? Is it better to receive it through a third-hand translator, or are we nearer what the author is saying by reading him first hand in English which he has in any case, "bent" himself? What, for example, would *Things Fall Apart* have read like, had Achebe first published it in Igbo and we received it through a translator's endeavours? The debate on language use in African literature is still a heated one and no attempt is made to resolve it or any other issue in this volume.

The multitudinous nature of African literature has always been an issue but really not a problem, although its oral base has been used by expatriate critics to accuse African literature of thin plots, superficial characterization, and thin narrative structures. African literature also, it is observed, is a mixed grill: it is oral; it is written in vernacular or tribal tongues; written in foreign tongues—English, French, Portuguese—and within the foreign language in which it is written, pidgin and Creole further bend the already bent language, giving African literature a further taint of linguistic impurity.

African literature further suffers from the nature of its "newness" and this creates problems for the critic. Because it is new, and because its critics are in simultaneous existence with its writers, we

---

[4] Quoted by Emmanuel Ngara, *Art and Ideology* (London: Heinemann, 1985), p.40.
[5] Achebe, p. 59.
[6] Quoted by Phanuel Egejuru in *Towards African Literary Independence* (New York: Greenwood Press, 1980), p.14.

confront the problem of "instant analysis" which provides expatriate, critics with the divine afflatus to impose their supercilious and, some say, arrogant critical standards on the criticism of African literature; which further denies the advantage of hindsight to our criticism; which fails to distance sentiment and subjectivity from objective analysis. And sentimental attachment to a living author often leads to vague hymn singing due to friendships or, on the other hand to vitriol owing to clash of personalities or ideas.

Around these issues also accrete the idea of who should be the rightful or acceptable critic of African literature. Must he be an African,[7] as Ernest Emenyonu tried once to urge us, because African literature must be evaluated on criteria based on values imbibed by an African critic who must perhaps think black, write black and possibly wear black? Or must African literature bare its bosom to the expatriate critic who fails to understand the culture, the traditions, the national ethos and even the intention of the writer and is thus likely to misapply the tools of his art as a critic? In the above is the great divide—the Afrocentric critic urging the uniqueness of African literature, away from which the expatriate critic must turn, versus the Eurocentric, expatriate universalist critic who argues that African literature is part of world literature and that there should be no special *ichor* in its veins that distinguishes its vital juices from the literature of Europe.[8] Hanging on our lips is an answer to the question: "what is the best approach to the criticism of African literature?

II

In the light of the above, this volume continues the debate and tries to clarify contemporary burning issues in African literature, by focusing on particular areas where the debate has been most concentrated or around which it has hovered and been persistent. Most of the essays published here had appeared in far-flung journals which may not be available to the average student or scholar. One

---

[7] Ernest Emenyonu, "African Literature: What Does it Take to Be its Critic?" *African Literature Today*, No.5 (1971), pp.1-11.

[8] Donatus Nwoga, "Plagiarism and Authentic Creativity in West Africa", in *Critical Perspectives on Nigerian Literatures,* ed. Bernth Lindfors (Washington, D.C.: Three Continents Press, 1976), p.159, ff.

issue around which the debate has hovered is that of source and influence in African literature. The first act of apostasy started with a debate between Professor Sellin and Paul Flamand around the idea that Ouologuem's *Le Devoir de Violence* was plagiarized from another work *Le Dernier des Justes* and from Graham Greene's *It's a Battlefield*. Before we could catch our breath, Donatus Nwoga came out to openly charge Christopher Okigbo of plagiarism in the "Four Canzones" by copying from Miguel Hernardez's "El amor Ascendia entre Nostros", plus other poems Okigbo plagiarized from Yoruba salutation poems.[9]

The issue of source and influence is continued in this volume in the essay "A Source for Arrow of God" with an updated information since its publication in Research in African Literature.[10] Another study, "The Sons of Achebe: The example of John Munonye" extends the debate on the issue of source and influence. Raging still at almost all international conferences on African literature is the perennial topic of the African aesthetic in literature. The essay entitled: "Prolegomena to a Definition of the African Aesthetic in Literature" fully addresses this issue. Of equal currency in African literary circles is the issue of feminism which is addressed in the essay "A House Divided: Feminism in African Literature" and its implications further explored in two other essays. The rest of the essays speak for themselves: the place of mythology in our literatures, the "tradition" of the Nigerian novel; the challenges of criticism for the African critic, plus trends in that criticism; the issue of politics in the West African novel; the place of utopia in the African literary imagination, and the African concept of tragedy in the African novel as reflected in "Achebe's Tragic Heroes"

C. E. N.
University of Port Harcourt

---

[9] Ibid.
[10] See Letters to the Editor, *Research in African Literatures*, Vol.15, No.1 (Spring, 1984), pp.148-150).

1

A source for *Arrow of God**

With the exception of occasional remarks on oral or folkloric sources, scholars have said little about the literary materials upon which African authors have based their writings. My own research has not led me to any detective criticism reconstructing written sources for any long fictional prose works from Africa. What one is likely to find are vague conjectures and suspect theorizing of diffuse sources for, say, Okigbo's poetry. Many a critic, without painstaking efforts at proof, has made weak-kneed suggestions that. Achebe's novels owe a lot of Joseph Conrad. One possible reason for the vacuum existing in source study of African literature is, of course, complacency: we all assume that our writers, especially novelists, do not research their stories, that their material comes naturally to them like leaves to a tree and that all they did was merely to reconstruct their stories from the common petty-cash drawer of their culture. And a great writer like Achebe has consistently given the impression that all he did in *Things Fall Apart* and *Arrow of God* was merely to reconstruct Igbo culture from his own personal knowledge (which is irrefutable) and from stories told him by his father and grandfather (which must be taken with a grain of salt: either his grandfather told him more than ours told us or he began keeping a diary from the age of seven).

A few words about the normal problems of source-study art in order here. The aim of source-study, we are all aware, is to establish the nature of the ingredients that coalesced into a finished literary

---

* First published in *Research in African Literatures,* Vol. 8, No. 1 (1977), pp. 1-26.

artefact.¹ Every literary critic knows that the possible sources of a finished literary work are as diverse as the writer's whole experience, for the writer might have sketched his characters from people he has known in real life who serve him as prototypes; or he might have drawn the main events of his story from contemporary or past historical events, or from a visual impression or a dream or a story he has heard. But genuine source-study must demonstrate evidence that goes beyond mere echoes, by showing the *concrete testimony* of a printed page laid side by side with the original text. Above all, the source-scholar must try to transcend Douglas Bush's good-humoured definition of a scholar as "a siren which calls attention to a fog without doing anything to dispel it!"² With this in mind, let me get down to the task of demonstrating a source for Achebe's *Arrow of God*.

One of the rare original insights G. D. Killam came up with in discussing Achebe's *Arrow of God* is contained in the following passage:

> A cursory reading of the novel suggests that much of the background is there for its own sake, that it has come to dominate the book and has in a sense become the subject of the book. There is much in the novel which has little direct relation to the story the novel has to tell. Yet them gains made in terms of the overall tragic consequences the novel displays wherein a whole society is involved are obvious once Achebe's purpose is taken into account.³

Very true, for as will soon be demonstrated, Achebe was heavily shackled by his source. Although Achebe has never admitted it publicly, the single most important source—in fact, the only source—for *Arrow of God* is a tiny, socio-historical pamphlet published without copyright by a retired corporal of the Nigeria Police Force. His name was (he died in 1972) Simon Alagbogu Nnolim, and the title of his pamphlet was *The History of Umuchu*, published in 1953.⁴ It was while I was preparing a second, enlarged edition of this booklet⁵ that certain passages began to remind me of

---

[1] Richard D. Altick, *The Art of Literary Research*, rev. ed. (New York: W. W. Norton & Company, 1975).
[2] Ibid., p. 94
[3] G. D. Killam, *The Novels of Chinua Achebe* (New York: Africana Publishing Company, 1969), p.61.
[4] By Eastern Press Syndicate, Depot Road, Enugu, Nigeria,
[5] Published by Ochumba Press, Ltd., Enugu, Nigeria, 1976

Arrow of God. One such passage was the story of the priest who refused chieftaincy, was imprisoned, and stubbornly refused to roast the sacred yame. As it turned out, this happened in my own village, Umuchu, in Awka Division, Nigeria, in 1913. The District Commissioner who is called Winterbottom by Achebe in his fictional work was, in history, J. G. Lotain. The High Priest called Ezeulu by Achebe was, in the history of Umuchu, Ezeagu, the High Priest of Uchu. He was actually imprisoned for two months at Awka by J. G. Lotain; and the Seed Yam Festival (changed to New Yam Festival by Achebe), which usually fell during the harvest months of November and December, began to fall—and still falls to this day— in February and March, because he refused to roast two sacred yams in one month. As I began to collate the two texts, I found out to my amazement that Achebe did not merely take the story of the High Priest and blow life into it, as Shakespeare did when borrowing material for *Julius Caesar* from Plutarch's *Lives of the Noble Grecians and the Romans;* Achebe went much further. He lifted everything in *The History of Umuchu* and simply transferred it to Arrow of God without embellishment. One must admit, of course, that he fictionalized his source, created characters other than that of Ezeulu, and provided thematic and dramatic centres.

My first impulse was to take up the phone and call him, since we were not more than sixty miles from each other, but I resisted the impulse: he would think it sheer effrontery. But when I met Achebe at the First African Literature Association Conference in Austin, Texas, in March of 1975, I felt encouraged to approach him. Did he know one Simon Nnolim, a former policeman in Enugu, I ventured to ask, and did he read his book entitled *The History of Umuchu* from which much of *Arrow of God* seems to have been drawn? Yes, he said, he knew him. He went further: he admitted that while working for the Eastern Nigeria Broadcasting Service he interviewed Nnolim in 1957. He was visibly shocked to hear of his death. He reminisced that Nnolim and one Mr. Iweka who wrote *The History of Obosi* (to which Nnolim himself alluded as the source of his inspiration to write a similar book) were rare people who collected invaluable information that was of historical and anthropological interest. Nnolim had never mentioned the writer of *The History of Obosi* by name. Achebe filled in that gap for me. Achebe also added that he and the officers of the E.N.B.S. interviewed Nnolim in our hometown, Umuchu; that the object of the interviewer was Night Masks who performed for them; that they stayed about three nights in Umuchu. But he did not remember reading Nnolim's book. However, as will be demonstrated, the internal evidence is overwhelming that he had Nnolim's book before him as he wrote *Arrow of God*. It is very probable that Nnolim, being a generous man, had made a present of his book to Achebe. Let us turn now to the textual evidence.

Since Nnolim's *The History of Umuchu* predated *Arrow of God* by thirteen years, and *Things Fall Apart* by five, and since the discussion that follows will make clearer sense if organized around Nnolim's chapters, I shall discuss Achebe's borrowings under Nnolim's subheadings, where appropriate. A running commentary will be carried on as the two books are laid side by side, but the reader must be warned that, for the purposes of clarity, the order of events in both works could not be adhered to here. One more preliminary remark: it is surely more than coincidence that Achebe's Umuaro is Nnolim's Umuchu; that Achebe's Umuaro is Nnolim's Umuchu; that Achebe's Ezeulu is Nnolim's Ezeagu; that Achebe's god, *Ulu*, is Nnolim's *Uchu*; that Achebe's six villages which sought amalgamation are Nnolim's six villages in Umuchi; that Achebe's New Yam Festival is Nnolim's Seed Yam Festival; that Achebe's missionary, "Hargreaves," is no more than Nnolim's anthropologist, "Hargroves:"[6] that Achebe's story of Umuama and the sacred python is Nnolim's Umunama and the sacred short snake; that Nnolim's Gun Breaker, J. G. Lotain, is Achebe's Gun Breaker, Winterbottom; that Achebe's "The Festival of the Pumpkin Leaves" is Nnolim's "The Feast of Throwing First Tender Pumpkin Leaves"; that Achebe's ceremony of Coverture is Nnolim's ceremony of *Nkpu*; that the main market in Achebe's Umuaro and Nnolim's Umuchu is Nkwo, where the Ikoro and the amalgamation fetish in both sources are located.

S. A. Nnolim began his *History of Umuchu* with the story of the amalgamation of the six villages for the sake of mutual protection against Abam warriors. He writes in Section IV:

---

[6] See Chinua Achebe, *Arrow of God* (New York: Anchor/Doubleday, 1969), p.52, and S. A. Nnolim, *The History of Umuchu* (Enugu: Eastern Syndicate Press, 1953), pp. 32-33. All quotations are taken from these editions. A few minor typographical errors in Nnolim's book have been corrected, but no words have been changed. Anything added to the original text has been placed in brackets.

This history of the town is really a study of the different sets of people who now inhabit the area known as Umuchu. The town, though a unity today, is beyond all doubt the Union of a number of towns, which necessitate the individual procedure in discussion herein adopted. This method has been carefully followed up to help those who will find the booklet useful in the course of their study. In dealing with the matter in hand certain questions will naturally crop up:

1. What towns unite to make Umuchu?
2. How and why did they so unite?

Well, reference to question (1), the present day Umuchu is composed of:

Ihite; Ogu; Osete; Ogwugwu; Ibughubu and Achalla. With exception of Ogu, whose origin at the moment can not be traced, each of the other five towns have their different lines of origin. Ibughubu traces its genealogy to Osete, but still it may be maintained quite consciously that there are no rigid lines of demarcation to this originality, since the ties of inter-relationship directly or otherwise are noticeable among the towns. Their union in answer to question two was brought about by a crave for defence during the days of repeated warfares and gross brutality. The story of the amalgamation is clearly portrayed in that which gives the authentic origin of the name.

Local amalgamation: the origin of name

For the purpose of this booklet, the term local amalgamation is employed in distinction from the kindred amalgamations which obtained in Nigeria due to European influence. The local amalgamation took place round about the time when Abriba, Abam, Ohafia, and Adda menace was at its highest, the above named warriors of old time used by "Arochukwu" to subdue any town which may by that time disobey their orders, but before the union of the towns (now villages) they were each quite independent of the others and each had its own name, customs, and its annual festivals; defence was likewise resigned to individual towns concerned; thus when they were attacked by warriors from Arochukwu called by then "Agha" Abam, Abriba or Umuada, the wretched town often put to flight and captives among them were carried off into slavery.

The warriors of those days whose story are still in the heart of many through out the Eastern Nigeria were strong black and brave men of huge size; they often marched into the victims at the dead of night armed with long heavy bow shaped swords with brass hilts; their number was never below hundred in a batch. When in the enemies' territories they generally began their slaughter early the following morning, thus the then sparsely people towns being unarmed and outnumbered, offered little or no stout resistance and the Abriba kept on preying on and diminishing the number of the scanty few.

This state of affairs lingers on around the neighbouring towns till the six friendly towns sensed their complete annihilation. Should the old individual protection which was useless before the huge number of Abribas continue? A united front therefore against these common foes was the primary craving of every one. Heaven knows what source of terror their adversaries are to them and sure as death, their night rests are nothing but dreams of illusive means of freedom.

They met and agreed to unite; to do this effectively they invited a strong team of qualified native doctors who prepared a medicine known as "*Ichu*" meaning Antidote, in other words to render null and void the attempt of any aggressors to cause them more harm by means or by violence. Though the legendary "*Ichu*" meaning antidote was supposed to be the goddess, after the medicine had been prepared, the united towns dedicated themselves to and called themselves the children of "*Ichu*" (Umu-Ichu); the medicine was parcelled in two; one buried in the heart of the meeting place now called Nkwo Uchu, the other parcel was buried into a lake formerly known as Odere; the lake's name automatically became Ichu Stream; the meeting place became the seat of the goddess protectoress of the town. A market was also erected there to keep in living memory the idea of the meeting and local amalgamation therein engendered. The market and Odere lake are still called Nkwo-Uchu, and Uchu lake respectively. (pp. 7-8)

Below is how Achebe fictionally reacreates this passage:

> In the very distant past, when lizards were still few and far between, the six villages—Umuachala, Umunneora, Umuagu, Umuezeani, Umuogwugwu and Umuisiuzo—lived as different people, and each worshipped its own deity.
>
> Then the hired soldiers of Abam used to strike in the dead of night,

set fire to houses and carry men, women and children into slavery. Things were so bad for the six villages that their leaders came together to save themselves. They hired a strong team of medicine men to install a common deity for them. This deity which the fathers of the six villages made was called Ulu. Half of the medicine was buried at a place which became the Nkwo market and the other half thrown into the stream which became Mili Ulu. The six villages then took the name of Umuaro, and the priest of Ulu became their Chief Priest. From that day they were never again beaten by an enemy. How could such people disregard the god who founded their town and protected it? (pp.16-17)

The above defies commentary. Of the six villages, Achebe discarded four and retained two, as he found it in his source. With a little fictional engineering, he changed Nnolim's Uchu goddess to Ulu goddess. The rest is set down almost verbatim. Another important passage Achebe lifted from Nnolim is the story of Umunama and the sacred python. My town does have an uninhabited, fertile farmland called Umunama. To date, no one lives there, even though villages surround it on all sides. My own family still has a rich farm patch in Umunama, but it is in a valley and subject to floods, which frequently wash away the yam mounds. Here is how Nnolim tells the story, or rather the legend, of Umunama (pp. 16-17).

UMUNAMA

The legend about Umunama in my opinion seems to be useless so far none of them could really be traced. It came about that they killed a short snake (Eke) and gave to one man Eweshi by name to cook for them, each of them contributed a piece of yam, and small pot full of water (Okwu Ite); these were collected in a wooden bowl (Ikpo) for making stew with the short snake (Awayi); before that, each person marked his yam. When it is done each person again took his remarked yam, and also filled his small pot with the amount of water he gave out for the cooking. Funny as it were; at last Eweshi and his brother found that there was no water remaining in the cooking pot to fill their own small pots.

The rest of the Umunama inhabitants then evacuated and settled in Okigwi area where we get Umuna today in Owerri Province. The neighbouring towns who saw the disorder caused by the killing of the short snake made a law that anybody killing the short snake will be punished as though he killed a human being. From this also we have a common proverb in our town "Ibu Ikpo Awayi Eweshi" because he suffered to make the stew, but never tasted a drop of the pottage. The land formerly occupied by Umunama still bears the name to this date. (pp. 16-17)

And here's how Achebe tells the same story:

Mr. Goodcountry's teaching about the sacred python gave Moses the first opportunity to challenge him openly. To do this he used not only the Bible but, strange enough for a convert, the myths of Umuaro. He spoke with great power for, coming as he did from the village which carried the priesthood of Idemili, he knew perhaps more than others what the python was...He told the new teacher quite bluntly that neither the Bible nor the catechism asked converts to kill the python, a beast full of ill omen.

"Was it for nothing that God put a curse on its head?" he asked, and then turned abruptly into the traditions of Umuaro. "Today there are six villages in Umuaro; but this has not always been the case. Our fathers tell us that there were seven before, and the seventh was called Umuama." Some of the converts nodded their support, Mr. Goodcountry listened patiently and contemptuously.

"One day six brothers of Umuama killed the python and asked one of their number, Iweka, to cook yam pottage with it. Each of them brought a piece of yam and a bowl of water to Iweka. When he finished cooking the yam pottage the men came one by one and took their pieces of yam. Then they began to fill their bowls to the mark with the yam stew. But this time only four of them took their measure before the stew got finished...

"The brothers began to quarrel violently, and then to fight. Very soon the fighting spread throughout Umuama, and so fierce was it that the village was almost wiped out. The few people that survived fled from their village, across the great river to the land of Olu where they are scattered today. The remaining six villages seeing what happened to Umuama went to a seer to know the reason, and he told them that the royal python was sacred to Idemili; it was this deity which had punished Umuama. From that day the six villages decreed that henceforth the python was not to be killed in Umuaro, and that anyone who killed it would be regarded as having killed his kinsman." (pp. 53-54)

Again, the above defies comment. Achebe hardly garnished his material beyond changing the name of the village Umuna to the fictional Olu, Nholim's Eweshi who made the stew simply becomes Achebe's Iweka!

A source for Arrow of God

On the same page, immediately following his legend of Umunama, Nnolim discusses the function of the *Ikoro:* a mighty wooden tom-tom carved out of the trunk of a tree and used by Umuchu to summon her people in times of danger or when matters of urgency arose. He writes:

> **UMUCHU AFTER 1486**
>
> Before 1486 there was practically no marked improvements in the segregated towns, due to insecurity of life and property. It follows, then, that security of life was of prime importance and needed prompt attention. Hence a reliable device of call was introduced: "Ikoro." After the local amalgamation Umuchu people anxious about self defence decided together on the establishment of a permanent system of call in cases of danger or otherwise, to this end, "Ikoro" was introduced.
>
> It was a wooden bell carved out of a strong heavy log of wood and measured eighteen and half feet long, five and half feet high, and carved in about two and, half feet deep. When beaten with the short lengths of wood it gives a deep note that carries for a distance, that it could be heard in any part of the town. Certain danger, urgent call, unexpected occurrence and merriment after conquest or festival. It still exists in a much reduced size and can now be seen at the southern end of the market square. Its sound invigorates and stirs up the people to mad action irrespective of consequences, especially when the beater causes it to vibrate the gallant names of persons, age-grades, villages and the town at large. In the old times the skulls were hung around the "Ikoro," that was the reason why it was destroyed by the order of the Government during the invasion of Umuchu; since then the use of "Ikoro" ceased.
>
> At any rate, during this day of enlightenment and culture, sons of Umuchu, at the request of the elders, approved the reconstruction of the "Ikoro" during the annual conference of January 1952, when it was definitely clear to all that it was never intended for evil purpose but rather for a medium of general information for the town's interest. (pp. 17-18)

In *Arrow of God*, Achebe writes of the *Ikoro* (which he changed to *Ikolo)* thus:

> The Ikolo was fashioned in the olden days from a giant iroko tree at the very spot where it was felled. The Ikolo was as old as Ulu himself at whose order the tree was cut down and its trunk hollowed out into a drum. When the Ikolo was beaten for war it was

decorated with skulls won in past wars. But now it sang of peace (pp. 79-80).

One other minor detail must be noted here. My town, Umuchu, about which S. A. Nnolim wrote, was invaded by Europeans around 1912. When the town was subdued, according to oral sources, J. G. Lotain, who was the District Commissioner living in Awka, invited the town to bring in their spokesmen so that peace terms could be ironed out. As it turned out, when the elders and leaders were assembled, instead of discussing peace terms, they were handcuffed, shaved, carted to Awka, and forced to collect heavy fines in addition to collecting all guns in the village. The alternative to surrendering all arms was death in prison. This last threat thoroughly alarmed the town, which complied in every detail. (A similar situation is described in *Things Fall Apart* when Okonkwo and other leaders are manacled and detained in jail.) The elders of Unauchu then began to refer to J. G. Lotain as the "Gun Breaker." Below are two versions—first Nnolim's, then Achebe's:

On page 10 of his book, Nnolim says:

> The outward might of a nation comes from the inward strength of its people. Before and after the local amalgamation, Umugama and Ugwuakwu were exceedingly. feared; the former were hard hearted gunners, Nkeregbe, often appealed to and hired by oppressed persons, villages and towns against the adversaries. It is they who surrendered their cap guns as well as other villages for destruction at the order of Mr. J. G. Lotain District Commissioner.
>
> Awka about 1913: their method was to lay ambush in the enemies' quarter bynight and open fire at their first sight of them.

And on page 18, he adds:

> For the purpose of immediate defence all bold youths liable to stand firm or march forward to the rescue of the town must own or purchase arms of precision, matchets, swords or flint lock guns; these were used in place of the unreliable and risky clubs, bows, and arrows, shield and spears. These arms were latter collected for destruction at the order of Mr. J. G. Lorain, District Commissioner in 1913. This was done in the presence of all the people concerned or their respective headmen, and some three thousand arms of various descriptions plus over two thousand flintlock guns received from the

available males were thus treated.

For Achebe's own fictional purposes and to provide for some continuity in the story he began telling in *Things Fall Apart* about the District Commissioner who was writing a book on *The Pacification of the Primitive Tribes of the Lower Niger*, he represents Winterbottom as destroying the guns in Umuaro to prevent further conflicts between Umuaro and Okperi. But the story that Nnolim tells is part of that pacification—destroying all the guns in Umuchu and similar towns, the white man made sure of total conquest and total subjugation of the entire Southern Nigeria: On page 153 of *Arrow of God*, Achebe refers to Winterbottom as "The Destroyer of Guns." Elsewhere he had said that Winterbottom "gathered all the guns in Umuaro and asked the soldiers to break them in the face of all, except three or four which he carried away" (p.31).

The Festival of the Pumpkin Leaves

As far as I know, Umuchu, my hometown, is the only village that celebrates publicly, and with a great deal of fanfare, the feet of throwing the first tender pumpkin leaves at its Chief Priest. People from surrounding towns—Achina, Uga, Akokwa, Umuomaku, Akpo, Amesi, and so on—troop to Nkwo-Uchu (our local market—held on the same market day in *Arrow of God)* to observe this curious phenomenon. In relating the Festival of the Pumpkin Leaves, Achebe was artlessly faithful to his source—Nnolim's *The History of Umuchu*. This is how Nnolim writes of "The Feast of Throwing First Tender Pumpkin Leaves":

> This is one of the general feasts performed by the whole Umuchu annually It usually takes place in April or May according to native method of calculation. The feast must be on Nkwo Uchu Market Day, being the seat of the amalgamation, and the appointment is pronounced by the Uchu juju priest and his messengers will ring the Ogene in the Nkwo market to the hearing of all, pointing out the feast "Ta-Bu-Ato" meaning 8 days from the date of announcement. On the day, as women were the only people to throw the leaves, all the women will dress very attractively in their best dresses, plait their hair, and each when coming to the market that day must have in her possession, two or more pumpkin leaves tied together. The

men also will wear their best clothes and each with one or more pots of palm wine. Every grown-up Umuchu must attend market that day. Immediately each person enters the market they start drinking with friends and in-laws, etc. When it is known that every one is well satisfied and the market is well filled, the juju priest and his messengers will start beating the famous "Ikoro" (wooden drums) and also start making a big hollow square around the market to enable all the attendants to watch the ceremony.

When a sign is given that juju priest is approaching to run across the square, all the women, men, and spectators, as it always happens, will fall in lines around the market square; the women each carrying the pumpkin leaves in their right-hand, flagging them across her head and murmuring several words of prayers to Uchu juju individually.

Head of Priest's Arrival: On the arrival of the head juju priest from Ugwuakwu side as it usually happens, he will dress in the official juju dress as follows: Big staff called "Nne Ofo," Ojii sword, in his two hands, part of his face and both his eyes rubbed with white chalk, with an eagle's feather on his head. The head juju priest jumps out half dancing, half leaping, and half running; he starts going round the market square. Each woman aiming at him will throw her tender pumpkin leaves in such a way as not to touch his body; these will continue till he goes round the square, and by then all the women will throw out all the pumpkin leaves in their hands, and at the same time the juju messengers will pick very few leaves for purpose of ceremony. Afterwards, the rest [of the] leaves [are] trodden by people at the close of [the] head juju priest's appearance. Women then begin to run merrily in the market square, each town at its own scheduled time. Ugwuakwu, Umugama, and Akukwa will run first called "Ihite Nato," then comes Amanasa and Okwu na Achalla, called "Ezinato." No town contravenes its neighbours' time and the atmosphere seems happy throughout. The feast lasts till night, and that marks the full start of the farming season.

It is noteworthy to understand that the feast is still in progress to this present time. It is also important as it commemorates the unification of the town. From my youth I have for times without number been an eye witness to this feast and I strongly recommend the continuation of this feast. (pp. 24-25)

Achebe began discussing the *Festival of the Pumpkin Leaves* on page 3 of *Arrow of God*. Here he says: "The festival of the Pumpkin Leaves would fall on the third Nkwo from that day" (a transliteration of Nnolim's TA-BU-ATO: third market day or 8 days). Under the exigencies of fiction, Achebe spreads out his description of the festival, but he still follows his source faithfully. On page 78 he mentions in detail how Nwaka's wives decorated themselves and on their legs wore "enormous rollers of ivory" so that "their walk was perforce slow and deliberate, like the walk of an Ijele Mask lifting and lowering each foot with weighty ceremony." He adds that, when Ugoye was prepared for the market, "she went behind her but to the pumpkin which she specially planted after the first rain, and cut four leaves, tied them together ... and returned to her hut" (p. 77). Then Achebe continues:

> Soon after, the great Ikolo sounded. It called the six villages of Umuaroone by one in their ancient order: Umunneora, Umuagu, Umuezeani, Umuogwugwu, Umuisiuzo and Umuachala.
>
> The Ikolo now beat unceasingly; sometimes it called names of important people of Umuaro ... but most of the time it called the villages and their deities Finally it settled down to saluting Ulu, the deity of all Umuaro. (p. 79)
>
> A big *ogene* sounded three times from Ulu's shrine. The Ikolo took it up and sustained an endless flow of epithets in praise of the deity. At the same time Ezeulu's messengers began to clear the centre of the market place.
>
> Although they were each armed with a whip of palm frond they had a difficult time. The crowd was excited and it was only after a struggle that the messengers succeeded in clearing a small space in the heart of the market place. From this central position they worked furiously with their whips until they had forced all the people back to form a thick ring at the edges. The women with their pumpkin leaves caused the greatest difficulty because they all struggled to secure positions in front. The men had no need to 'be so near and so they formed the outside of the ring.
>
> The *ogene* sounded again. The Ikolo began to salute the Chief Priest.
>
> The women waved their leaves from side to side across the face, muttering prayers to Ulu, the god that kills and saves.
>
> Ezeulu's appearance was greeted with a loud shout that must have been heard in all the neighbouring villages. He ran forward, halted abruptly and faced the Ikolo....
>
> He wore smoked raffia which descended from his waist to his knee. The left half of his body—from forehead to toes—was painted with white chalk.
>
> Around his head was a leather band from which an eagle's feather

pointed back wards. On his right hand he carried Nne Ofo, the mother of all staffs of authority in Umuaro, and in his left he held a long iron staff which kept up a quivering rattle whenever he struck its pointed end into the earth. He took a few long strides, pausing on each foot. Then he ran forward again as though he had seen a comrade in the vacant air. (p. 80)

By now Ezeulu was in the centre of the market place. He struck the metal staff into the earth and left it quivering while he danced a few more steps to the Ikolo which had not paused for a breath since the priest emerged. All the women waved their pumpkin leaves in front of them.

Ezeulu looked round again at all the men and women of Umuaro, but saw no one in particular. Then he pulled the staff out of the ground, and with it in his left hand and the Mother of Ojo in his right he jumped forward and began to run around the market place.

All the women set up a long, excited ululation and there was renewed jostling for the front line. As the fleeting Chief Priest reached any section of the crowd the women there waved their leaves round their heads and flung them at him It was as though thousands and thousands of giant, flying insects swarmed upon him (p. 82)

The six messengers followed closely behind the priest and, at intervals, one of them bent down quickly and picked up at random one bunch of leaves and continued running.........

As if someone had given them a sign, all the women of Umunneora broke out from the circle and began to run round the market place, stamping their feet heavily. At the beginning it was haphazard but soon everyone was stamping together in unison and a vast cloud of dust rose from their feet....

When they had gone round they rejoined the standing crowd. Then the women of Umuagu burst through from every part of the huge circle to begin their own run. Then others waited and clapped for them; no one ran out of turn. By the time the women of the sixth village ran their race the pumpkin leaves that had lain so thickly all around had been smashed and trodden into the dust (pp.83-84).

To add comment to the above is to gild gold. Achebe did not miss one detail, including such minute observations as the *Nne Ofo* (which he did not care to change or translate in the first instance). Nor did he miss the eagle's father, the white chalk with which the priest paints his body, the flinging of pumpkin leaves by women, the "half dancing, half leaping" that Nnolim describes, and the picking up of a few leaves for ceremony by the priest's attendants, or even the run around the market by women of the six villages.

The Sacrifice of Coverture

One of the ceremonies performed on behalf of a newly wedded woman in Umuchu is, according to S. A. Nnolim, the *Nkpu* (or covering-up) ceremony wherein all evils committed by her as a single girl are covered over in order to give her a clean slate as she enters the married state. This is what Achebe translates as the "Sacrifice of Coverture" in *Arrow of God*. As a prefatory remark I will say this: the words pronounced by the priest during the Nkpu ceremony are written in Igbo by S. A. Nnolim. I have taken the liberty to translate them, after rendering the Igbo words as Nnolim wrote them. The reason for my translating these words is to show how faithfully Achebe followed his source: he actually renders his source *verbatim*. At the end, Nnolim says that the hen used for the sacrifice is at the discretion of the priest "either to bury or take to his house". It would be interesting to see how Achebe treats this episode: he makes Obika raise a doubt about the propriety of the priest taking the hen home, and his mother tries to resolve it by saying it is done, although she had never seen it happen before.

Now, to Nnolim:

> Once the woman goes to live as wife to her husband she must perform a ceremony or sacrifice called (*Nkpu*). It is a sacrifice done by woman after she had been married and the attached likely meaning is to cover all the probable evils that might follow or might have followed her from youth to the state of married life.
>
> This is done towards the direction of the road or lane leading to where it came from, and is performed in the evening time when sure that she will not come out through that path till the following morning. In this case a hen, 4 small yams, 4 cowries that is 24 cowries known as (*ego nano*), tender palm leaves, 4 white chalks, one native pot, the "Olodu" flower, and etc., etc., form the ingredients of the sacrifice. A Juju priest officiating together with the woman and husband must be present with another small pot water.
>
> When all are ready, a hole will be dug in the centre of the path and with various appeasing words being pronounced by the juju priest thus- "*Ife ijili anya fu; nke ikwutelu na onu; nke inutalu nanti mobu*

nke izotalu na ukwu; nke nne metalu; Ekpudom fa nebea." The whole articles will then be buried in the hole with the exception of the hen which will be at the discretion of the juju priest either to bury or take to this house, though it must be killed. It will be buried that the back of the pot will be seen outside; after this, the woman will retire to her room and will not pass through that path till next day. (p.22)

In Igbo the word *Nkpu* means *Covering Up* and the word "Olodu" flower means *Lily* flower. My translation of the priest's "appeasing words" reads:

> Whatever (evil) you might have seen with your eyes, or spoken with your mouth, or heard with your ears, or trodden with your feet; whatever evil else your mother might have committed, or your father might have committed, I cover them up here.

In *Arrow of God* the sacrifice of Coverture was performed for Okuata, Obika's new wife. This is how Achebe tries to fictionalize his source:

> Her mother-in-law took her away into her hut where she would stay until the Sacrifice of Coverture was performed.
>
> The medicine-man and diviner who had been hired to perform the rite soon arrived and the party set out. In it were Obika, his elder half-brother, his mother and the bride...
>
> They made for the highway leading to Umuezeani, the village where the bride came from. It was now quite dark and there was no moon...The bride had a bowl of fired clay in one hand and a hen in the other. Now and again the hen squawked the way hens do when their pen is disturbed by an intruder at night...
>
> On his left hand Obika held a very small pot of water by the neck. His half-brother had a bunch of tender palm frond cut from the pinnacle of the tree.
>
> Before long they reached the junction of their highway and another leading to the bride's village along which she had come that very day. They walked a short distance on this road and stopped. The medicine-man chose a spot in the middle of the way and asked Obika to dig a hole there....
>
> While Obika was scooping out the red earth with both hands the medicine-man began to bring out the sacrificial objects from his bag.

First he brought out four small yams, then four pieces of white chalk and the flower of the wild lily.

"Give me the omu." Edogo passed the tender palm leaves to him He tore out four leaflets and put away the rest. Then he turned to Obika's mother.

"Let me have ego nano [four cowries]." She untied a bunch of cowries from a corner of her cloth and gave them to him He counted them carefully on the ground as a woman would before she bought or sold in the market, in groups of six. There were four groups and he nodded his head.

He rose to his feet and positioned Okuata beside the hole so that she faced the direction of her village, kneeling on both knees. Then he took his position opposite her on the other side of the hole, with the sacrificial objects ranged on his right. The others stood a little back.

He took one of the yams and gave it to Okuata. She waved it round her head and put it inside the hole. The medicine-man put in the other three. Then he gave her one of the pieces of white chalk and she did as for the yam. Then came the palm leaves and the flower of the wild lily and last of all he gave her one group of six cowries which she closed in her palm and did as for the others.

After this he pronounced the absolution:

"Any evil which you might have seen with your eyes, or spoken with your mouth, or heard with your ears or trodden with your feet; whatever your father might have brought upon you or your mother brought upon you, I cover them all."

As he spoke the last words he took the bowl of fired clay and placed it face downwards over the objects in the hole. Then he began to put back the loose earth. Twice he eased up the bowl slightly so that when he finished its curved back showed a little above the surface of the road...

"Do not forget", said the diviner [to Okuata]..."that you are not to pass this way until morning even if the warriors of Abam were to strike this night and you were fleeing for your life."

"This hen will follow me home," he said as he slung his bag on one shoulder and picked up the hen by the legs tied together with banana rope..."I alone will eat its flesh. Let none of you pay me a visit in the morning because I shall not share it.... Even diviners ought to be rewarded now and again...Do we not say that the flute player must sometimes stop to wipe his nose?"

As soon as he was out of earshot Obika asked if it was the custom for diviner to take the hen home.

"I have heard that some of them do," said his mother. "But I have never seen it until today. My own hen was buried with the rest of the sacrifice." (pp. 132-36 passim)

The Arrest of Ezeulu and Offering a Seed Yam Feast

There are two dramatic centres in *Arrow of God*: first, the arrest and detention of Ezeulu by the District Commissioner; and, second, Ezeulu's refusal to roast two sacred yams in one month. As will soon be demonstrated, S. A. Nnolim's *A History of Umuchu* provided both to Achebe. Achebe was so carried away at this point in his novel that he forgot even to attempt to disguise his source. As usual, I shall begin with Nnolim's story of "Offering a Seed Yam Feast" and lead up to the arrest of Ezeulu, which he discussed under the heading, "Method of Recording the Months":

OFFERING A SEED YAM FEAST

Offering of the seed yam feast is the second general feast performed by the whole town: the pumpkin leaves are done by women while the seed yam feasts are done by men. Every grown up man who would be able to discharge a gun must offer one seed yam annually. This feast is done always in January or February according to the native method of months calculation. The feast is done on Nkwo-Uchu market day and the announcement is also made eight days in advance. On the day of the feast, Well Dinner Parties are common, because since Adam and Eve ate the forbidden fruit, much depends on dinner; men will invite their kindreds and benefactors, early before the time of going to the market. Each man will put on his best clothes; young boys even decorate their bodies with dyewood (Uli). The women on the other hand will appear in the best robes and ornaments, plait their hair, decorate all their bodies with "Uli", Ogalu, and "Nkirisiani", they always appear very attractive on such occasion.

No importance is attached to any article of trade on this day; the only articles of trade carried by women are corn cake, melon cakes and women portable calabash for their drinking purposes (Nwonya). The feast is most enjoyable and interesting because of the occasion that favours its performances. (a) It is done in dry season and at times even every one has less work to do. (b) It is done when everyone is at ease and when palm wine is produced in abundance in the town. Inside the juju seat, the six towns have their stalls in the round wall where the Uche seat stands. Inside there each village comes in turn to offer one seed yam. As one puts down his yam, prayers are muttered to the Uchu juju, touching his forefinger on the ground chalk in a pot and rubbing same on his forehead and went away. This will be going on till the whole towns laid their yams down, and the Place will be full of seed yams carefully arranged in groups.

When this is finished almost in the afternoon, drinking will be going on in almost every corner of the market till the famous IKORO is sounded. The trumpeters of each section of the villages will be busily engaged in calling brave men and noble women of the town. The Town Announcer, the women singers (Elile), the flute blowers all will be busy keeping the occasion warm.

The eldest daughter of the juju priest will appear in a hand bell and one line of leopard skin across her belly, from one place' 'lb another with [a] lot of women servants following her and addressing her in various honourable names.

There were men who act as cavalry in the market, who will dress in some gorgeous and peculiar war dresses, and will jump out from one section of the market to another in merriment, after being addressed by various men and women war singers.

DOLLS AND STATUES

The dolls and statues from all other juju seats in those six villages will be lined up with carriers who will fall in behind them at Ugwuakwu lines of stalls. These dolls receive the presents from the interested parties; the presents were some times four cowries, and some times chalks, and, etc. Then after several number of beating Ikoro wooden drum, the Ihite nato will start [the] merry run, as that usually happens, with both their wives and daughters, those who have, of course, done the marketing ceremony. They will in addition sing several traditional war and civil songs and dance. Then followed Okwu na Achalla and Amanasa.

After all these the feast will continue till many foreign friends followed their invitees home. While all these were going on, the two sided juju priests from Ugwuakwu and Osete who were already in the juju seat, when yams were being offered, will then count the yams of each village separately and keep the number secret until another four days time when a sacrifice consisting only the juju priests and one of the elders from each of the six villages. On that day the head of the Uchu juju priest will reveal to each man the number of grown up men in his quarter for the past year, after the sacrifice. They renew their loyalty to their goddess in harmony.

THE YAMS—Twelve yams will be selected by the elders and handed over to the head juju priest; he will keep those twelve yams very carefully because he will use [them] in counting the moons of the year. Other seed yams which usually number several thousand will be kept and planted for Uchu juju under communal and voluntary labour at the juju priest supervision.

METHOD OF RECORDING THE MONTHS

First, new moon the head juju priest will see on the sky after the seed yam feast, he removes one yam from those twelve yams and roasts it in the fire and eats without oil. When that moon Arishes, he watches for the next new moon he again removes another yam from the remainder and roasts it as explained above. When he sees that the yams remain eight, he pronounces first pumpkin leaves. These he uses to count the moon throughout the year, and on the month he eats the last of the yams, he pronounces the seed yam feast, and marks the end of Umuchu one calendar year.

There was confusion in the year about 1913, during the contact with Europeans when our head juju priest named "Ezeagu Uchu" met Mr. J. G. Lotain D. C., and started to claim superiority above the D. C. on account of his Uchu goddess. The District Commissioner as they were called by then did not understand him, and ordered escorts to bring him to Awka for official interrogation as to know whether he was entitled to be a chief. He remained at Awka for two months and bluntly and blindly refused to accept the appointment of a warranted chief. He said that such would be contrary to the wishes of his goddess. While at Awka for two months, the two yams he would have roasted remained untouched. On his return, he refused to roast two yams in a month, saying that such has never been done to his hearing in the history of his goddess; then from that time the first month of Uchu instead of falling on January each year some times falls on February. At the same time too one carved doll, known as Nwobiala Uchu, was carried away by soldiers and destroyed (pp. 25-27).

Now to Achebe. It must first be pointed out that Achebe changed Nnolim's "Offering a Seed Yarn Feast" to the "Feast of the New Yam," for his own fictional purposes. It must be emphasized, too, that the strong, stubborn character of Achebe's Ezeulu is a mere carryover from the stubborn EzeaguUchu in. Nnolim's *History*—a man who would neither kowtow to the District Commissioner nor accede to his own people's advice that he roast two sacred yams in one month. For fictional purposes, Captain Winterbottom's illness becomes the motivation or fictional excuse to keep Ezeulu at Okperi (which, in reality, is Awka divisional headquarters). But where Nnolim says that Ezeagu-Uchu was detained for two months, Achebe reduces it to thirty-two days (which, technically, will still leave Ezeulu two yams to roast in one month!) I must point out, also, that in my town, Umuchu, offering the Seed Yam Festival marks the end of the year, a point Achebe did not miss; nor did he fail to include Nnolim's account of the gifts given: small and almost inconsequential dolls and statues.

Achebe's account of the Feast of the New Yam starts as follows:

> After a long period of silent preparation Ezeulu finally revealed that he intended to hit Umuaro at its most vulnerable point—the Feast of the New Yam.
>
> This feast was the end of the old year and the beginning of the new...It reminded the six villages of their coming together in ancient times and of their continuing debt to Ulu who saved them from the ravages of the Abam. At every New Yam feast the coming together of the villages was re-enacted and every grown man in Umuaro took a good-sized seed-yam to the shrine of Ulu and placed it in the heap from his village after circling it round his head; then he took the lump of chalk lying beside the heap and marked his face. It was from these heaps that the elders knew the number of men in each village. If there was an increase over the previous year a sacrifice of gratitude was made to Ulu; but if the number had declined the reason was sought from diviners and a sacrifice of appeasement was ordered. It was also from these yams that Ezeulu selected thirteen with which to reckon the new year. (p. 213)

And following rather too closely what he found in his source, Achebe goes on to describe the smaller gods and goddesses lined up during the ceremony. Where Nnolim says:

> The dolls and statues from all other juju seats in those six villages will be lined up with their carriers who will fall in behind them at Ugwuakwu lines of stalls. These dolls receive the presents from the interested parties. The presents were some times four cowries, and some times chalks...(p. 26)

Achebe says:

> If the festival meant no more than this it would still be the most

important ceremony in Umuaro. But it was also the day for all the minor deities in the six villages who did not have their own special feasts. On that day each of these gods was brought by its custodian and stood in a line outside the shrine in Ulu so that any man or woman who had received a favour from it could make a small present in return. This was the one public appearance these small gods were allowed in the year. (pp. 231-32)

The arrest of Ezeulu and what Achebe did with it need no longer take up our time here. As I mentioned earlier, it is at the core of the novel. But for purposes of demonstration, it is dealt with by Achebe, starting on page 156 of *Arrow of God*. The offer made to Ezeulu by the District Commissioner's deputy, Mr. Clarke, and Ezeulu's stubborn refusal to accept it, is recorded on page 196. But further dramatic interest is provided by the way Achebe depicts Ezeulu watching for the moon and playing games with it. How Ezeulu roasts and eats his sacred yams without oil is taken directly, and without garnishing, from Nnolim. Nnolim says on page 27: *"When he sees the yams remain eight, he pronounces first pumpkin leaves."* Earlier on the same page he said: "First new moon the head juju priest will see on the sky after the seed yam feast, *he removes one yam from those twelve yams and roasts it in the fire and eats without oil"* (italics mine).

Here is how Achebe recreates Ezeulu's watching of the moon, roasting and eating the yams, and using the yams to record the year's events. *Arrow of God* actually opens with Ezeulu looking for the new moon. When he found it,

Ezeulu went into his barn and took down one yam from the bamboo platform built specially for the twelve sacred yams. There were eight left. He knew there would be eight; nevertheless he counted them carefully. He had already eaten three and had the fourth in his hand...

As he waited for the yam to roast he planned the coming event in his mind. It was Oye. Tomorrow would be Afo and the next day Nkwo, the day of the great market. *The festival of the Pumpkin Leaves would fall on the third Nkwo from that day.* Tomorrow he would send for his assistants and tell them to announce the day to the six villages of Umuaro. (p. 3; italics mine)

But having used Nnolim to establish the month of the festival of Pumpkin Leaves, Achebe did not stop there. He felt he must explain also that the roasted sacred yams are eaten without oil, just as he found it in his source. On page 6 of *Arrow of God*, he lets us watch Obiageli, Ezeulu's little daughter, who looks steadily at her father in hopes he might give her a piece of the sacred yam he was consuming:

> She should have known by now that her father never gave out even the smallest piece of *the yam he ate without palm oil at every new moon*. (Italics mine)

Finally, it must be stressed that the fact that Achebe owes so much to Nnolim's booklet merits neither praise nor censure. My interest has been purely literary and in the service of criticism of African literature. This said, and with all the preceding discussion in mind, it would only be fair to conclude that Achebe's *Arrow of God* is little more than a fictional expansion of *The History of Umuchu* by Simon A. Nnolim; that the entire setting of Achebe's novel is Umuchu, which is not too far away from his own village, Ogidi; that the customs, ceremonies, and feasts he describes are those of Umuchu and not eclectically gathered from diffuse sources; and, finally, that his treatment of the night Mask he owes, by his own admission, to watching them perform for the team from E. N. B. S. which he headed.

But the above does not preclude other sources. His long oral interview with Nnolim must have yielded sources that are not traceable to one who has no access to Achebe's diary. Secondly, Nnolim mentions C. K. Meek's *Law and Authority in a Nigerian Tribe* (1937)[7] as one of the sources he used while preparing *The History of Umuchu*. It is only natural to expect that Achebe traced Nnolim's sources, including intelligence reports and social anthropologists' reports. For example, in his Introduction, C. K. Meeks speaks of "the widespread hatred of the system of Native Administration concluded through the artificial channel of Native Courts, the members of which, under the name of 'Warrant Chiefs,' had come to be regarded as corrupt henchmen of the Government,

---

[7] C. K. Meek, *Law and Authority in a Nigerian Tribe* (London: Oxford University Press, 1937).

rather than as spokesmen and protectors of the people" (p. ix).

Meek was writing, here, of the cause of the women's riots of 1929—a riot that seemed to have taken the administration, which had thought everything was going beautifully, by surprise. Meek, whose anthropological study of the Igbos was regarded as a very authoritative one, goes on to say that Indirect Rule was a mistake in Igboland where "there were no chiefs at all, and there was no higher unit of government than the commune or small group of contiguous villages" (p.x). The unfortunate result of Indirect Rule which created these *Warrant Chiefs,* Meek further admits, was the creation of "chiefs"; who were "armed with an authority far in excess of that possessed by the village-councils in former times. This and their venality as judicial officials had made them feared and disliked" (p. x), until the Secretary of State for the Colonies set up a Commission of Inquiry "with a view to setting up Native Administrations which would be more in accordance with the institutions and wishes of the people than the bureaucratic system which had so signally failed" (p. xi).

The point of the above is that it seems to have provided some fuel for Achebe's depiction of Winterbottom's discontent with the Lieutenant-Governor's memorandum because "the tragedy of British colonial administration was that the man on the spot who knew his African, and knew what he was talking about found himself being constantly overruled by starry-eyed fellows at headquarters" *(Arrow of God,* p. 63); hence, the Lieutenant-Governor, to Winterbottom's chagrin, reinstated the corrupt Warrant Chief Ikedi, whom Winterbottom had deposed.

Achebe seems to have owed further debts to Meek in writing *Arrow of God* and *Things Fall Apart.* As a native of Umuchu, which; is, the setting of *Arrow of God,* I must confess that *Ikenga is* not possessed by our people and by those surrounding towns, It is known only in Owerri Division, which is far removed from Achebe's setting. When, therefore, Akukalia split Ebo's *Ikenga* in two (p. 27), causing the latter to kill Akukalia, one must conclude that Achebe borrowed this peculiar custom from elsewhere. In explaining the cause of the war between Umuaro and Okperi to Clarke, Winterbottom felt obliged to explain why Ebo felt justified in killing Akukalia, for, in splitting his *Ikenga,* he had committed the worst sacrilege. Winterbottom says:

"I may explain that Ikenga is the most important fetish in the Ibo man's arsenal, so to speak. It represents his ancestors to whom he must make daily sacrifice. When he dies it is split in two; one half is buried with him and the other half is thrown away."

In C. K. Meek, the Ikenga is described thus:

"Ikenga is the personification of a man's strength of arm, and consequently of his good fortune. At Oweni the symbol occurs only...in the form of a forked piece of wood some 6 to 8 inches long, with a flat bottom...The owner offers sacrifice when he feels inclined, *and on his death the symbol is thrown into the 'bush of evil* (p. 39; italics mine)

The italicized words point a familiar trend we found in this study. Achebe must have looked at Meek's comprehensive study of Igbo culture before he wrote both *Things Fall Apart* and *Arrow of God*, as I shall try to demonstrate further with one more quotation. We are all familiar with the passage in *Things Fall Apart* where there is a rare exchange between the Masked Spirit—Egwugwu—and Uzowulu. It went on like this:

When all the egwugwu had sat down and the sound of the many tiny bells and rattles on their bodies had subsided, Evil Forest addressed the two groups of people facing them.
"Uzowulu's body I salute you," he said....
Uzowulu bent down and touched the earth with his right hand as a sign of submission.
"Our father, my hand has touched the ground," he said. "Uzowulu's body, do you know me?" asked the spirit. "How can I know you, father? You are beyond our knowledge."[8]

Compare this with Meek's record of such an exchange. Whenever a Masked Spirit appears before humans, Meek observes:

Falling down before the masker, he saluted by putting his hand to the ground and then to his forehead...murmuring: "Father, Owner of

---

[8] Chinua Achebe, *Things Fall Apart* (London: Heinemann, 1958), p.82.

land."

Meek continues:

> A member of the society brings a plantain stalk and begins beating it on the floor of the but and shouting "Egugu, oh!"...The summoner then hails the arrival of the ghosts, saying, "Our father, our father." The masker, speaking through his voice disguiser, says in reply, "Do you know the Mmo?" The summoner replies, "Nay, father, the Mmo can never be known." (p. 68)

Here, again, the similarities are incontrovertible, suggesting a borrowing by Achebe from Meek's work published in 1937.

In conclusion, the reader must be warned that the foregoing is in no way intended to denigrate the great artistic achievements of Achebe as a creative writer and novelist. But my study does establish a few facts about Achebe and his sources. First, we must admit that Achebe is a careful researcher of his facts, which shows great intelligence, for no one has been able to complain that his depiction of Igbo society is distorted or falsified. Secondly, one must admit that it takes painstaking and diligent research to organize and bring alive such complex material. Thirdly, though Achebe is a great observer of Igbo cultural life, the evidence tends to show that his sources are not solely oral; Achebe did not write from personal observation alone, nor merely from a combination of personal observation and the great stories told him by his father and grandfather. He definitely made use of printed sources in writing *Arrow of God*. Here is a diagram of what I term the "watering trough of ideas" that influenced him:

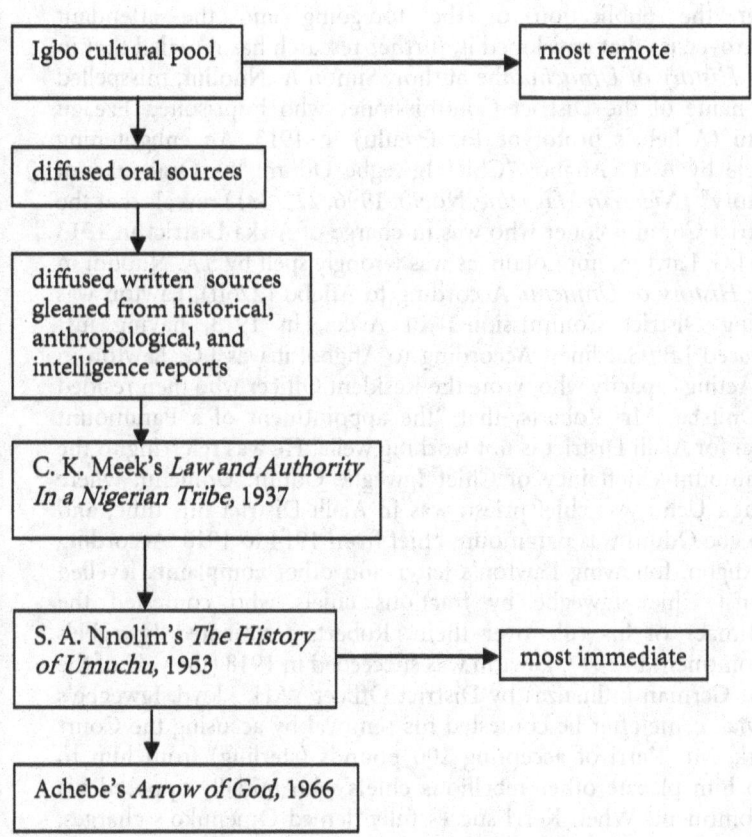

One more word: as I said earlier, G. D. Killam's remark to the effect that "much of the background in *Arrow of God* is there for its own sake, that it has come to dominate the book and has in a sense become the subject of the book," is a very perceptive one. As Achebe himself might have said, in writing *Arrow of God* he had his kernels half cracked for him not by his *chi*, but by Simon A. Nnolim.

Postscript

After the publication of the foregoing and the attendant controversies that enveloped it, further research has revealed that in *The History of Umuchu,* the author, Simon A. Nnolim, misspelled the name of the District Commissioner who imprisoned Ezeagu Uchu (Achebe's prototype for Ezeulu) in 1913. An enlightening article by A. E. Afigbo: "Chief Igwegbe Odum: the Omenuko of History" *(Nigerian Magazine,* No.90, 1996, 222-231) reveals that the District Commissioner who was in charge of Awka District in 1913 was J.G. Lawton, not Lotain, as was wrongly spelt by S.A. Nnolim in *The History of Umuchu.* According to Afigbo (226ff), Lawton was Acting District Commissioner of Awka, in 1913, having just replaced J.B. Gardiner. According to Afigbo, it was J.G. Lawton in his Acting capacity who wrote the Resident Officer who then resided at Onitsha, Mr. Roberts, that "the appointment of a Paramount Chief for Ajalli District is not working well." He was referring to the paramount chieftaincy of Chief Igwegbe Odum. Umuchu, where Ezeagu Uchu was chief priest, was in Ajalli District this time, and Igwegbe Odum was paramount chief from 1914 to 1918. According to Afigbo, following Lawton's letter and other complaints levelled against Chief Igwegbe by fractious chiefs who contested the legitimacy of his rule over them, Roberts terminated Igwegbe's appointment in 1917. Lawton was succeeded in 1918 (the year of the great German influenza) by District Officer W.H. Lloyd. Igwegbe's dowfall came after he contested his removal by accusing the Court Clerk, Mr. Kerri of accepting 100 pounds (sterling) from him to help him placate other rebellious chiefs who initially opposed his appointment. When Kerri successfully denied Omenuko's charges, the Inspector of Police, Mr. Dodson, made such an unfavourable report about Igwegbe Odum, *alias* Omenuko Aku ("he who displays largesse in times of great scarcity"), that Lawton, before handing over to Lloyd, terminated Igwegbe's warrant as the, local chief of Oneh. Chief Igwegbe was publicly reprimanded in front of other chiefs in 1918, and he retired discredited.

According to Afigbo, whose study we are still following, it was under this new District Officer, W. H. Lloyd, who succeeded Lawton in 1918, that Igwegbe Odum agreed to leave Oneh for good and go back to Arondizuogu, the village where he was born and from where he was chased out as a criminal after he sold his carriers into slavery to recover money for goods that perished in a raging river that those carriers were fording. The rise and fall of Igwegbe Odum is the subject matter of the Igbo classic novel *Omenuko,* by Peter Nwana—a book that is still read by Igbo scholars at all levels of the educational ladder.

How does all this concern us? First, Igwegbe Odum comes from Arondizuogu, a town near Umuchu, where Ezeagu Uchu of *Arrow of God* came from. Arondizuogu is no more than one kilometre from Umuchu, to the south (although it was a part of the old Owerri Province, which belonged to a different administrative arrangement entirely). Then, Oneh, where Chief Igwegbe made his headquarters and ruled until his forced retirement in 1918, is about three kilometres east of Umuchu. My wife's mother hails from Oneh. I, myself, know Omenuko's compound, and the hill overlooking that compound is called, even now, Ugwu Igwegbe, or Igwegbe's hill. The ruins of Igwegbe's compound, called to this day by natives of Oneh, Okpulo Igwegbe, or "the ruins of Igwegbe's compound," are still in existence.

Now, how does all this enlighten us further? There seems to be a missing link in Afigbo's study, an event that did not concern his article on Chief Igwegbe or was not recorded in his source, possibly because European intelligence reporters did not think it worthwhile to leave on record. The question that concerns us here is what happened immediately before Chief Igwegbe (who was a stranger to Ajalli by all accounts) was offered the paramount chieftaincy either later in 1913 or early in 1914. The missing link, the untold story, could be inferred thus: After Lawton reluctantly released the proud Ezeagu Uchu from detention in 1913 - a man whom he obviously found a dignified personage fit to be elevated to the high post of first paramount chief of Ajalli (Nnolim in his *History of Umuchu* writes on p.58, new edition: "I went with my father to Ezeagu Uchu when he performed purification ceremony on his return from Akwa")— he must have reluctantly turned to the flamboyant Chief Igwegbe who claimed to be speaking for all the people of Ajalli. When authenticated, all this will be history, not fiction. To fill this lacuna by discovering any intelligence records that actually show Ezeagu Uchu's appointment and his refusal to accept it is a challenge facing historians and literary scholars.

Trends in the criticism of African literature*

What have eventually emerged as trends in the criticism of African literature come from the conflation and coalescence of several critical judgements and from innumerable critical approaches enunciated by a plethora of critical pundits spread all over the African Diaspora. To begin with, the current state of African literature bears testimony to the fact that vigorous literary criticism thrives in Africa. The critic of African literature is invariably a university man using a book or a highbrow critical journal to devote attention to books, authors, or critical theories for the edification of students and fellow scholars about the nature of literature and the function of literature in society. The African literary critic has, in no small measure, helped determine the shape of African literature in this century.

The critic of African literature wears many garbs. Earlier in this century he was a mere chronicler, a journalist-cum-critic who doubled both as reviewer and critic. As a reviewer (a role in which he was more of a journalist) he believed his job consisted of describing the book before him to help the reader determine whether it was worth investment of his time and money. His praise helped sales, his censure often sealed the fate of a new book, and from his ranks emerged the earlier traditional group of critics, the sort that Rene Wellek would call "petty antiquarians."—This early

---

* First published in *Goatskin Bags and Wisdom: New Critical Perspectives on African Literature*, ed. Ernest Emenyonu. Trsnton, New Jersey. Africa World Press (2000), pp.3-15.

group happened to be dominated by European/American expatriates, those petty antiquarians who were rather fascinated by the anthropological curiosities and primitive social cultures revealed in African literary output, especially fiction. The indigenous African critic, as he found his feet, was more hostile than grateful to these expatriates. In retrospect, however, the African critic owes a lot to these earlier expatriate, who were indeed pioneers and pathfinders. If Gerald Moore (*Seven African Writers*, 1962), Margaret Laurence (*Long Drums and Cannons*, 1986), Anne Tibble (*African English Literature*, 1965), and Judith Gleason (*Novels by West Africans in English and French*, 1965) were fascinated by the quaint nature of the content of books by Africans, they were even more enthralled by our ability to put pen to paper and still make sense to an international audience. After all, weren't residual arguments still raging in their historical and social studies as to the African's claim to full humanity? If they did not indeed show us the critical path to follow, at least they pointed out to us the critical highways to avoid. In the process of reacting to the condescending dicta of the expatriate critic, the indigenous African critic found his feet. In retrospect, the indigenous African critic has come to understand that the expatriate critics were indeed slaves to the critical trends of their age, when the critic believed that his job was "to see literature in relation to life and life in relation to history." They knew no better and we need to re-evaluate our antagonism to their stance.

The real job of literary criticism started in Africa in the seventies with the emergence of those critics both foreign and indigenous who placed the aesthetic and artistic content of a book over and above its social and historical concerns. These were critics whose first mission was to make judgments about the faults and the beauties embedded in a work of art to see, according to Matthew Arnold (in "The Function of Criticism at the Present Time')" "the object as in itself it really is without the intrusion of any other values whatever." Axiology (the theory value) was edging out anthropology, as the critic saw the true mission of criticism as the pursuit of what the French term *le bien, la vrai, le beau* (the good, the true, the beautiful). Because ?-evaluation always ends in appreciation, in what arouses enthusiasm, in what engages full attention, in what reveals worth (especially the purely literary value), critics who so engage themselves in it are regarded as the authentic evaluators of African literature. While the critic who looks at literature from its intrinsic properties continue to be valued, according to the formalist critic, it must be agreed that the best critic is the one who brings to bear upon the literary artefact every possible field of knowledge which helps to illuminate the text, for there is no limit to the varieties of curiosity that literature may stimulate. F. R. Leavis thus speaks of the "inevitableness with which serious literary studies lead outside themselves and of the cogency with which they ask to be associated with studies outside the strictly literary critical field."⁴ But the critic must keep his nose to the literary artefact lest he will come to resemble those people who go to the theatre just to watch the audience.

In this century, we have observed several identifiable trends in the criticism of the literature of Europe and the West, about which the critic of African literature dare not claim ignorance. So, while certain trends in the criticism of African literature echo certain aspects of the major trends in Europe, there is no deliberate attempt to copy or follow trends in the criticism of European literature. The Marxist trend was led by Georg Lukac and Plekhanov. In *Goethe and His Age*, 1947, and *The Historical Novel*, 1955. Lukac interprets literature in terms of social realism, urging the writer to be a social realist who uses socialism, Marxism, and communism to toe the party line—and the party spirit, since writers are engineers of the human soul. Sigmund Freud became the inaugurator of psychoanalytic criticism symbolized in dreams, myths, and fairy-tales, using the Oedipus Complex phenomenon to interpret Shakespeare's *Hamlet* and Dostoyevksy's *Brothers Karamazov*. Freud's disciple William Ernest Jones also used the Oedipus Complex idea in a reinterpretation of *Hamlet* that has become a classic in its own right. Edmund Wilson in *The Wound and the Bow* successfully borrowed from Freud depicting literature as the storehouse of man's sub-consciousness.

Freud's erstwhile partner Carl Jung, in *The Archetypes and the Collective Unconscious*, opened new windows into literary interpretation by the use of mythology and cultural anthropology, urging on us terms like archetypal patterns, the universal symbols; he saw in man's deepest unconscious the reason for sacrifice and the scapegoat figure. Borrowing from Jung's work (and of the nineteenth century anthropologist Sir James Frazer), Joseph Campbell in *The Masks of God: Primitive Mythology* became interested in the biographies of gods, prehistory, and myth as symbolic projections of a people's hopes and values and the essential substructure of all human activity. Northrop Frye borrowed a large page from the above authorities in writing his influential *Anatomy of Criticism*.

The existential movement in Europe, advanced by the likes of Jean Paul Sartre, Camus, and Kierkegaard, nudged European criticism towards absurdism. Frank Kafka (in the novels, *The Trial and Metamorphosis*) and Albert Camus (in the novel *L'Etranger* and the essay *The Myth of Sisyphus*) gave concrete (if imaginative) expression to this world view, depicting man as a victim of the human condition in a universe that is fragmented, darkened by illusion, where man feels himself to be a stranger whose movement is from nothingness whence he came toward the nothingness where his life must end, so that human life, in the main, is both anguished and absurd. Characters in plays and novels of the absurd find themselves in a fantastic and nightmarish world, grotesquely comic and irrational, where absurd, comic, horrifying, and irrational occurrences are enacted. We find these, characters in Kafka's *The Metamorphosis*, Beckett's *Waiting for Godot*, and Tom Stoppard's *Rosencrantz and Guildenstern Are Dead*. These form part of the critical movement termed modernism and postmodernism that involves a radical break with the traditional bases of Western culture—a radical break which questions the certainties that championed, advanced, and supported the West's religious, moral, and social organization of earlier centuries. The works of James Joyce (especially Finnegan's Wake), Eliot's The Waste Land, and twentieth-century literary movements such as Cubism and Surrealism became prominent features of modernism and existentialism.

At present, literary criticism in Europe and the West still hovers around linguistic aspects of literature, with far-reaching tentacles in semiology, structuralism, and deconstruction. It started with Ferdinand de Saussure's *Course in General Linguistics* (1916) with his important distinction between *langue and parole*, and bloomed into the linguistic implications of semiology (with the signifier and the signified claiming special attention). It soon caught the attention of Russian formalists (such as Roman Jacobson) and the French cultural anthropologist Claude Levi-Strauss, as structuralist criticism began to view literature as a second-order system which uses language as its medium where a literary work is a mode of writing (*ecriture*) in which factors within the literary work generate literary effects without reference to a reality existing outside itself. The Russian structuralist Valdimir Propp in *Morphology of the Folktale* and the French critic Roland Barthes, together with Tzvetan Todorov, Gerard Genette, and Julia Kristeva, have indeed moved to what is termed *post-structuralism* along with Jacques Derrida of the *Tel Quel* Group. These have now pushed structuralism into deconstruction, which they like to term a dismantling of literary structures by demonstrating how the literary structures have already dismantled themselves. As we can clearly see, this last trend reveals how far Europe, with its much older written traditions, has moved in the criticism of its own literatures. It is only in criticism, according to Matthew Arnold, that the thought of an era becomes articulate and crystallized.

As we face trends in the criticism of African literature, the above summary of critical trends in the West is seen as inevitable, because African literature and its criticism have not weaned themselves away completely from the literary breast of Europe. We may have argued, and quite successfully, the Africanness of African literature and its uniqueness as distinct from any other (especially in our myth-making) as a way of shunning Western rationalism, in our use of African orature as the foundation of our literary endeavours; in our emphasizing a rural rather than an industrial way of life; in our emphasis on communal and collective existence, in our group solidarity rather than pursuit of individualistic endeavours; in adherence to ritual observance such as ancestor worship rather than following Europe's clockwork ideas of progress and regression. But then we must submit to the humiliating admission that the language of expression of our literatures is most often in European tongues and we were fed on the breast of European literary tenets.

It came as a complete surprise to the Western critic that when the African critic woke up to take control of the criticism of his own literatures, he started angrily by attacking expatriate critics whom, he believed, brought their supercilious and arrogant attitudes to bear on all things African, including African literatures. In *African Literature Today*, No.5, 1971, with the spirited lead article by Ernest Emenyonu captioned "African Literature: What Does it Take to be Its Critic?" the author's righteous indignation and the debate surrounding it may have finally silenced expatriate critics such as Judith Gleason and Margaret Laurence, but it failed to daunt the main object of its attack, Bernith Lindfors, who came up with a taunting response in *African Literature Today*, No.7, 1975. In "The Blind Men and The Elephant," Lindfors warned xenophobic champions of criticism of African literature that "common sense just does not allow a single tribe of critics to claim a monopoly on clear vision" and that "indeed, if all interpretation were left to native critics, truth might be sought principally on a local level, its universal dimensions all but forgotten". (54).

The issue which Emenyonu's article spearheaded was the question of identity for Africans and the authenticity of their literatures. Emenyonu's open resentment was against "colonialist critics" whose hobbyhorse was finding "masters" for African writers, attempting in the process to overturn the "depreciation of the African image" by expatriate critics. He went for Lindfor's jugular, asserting that Cyprian Ekwensi "obtained his stimulation from third rate American movies and fourth rate British and American paperback novels", preferring that no "literary godfathers" outside Africa, be found for African Ayi Kwei Annah attacked Charles Larson (*The Emergence of African Fiction*), accusing him of "Larsony" or the use of fiction, while others descended on Gerald Moore (*Seven African Writers*) for tracing Tutuola's masters to Dante, Bunyan, and Blake; Achebe's to Joseph Conrad, and Soyinka's Clark's, and Okara's (poets all) to Hopkins, Eliot, Yeats, Dylan Thomas, and others. And the gentle Achebe had grumbled about "getting a little weary of all the special kinds of criticism which have been designed for us by people whose knowledge of us is very limited."[2]

But the finishing blow which ended the attacks on colonialist criticism and the expatriates, came from the most influential book on the criticism of African literature of that period: *Toward the Decolonization of African Literature* (Enugu: Fourth Dimension Publishers, 1980) by the maverick critics Chinweizu, Jemie, and Madubuike In language as crude and vulgar as their adopted "Bolekaja critics", they asserted that "the cultural task in hand is to end all foreign domination of African culture" and to probe "the ways and means whereby western imperialism has maintained its hegemony over African literature" (1, xiii). They went further, insisting that African literature is not and should never be made to be an extension of European literature, either in form or content; that foreign forms and metaphors should be expunged from the corpus of African literature; and that those who interpret African literature as an extension of European literature are traitors chasing after foreign literary gods.

The major achievement of *Toward the Decolonization of African Literature*—what was new, what made it such an influential book—was the attention they turned to African writers and critics who mimicked and copied European literary modes and writers. Not satisfied with attacking colonialist and expatriate critics (who were already receiving hammer blows from Emenyonu *et al.*), Chinweizu and company went for the throats of fellow African writers and critics in an effort to complete the task of fully decolonizing African literature. They asserted that the literature written by African writers was "the literature of imitation and adaptation, not a literature of imagination and invention" (6). In what was clearly a case of overkill, the authors of *Toward the Decolonization of African Literature* succeeded in shocking us into an awareness of how deeply and pervasively most indigenous African writers and critics were tied to the European literary apron strings, how they were never weaned away from the European literary breast. This is where *Toward the Decolonization of African Literature* carved its niche in the annals of criticism of African literature in their efforts to finally cure African literature and its indigenous writers and critics of their colonial hangover. After the troika, the debate over the influence of expatriate criticism of African literature died completely. And the time had arrived which justified Joseph Okpaku's insistence that "the primary criticism of African art must come from Africans using African standards."

What those "African standards" were became the subject of numerous debates on the pages of very influential journals devoted to the criticism of African literatures. Prominent among these journals were *African Literature Today, Research in African Literatures, The Journal of Commonwealth Literature, Black Orpheus, Transition, Matatu, Okike, Kunapipi*, and a host of in-house journals emanating from various English and Literature Departments of African universities. But because of the poor economic situation in many African countries, many of the in-house journals appear peripatetic or have disappeared completely from circulation, the saddest case being the death of *Calabar Studies in African Literature*, which had thrived in the 1980s with Ernest Emenyonu as General Editor.

But all the debates in these various journals never resolved the burning question of what constitutes the African aesthetic in literature, what makes African literature so unique that one could easily distinguish it from other world literatures. The various debates, on-going and unabated, seem to have gravitated around certain key ideas that remind us of the various exclamations of the blind men and the elephant. Critics argue vigorously about the accuracy of their perspicacious insights, but the issue of an African aesthetic in literature remains largely unresolved. And the issue may remain unresolved in spite of the amount of ink spilt on what constitutes African literature and its definition; on the "newness" of African literature on the world scene; on the problem of the appropriate language suitable for its propagation (European or indigenous); on who constitutes the audience of that literature, on its oral base or orature; on the critical standards by which it should be judged; on who should be its accredited critics (indigenous critics or European); on its ideological orientation; on what constitutes its appropriate theory; and on the function of African literature (utilitarian or aesthetic); on its Negritude aesthetic. These unresolved issues were the main critical preoccupations of the 1980s.

Toward the Decolonization of African Literature, as I mentioned earlier, addressed the issue of the African aesthetic in literature by drawing our attention to how deeply Eurocentric rather than Afrocentric our African critics and writers were. The major flaw in their thesis was the myopic view that their work was done once African literature and criticism were decolonized. Their avowed irreverence and quarrelsome stance failed to address where we went from there once we ceased to be Eurocentric, or in what new directions in the theory of African literature we should turn. A few other attempts, most of them unsuccessful, were made in the late 1970s and the early 1980s to address the question of the African-aesthetic in literature. The most uncoordinated of these efforts was a medley of unrelated and misaddressed essays edited by Lemuel Johnson et al. entitled *Toward Defining the African Aesthetic* (1982). Most others took the traditional view summarizable in the words of Kwasi Wiredu:

> African nationalists in search of an African identity, Afro-Americans in search of their African roots, and foreigners in

search of exotic diversion...all demand an African philosophy fundamentally different from Western philosophy, even if it means the familiar witches' brew.[5]

In the above is the circumambient presence of the Negritude aesthetic, a movement that is now behind us but which constituted a vital road through which all people of African descent had to pass in their collective search for authenticity and the restoration of the innate dignity of the African personality. But since the informing spirit of the Negritude aesthetic in African literature is Africa's continuing search for identity, that movement may be behind us but not quite forgotten in our many-sided approach to autochthony. Respect for our identity was uppermost in Emenyonu's mind when he asked Lindfors to cease searching for literary godfathers for our writers. It was uppermost in the troika's minds when they roundly condemned Adrian Roscoe and others as expatriate critics who are denigrating the genuine Africanness of our literatures while they turned around to condemn fellow African writers who were Eurocentric in their output. The Negritude aesthetic still hovers around our continuing debate about language-use in our literatures. It seems now axiomatic that so long as we don't forget our colonial past, so long shall the African personality hang on to the Negritude aesthetic as a reassuring counterweight.

Before moving on, we must draw attention to a book that had tried to fill a much-needed gap in our quest for a theory of African literature. It is Chidi Amuta's ambitious work, *The Theory of African Literature* (London: Zed Books Ltd., 1989). But those who rush to this book to satiate their hunger on the aesthetic and theory of African literature will surely be let down; for Amuta's book looms like a large covered dish to which a hungry man rushes to dull his hunger and finds only a slice of yam oiled on one side with no salt. The fault is not that f he book lacks intellectual sinews or is bankrupt on ideas. The problem is Chidi Amuta's intellectual arrogance arising from predictable clichńs about his own approach which is predicated on a "radical dialectical criticism" enthroning a "dialectical theory of literature" in language that is full of exegetical turgidity that needs the services of Derrida for proper deconstruction. In the Preface, Chidi Amuta was in his most arrogant posture:

> The ideas set out here simultaneously constitute an act of rebellion, a political statement, a personal testimony and an intellectual intervention in that order. This book is the culmination of my efforts...to confront the ignorance of the, last ten years on the

nature of African literature and its relationship to the society that informs it. (vii)

To make his point, Amuta in his Introduction accuses those he condescendingly addresses as "bourgeois critics" (with their traditional propensities in the criticism of African literature) of suffering from "a disturbing theoretical anaemia" as they have remained "tangential and irrelevant" in current criticism of African literature (5). He then urges on his readers' acceptance of his own "emergent Marxist criticism" because "literary criticism must be predicated on a theoretical outlook that couples cultural theory back to social practice", since human existence and proceeds therefrom to proffer a scientific theory of society that rejects exploitation and inequality" (9-10). It was not that Amuta did not write a solid book based on the Marxist sociological approach to criticism, but rather, in his quest to establish a theory of African literature, he may have blindly grabbed just one leg of the elephant and proclaimed it a tree. In yoking hindsight to current realities in the criticism of African literature, Chidi Amuta may have to bite his tongue if he still has any. Since the collapse of communism, Amuta may have learnt how ephemeral certain trends are, whether in artistic fashions or the movement of ideas. After condemning bourgeois and traditionalist critics before him, he may now be dismayed to realize how soon his own critical ideas have become "tangential and irrelevant" like those of his fellow critics he denigrated. There are many approaches to literary criticism. Each approach adds to the corpus of knowledge in our intellectual history a fact that should teach some of us humility

Chidi Amuta's *The Theory of African Literature* has further implications for the Marxist/Sociological brand of criticism which flourished in the 80s. He had, in 1986, published *Towards A Sociology of African Literature* (Oguta: Zim Pan-African Publishers). Both books gave teeth to disparate but strident critical voices championed by Biodun Jeyifo (editor of *Positive Review*) and ably assisted by G. G. Darah, Yemi Ogunbiyi, Kole Omotoso, Femi Osofisan, and Eddie Madunagu. This group of the intelligentsia flaunted their ideological leanings insisting (vulgar Marxist style) that literature, as part of ideological superstructure, must ally itself with the Marxist dictum that art, as an instrument in the class struggle must be a reflection of the social structure. The proletarian propensities in their critical essays carried with it the usual

revolutionary ring and brought new critical tools for interpreting African literary works. They urged social relevance as the measuring rod of our criticism, which must be sensitive to the affective nature of art, insisting that artistic output must be part of social engineering. As soon as this group found their feet, the "Komfess artistes," led by Femi Osofisan, Bodo Sowande, and Kole Omotoso, emerged to produce literary works that lent themselves to critical analysis using the tools already sharpened by their ideological bent. Festus Iyayi's *Violence, The Contract Heroes*, Femi Osofisan's *Kolera Kolej*, Kole Omotoso's *The Edifice*,
Bode Sowande's *Our Man the President*, Ousmane Sembene's *God's Bits of Wood*, and Ngugi wa Thiong'o's *Petals of Blood* and *Devil on the Cross* became critical quarries for the Marxist-sociological brand of criticism. Amuta's *The Theory of African Literature* and *Towards A Sociology of African Literature* at once presented a critical overview to the various ways in which this group looked at literature.

While Biodun Jeyifo and Amuta and their group shouted themselves hoarse, a quiet trend unfolded itself using the mythic approach to look at our literatures. *African Literature Today*, No.11 (1980) was a special issue on Myth and History. Predictably, Isidore Okpewho, a powerful voice in myth criticism in Africa, contributed the lead article in this is,- Que. "Rethinking Myth," which was more theoretical than practical. Other important articles in that volume discussed the role of the gods in Elechi Amadi's novels (Niyi Osundare. "As Grasshoppers to Wanton Boys: The Role of the Gods in Elechi Amadi's Novels") and the Role and myth and ritual in Achebe's Arrow of God (Bu-Buakei Jabbi: "Myth and Ritual in *Arrow of God*"). Okpewho's contributions to myth criticism in African literature cannot just be dismissed in passing. His works *The Epic in Africa* (1979) and *Myth in Africa* (1982) have made invaluable contributions to our understanding of the circumambient role of myth and ritual in African life and art. Africa is a continent famous for its rich folkways, and her myths and folkways have always stimulated her artists—and continue to do so—while at the same time providing her critics with concepts and patterns which they use to their advantage in interpreting her works of art, especially her literatures.

Still raging and making waves is the feminist trend in the criticism of African literature. One of the avowedly imported ideologies like Marxism, feminist criticism took root in Africa through our female writers like Flora Nwapa (*Efuru, One is Enough*), Mariama Ba (*So Long a Letter*), Buchi Emecheta (*The Bride Price, Second Class Citizen, Destination Biafra*), and Bessie Head (*A Question of Power*). These African female writers, including Ama Ata Aidoo, after gorging themselves on a diet of ideological works from European and American feminists like Kate Millett (*Sexual Politics*), Betty Friedan (*The Feminine Mystique*), Simone de Beauvoir (*The Second Sex*), and Germaine Greer (*The Female Eunuch*), started a steady ideological warfare whose battle cry was equality for African women in the political, social, marital, economic, and legal areas of life's endeavors. Terms like empowerment, reification, self-actualization, and liberation of African women came to be proclaimed, published in journals, and debated in conferences organized solely by women *African Literature Today*, No.15 (1987) was devoted entirely to feministic issues and women in African literature. Books have emerged recently authored or edited by African female writers and critics. Helen Chukwuma edited *Feminism in African Literature* (Enugu, New Generation Books, 1994); Oriaku Nwosu came out with *The African Woman* (1993); and Theodora Ezeigbo just published *Gender Issues in Nigeria: A Feminine Perspective* (Lagos: Vista Books, 1996). And not to be forgotten is an earlier collection of essays entitled *Nigerian Female Writers* (Lagos: Malthouse Press, 1989) and edited by H. Otokunefor and O. Nwodo. The feminine point of view has taken centre stage in our literary discourse.

On a brief but final note we shall cast a glance on the problems of Language use in African literature. Critical response to issues raised by B. I. Chukwukere in "The Problem of Language in African Creative Writing" (*African Literature Today*, No.3), on whether the African writer should or should not write in a foreign language, and if he does, what variety of that language should he adopt, seems to have abated since Obi Wali's dire prediction that writing in English or other foreign languages by Africans could only lead to "sterility, uncreativity, and frustration." On the contrary, African creative writing under Achebe, Soyinka, Munonye, Camara Laye, Peter Abrahams, Okot p'Bitek, Ayi Kwei Armah, and a host of ethers seems to be waxing stronger in foreign tongues. The debate about which language to use moved from engaging drama to side-show freakishness as critics of African literature turned their attention to how far the African writer should exploit the writer uses standard English, which standard (Nigerian, or West African variety)? If he adopts pidgin, should he stay on pure pidgin, or "broken" English? Different "Englishes" or varieties of English have been suggested—"been-to", Queen's, etc. Since African writers "bend" English usage, how far can they go and remain acceptable?

But none of the above debates established a trend in the criticism of African literature. Emmanuel Ngara in *Stylistic Criticism and the African Novel* (London, 1982) dangled an apple, but there were no takers. In our review of trends in the criticism of European literature, we concluded that issues of language in criticism have been pushed from linguistics to structuralism to deconstruction. The challenge facing the critic of African literature today is that posed by Emmanuel Ngara, to move on to serious stylistic criticism by using in his craft both linguistic features and paralinguistic affective devices—such as symbolism, myth, allusion, allegory—which are not analysable in terms of normal linguistic description. To quote Ngara more fully:

> stylistic critic qua critic...must use the analytic tools of the linguistic and stylistician; he must, to some degree concern himself with minute details of grammar, lexis, phonology, prosody, meaning, as well as with the wider issues from the norm, the relationship between the author and his audience. But more than that he must relate his analysis of linguistic features to considerations of content value andaesthetic quality in art...The stylistic critic, in our definition is meant to bridge the gap between the stylistician and the critic...He is as much interested in questions of value as the conventional critic, while at the same time he seeks to assimilate as much of the insights of stylistics as possible. (12)

With the above as challenge to the critic of African literature, we end this study. The critic of African literature needs to catch up with the exploits of European critics in stylistic and linguistic analysis of literature. Catching up with the like of J. Austin and John R. Searle (Speech-Act theory); Claude Levi-Strauss, Roland Barthes, and Michel Foucault Kristeva (deconstruction) is a challenge that must be met by the critic of African literature. Those who have hitherto ignored Sunday Anozie's freshman appearances in structuralist discourses may have to take a second look at his contributions in this area.

Works cited

F. R. Leavis, "The Literary Discipline and Liberal Education," *Sewanee Review* LV, No. 3 (Autumn, 1957), p.586.

Chinua Achebe, "Where Angels Fear to Tread", *Morning Yet On Creation Day* (London: Heinemann, 1975), p.46.

Joseph Okpaku, "Tradition, Culture; and Criticism," *Presence Africaine* 70 (1969); 141. Others were Stanley Macebuh in "African Aesthetics in Traditional African Art" (*Okike* 5, [1974]); Charles E. Nnolim, "An African Literary Aesthetic: A Prolegomenon" (*Ba Shiru* 17 [1976]); Isidore Okpewho, "The Aesthetics of Old African Art" (*Okike* No. 8 [1975]).

Kwasi Wiredu, *Philosophy and African Culture* (Cambridge: Cambridge University Press, 1980), p.30.

Emmanuel Ngara, *Stylistic Criticism and the African Novel* (London: Heinemann, 1982), p.17.

3

Utopian literature and the African world view*

In [African] traditional religions there is no prophetism and no future paradise. For time ... recedes rather than progresses and the Golden Age—that era of the black man's greatness—the era of Timbuctoo and Benin, the era of the Yoruba and the Zulu, of Shango and Chaka, lies in the Zamani period. The Sasa is an ever-constant construction of the past and not of the future. Utopia exists in the past.[1]

Man writes utopian literature, it seems, either as a personal revolt against the human condition (i.e. against things as they are) or in his perpetual search for a heaven on earth—an earth that partakes of the Kingdom idea, namely: fullness, richness, manifoldness, satisfying individuality, paradise on earth. Utopian literature has always expressed man's longing for things as they might or ought to be, for it is the aim of utopian literature to invite the wretched of the earth to partake, even if vicariously, of the delights and satisfaction denied them in this valley of tears. The quest for an ideal society on earth for man first found expression in Plato's *The Republic* where the society is based on the idea of justice and division of labour: every man does the job for which he is best suited, and there is a community of wives and children in an environment where private property is also abolished. In *The*

---

* First published in *Nka: A Journal of the Arts*, No.1 (1983), pp.3-13.
[1] Frederick Ivor Case, "Negritude and Utopianism," *African Literature Today*, No.7 (1975), p.70.

Republic, philosophers rule the state, warriors defend it, and the producers—farmers, artisans, tradesmen—satisfy its economic needs. *The Republic* was thus the first attempt in literature of the West to provide a plan or a programme of living for a just society.

Thomas More, championing the humanistic view during the Renaissance and taking a Christian view of the just society on earth, pictures for us in his famous *Utopia* a state where all is well ordered, for the best, for all mankind. In the just society which he created, evils and deprivations such as poverty and misery are absent, as he demonstrates what utopia would Bite if the natural virtues—justice, temperance, fortitude, prudence—were encouraged and allowed free play and free expression. The popularity of More's book has since given the generic name—Utopia--to all such concepts of the ideal state on earth created by novelists, social philosophers, and visionaries.

Since the appearance of More's work, the word "Utopia" (coined from two Greek words: *outopia* (no place) and *eutopia* (the good place) meaning: "the good place in no place", has deeply etched itself in our literary imagination. Since then we have had many versions of utopia on the literary scene, prominent among which are what we have come to call and Categorise as "utopia of escape" and "utopia of reconstruction." The former presents a dream projection of a perfect and perfected world, no matter how remote from realization (Tomasso Campanella's *The City of the Sun*, Bulwer-Lytton's *The Coming Race*); and the latter attempts to provide a plan and a programme of living for a better society on earth (Cabet's *Voyage to Karia*, Bellamy's *Looking Backward*). In between we have had what has come to be called technological utopian satire (Samuel Butler's *Erewhon*) and utopian romance (William Morris's *News from Nowhere*). In the present century, a reaction to these utopian romances visualizing golden ages of the future or societies assumed to be ideal or better than what we have, has resulted in works that have come to be called dystopia or the bad place, which project in the future a hell on earth created by man, a very unpleasant imaginary world such as we have in Aldous Huxley's *Brave New World* and George Orwell's *1984*.[2]

Every utopia is but one manifestation of what man has as an

---

[2] See Charles E. Nnolim, "African Utopia and Ali Mazrui's The Trial of Christopher Okigbo," *New Literature Review*, No.11 (1982), pp.63-73.

inner aim and what he must have for fulfilment as an individual. To deny that man needs promise of a better future to exist is to reject utopia, to deny the truth about man's essence. According to Paul Tillich, it is impossible to understand history without utopia, for neither historical consciousness nor action can be meaningful unless utopia is envisaged both at the beginning and at the end of history. He further asserts that utopia has one positive characteristic: its fruitfulness—its ability to open up possibilities for man which would have remained lost to him if not envisaged by utopian anticipation, for every utopia is an anticipation of human fulfilment.[3] And many things anticipated by man in utopian literature have turned out to be real possibilities. Without this anticipatory inventiveness, countless possibilities would have remained lost to man and remained unrealized. And where no anticipatory utopia is created to open up possibilities for man, we find a stagnant, sterile present: we find a situation in which not only individual but cultural realization of human possibilities are inhibited and remain un-fulfilled. As Tillich continues to assert, for a culture which has no utopia the present is inhibiting, the future holds no promise and the danger of cultural retrogression is very much there, along with the danger of falling back on its past.[4]

Allied to what has been termed the fruitfulness of utopia is the power of utopia: its ability to transform dreams into reality. And over the years, Western writers on utopia, writers I term the bearers of utopia, have amply demonstrated these positive powers of utopia: its power and its fruitfulness, for these bearers of utopia always look forward to a dynamic present that keeps breaking into a better future, recognizing that the origin of utopia is man's ontological discontent with his lot in life and determined order to transform his dreams into reality. For all of us, the Israelites symbolize a people for whom a fanatic longing for God's kingdom on earth and at the end of time has transformed impossibilities to possibilities, in their quest for the promised land flowing with milk and honey on earth, for the New Jerusalem; and outside history at the end of Time, for a time of apocalyptic visionary unveiling in God's Kingdom, as clearly envisioned in the New Testament. This transformation of an earthly

---

[3] Paul Tillich, "Critique and Justification of Utopia," in Utopia and Utopian Thought, ed. Frank E. Manuel (Boston: Houghton Mifflin Company, 1966), p.296.
[4] Ibid., p. 298.

kingdom to a heavenly kingdom at the end of Time has thus become the Judaic legacy to the world. The Judaic supreme literary gift to the world—the Bible—is thus utopian literature par excellence, depicting for mankind the two most powerfully recognized types of utopian literature; utopia of the past—Eden—(the good old days) and utopia of the future—the coming Kingdom under God, the Millennia looked for at the end of time.

With the foregoing in mind, this study will argue that a people's world-view is reflected in its concept of utopia and this concept can help determine its future. It will further 'highlight What it views as the basic difference between the Western and African concepts of Utopia as reflected in their literatures and will go on to conclude that a forward-looking, future-oriented people first reflect this orientation in their utopian literature While a backward-looking conception of utopian literature depicts the world-view of a people who either love to revel in a glorious past or are satisfied with the present. Europe and the West, it will be argued, represent the former while Africa and Africans in the Diaspora represent the latter. This will inevitably force this study to raise certain disturbing questions at the end about the future of Africa in its continuing encounter with the West in a universe in which the survival of a people will be deter-mined more and more by the people's ability to map out strategies for survival in a technologically-oriented society of the future.

Under healthy circumstances, society and the culture provided by that society are friends, not enemies with the individuals within the society, for society will then provide the raw materials with which the individual builds, enriches, and makes something of his life. If one's culture is meagre, the individual is deprived; if it is rich, the individual could rise to unimagined heights. Furthermore, whenever there is a good marriage between the individual and society, the genius of certain individual (if the culture is rich) is certain to rise to the expectations of that culture. So in the final analysis, it was not the prophet Jeremiah (or Elijah or Isaiah) alone to whom the gift of prophecy in Judea belongs, but to an amalgam of circumstances inspired by the cultural milieu of the Jewish state—a state that thrived on a utopia geared to an apocalyptic future, a time of visionary unveiling when, with the intrusion of the Divine, the Kingdom of God will be achieved. Prophecy inevitably became the gift of those individuals in society who viewed most intensely this future in the New Jerusalem which St. John sketches most vividly in the book of the Apocalypse. By prophecy, by sheer intense imaginative projection and effort of the will, the Jew, an exiled and persecuted people in Egypt saw themselves back in Jerusalem (the land of their fathers) thus realizing their dream (even if it meant crossing the Red Sea with no ships and seeing the destruction of Pharaoh's army in the process!). The realization of the Jewish dream by the intervention of the Divine is the epic story of the Bible.

One could argue further, that it was not Caesar or Napoleon to whom martial prowess belonged in the abstract but to the marriage of their individual geniuses with the possibilities provided by a highly organized military machine tuned and oiled perennially for war. Nor is it the individual philosopher—Plato, Socrates, Aristotle—in Greece to whom the love of wisdom belonged in the abstract, but to the society's questing mind, to Greece's love of wisdom and order in the universe. And in the pre-sent century, it is not the individual U.S. or Russian astronaut to whom technological superiority in space-exploration belongs over his Asian or African counterpart (a superiority that has landed the U.S. on the moon) but to the advantages made possible by the pulling together of the resources of a society for whom technological competence is a fetish. The legacy of Europe and the West is the legacy of a universe which is transformed and continues to be transformed through astounding breakthroughs in technology.

Astounding breakthroughs in technology have been possible only for societies which made the problems of the future the centre of interest today. In modern times, science fiction dominates the literary markets of Europe and the West, and much of science fiction is futuristic. Jules Verne, much earlier, had captured our imagination with his imaginary journeys to impossible places. We had thought that *From the Earth to the Moon would remain forever Thousand Leagues Under the Sea* was also an impossible dream until man conquered the depths, and Alvin Toffler writes now with confidence of "The New Atlantis" in his equally celebrated *Future Shock*:

> Within fifty years man will move onto and into the sea—occupying it and exploiting it as an integral part of his use of this planet for recreation, minerals, food, waste disposal, military and transportation operations, and, as populations grow, for actual

living space.⁵

To be able to adapt to sea life, he has begun suggesting Ova man will be fitted with surgically implanted gills to enable him live "naturally" in the depths of the sea. *Future Shock* which is futuristic literature par excellence, is concerned with "educating for change," "preparing people for the future" and warning that "unless man quickly learns to control the rate of change in his personal affairs as well as in society at large, we are doomed to a massive adaptational breakdown."⁶ This is the mind of the West at work and at its best. Dealing with the problems of the future and preparing for those problems now is at the core of much of modern science fiction in Europe and the West. Much of science fiction is utopian literature and this genre of writing has made and continues to make inventions possible. Furthermore, they help to warn us about the dangers of a technological era in the future. Aldous Huxley's *Brave New World* and George Orwell's *1984* might, in the long run, have helped man avoid taking the perilous direction in which Western civilization seemed once headed.

Before moving to the African scene, one final glance will be cast in the direction of America as a land of promise, as the last best hope for mankind. This view has always been sustained throughout its existence as a nation-state by her writers of utopian literature—those I have called the bearers of utopia. Archibald Macleish had written in "America Was Promises":

America was always promises
From the first voyage and the first ship
There were promises

I contend that today, America is a realized land of promise because from its inception America was born with a national dream. Called the land of opportunities, with its encouragement of talent and strong belief in the work ethic, America is a nation-state with a spirit of optimism and a strong belief in a better future for herself and for mankind. The American experiment believes strongly in the transformation of this world into a heaven on earth. For her, the coming kingdom under God is here. More books on utopian literature envisaging a Golden Age have been written in America than in any other country. Mark Twain's *The Gilded Age*, William Dean Howell's *A Traveller from Altruria*, Bachelder's *A. D. 2050*, Hawthrone's *The*

---

⁵ Alvin Toffler, *Future Shock* (New York: Random House, Inc., 1979), p.188.
⁶ Ibid., p.2.

Blithedale Romance, and Bellamy's *Looking Backward*—all project a Golden Age in the future. And today America remains for many a symbol of human hope, a utopia looked for on earth. In *Looking Backward*, the author, Bellamy, writes in a postscript:

> All thoughtful men agree that the present aspect of society is portentous of great changes. The only question is, whether they will be for better or the worse. Those who believe in man's essential nobleness lean to the former view, those who believe in his essential baseness lean to the latter. For my part, I hold to the former opinion. Looking Backward was written in the belief that the Golden Age lies before us and not behind us, and is not far away. Our children will surely see it, and we, too, who are already men and women, if we deserve it by our faith and by our works.[7]

II

Utopia of a Golden Age in the past is also a well-recognized genre of Utopian literature. The Good Old Days and how to return to it have always captured the literary imagination of those who look back with nostalgia to a golden era that has been lost to us, to a pristine, prelapsarian Eden that has been spoiled by modern inventions and the artificialities of city life. The pastoral romance, Arcadia by Sir Philip Sydney, calls to mind a genre of utopian romance whose ancestry runs through Sydney to Jacopo Sannazaro to Virgil to Theocritus and became synonymous with an ideal land where peace and simplicity reigned as in the Golden Age, exhibiting an idealized rural beauty, simplicity and contentment where idealized shepherds sang their songs against a dream-like background of mountains, groves, and simon-pure streams. This genre of utopian literature has somehow influenced African writers who, in protest against the damages and ravages of colonial intrusion into their culture and way of life, have begun to return to a romanticized vision of their past with the ardour of a convert. And an important aspect of the Negritude movement involves a romanticized recreation of our culture which has been damaged and defaced through the colonial

---

[7] Edward Bellamy, *Looking Backward: 2000-1887*, (Boston: Houghton Mifflin Company, 1966), p.203.

intrusion.

In the light of the foregoing, one must recognize the Negritude movement among Africans and Africans in the Diaspora as the one clearly defined utopian and romantic movement in our literary history. And one unmistakable aspect of that movement is the *retour aux sources* or back to the sources trend or theme which strained alter a rediscovery of Africa's roots in order to recapture what the writers called the essential African reality. "To return symbolically to the source," according to Wilfred Cartey, "to abnegate the loss, the alienation, the confusion, will be the prime intention and motive of the Negritude poets as they search through their single selves for a communal African authenticity. Thus things remembered, that had been lost—the entry into infancy, something lost past—will link them, even as they seek a rebirth, to the beginnings of things."[8] The Harlem Renaissance in the U.S., Afro-Cubanism in Cuba, Indigenism in Haiti, Marcus Garvey's Return to Africa Movement, and the Rastafarian Movement in Jamaica—each was, along with the Negritude movement, a retour aux sources romantic longing for the past by writers for whom Africa remained a lost paradise, the Black Arcadia, the one place that will alone give back the displaced black man his roots, his humanity, his wholeness, his stability, his dignity. In modern fiction, Alex Haley's *Roots* looms large in this romantic nostalgia for a lost Africa. Chinua Achebe revels in ancestor worship. Camara Laye longs to return to his unspoilt childhood and unspoilt Guinea. The romanticizing of Africa's past by those I term her bearers of utopia thus wears many garbs.

One garb which this romanticism wears in the Caribbean is the cult of primitivism. Afro-Cubanism was a movement that was born in the 1920s in Cuba from the fashion for the cult of the primitive, out of a realization in Cuba of the role of the Negro in the overall life of the Cuban people. According to Coulthard, Negro primitivism was indulged in "as a corrective to the over-civilization of the white world with its unhappiness, frustrations, and inhibitions."[9] Overindulgence in sensuality, in sexual animality, in body gyrations in the dance as a way of releasing the over-abundant

---

[8] Wilfred Cartey, *Whispers from a Continent* (New York: Random House, Inc. 1969), p.217.
[9] G. R. Coulthard, *Race and Colour in Caribbean Literature* (London: Oxford University Press, 1962), p.30.

force of life in a frenzy of all the muscles in rhythmic harmony with rhymba music—these were manifestations of primitivism that elicited protests from Regino Pedroso:

> Are we nothing more than Negro?
> Are we nothing more than music and noise?
> Are we only rumba, black lust and carnival bands?
> Are we nothing more than grimaces and colour
> Grimaces and colour?[10]

The most celebrated retour aux sources writer in the Caribbean is, of course, Aime Cesaire whose Cahier d'un Retour au pays Natal celebrates his own form of primitivism in "heia for those who never invented anything/who never explored anything" and goes on to return symbolically to the Congo:

> noisy with forests and rivers
> where the whip cracks like a great banner
> where the water goes likwala, likwala,
> and to the Congo where the unspoiled African had the power
> to charm snakes to conjure up the dead
> voom roh oh
> to hold back the rains to cross the tides
> voom roh oh.[11]

Both the Harlem Renaissance in the U.S. and Indigenism in Haiti drove Black Americans (both in the U.S. and in Haiti) to a rediscovery of what was indigenous in their culture—to defend, present, and glorify the Afro-Haitian folk culture which had, till then, been neglected, relegated to the background or despised. Indigenism, with its folkloric realism, was a turning away from city life in order to return to rural Haitian life, to relive its peasant life, to use its folk language—Creole—and to celebrate its voodoo culture with its drum rhythms and sensual dances. And while Indigenism in Haiti tried to recapture the folkways of Afro-Haitian peasant life, Afro-Cubanism and Negrism aimed at recapturing Afro-Caribbean rhythms and Afro-Cuban peasant life long neglected by the civilizing process of colonialism.

"The Journey" as a recognized motif in literature invariably

---

[10] Ibid., p.33.
[11] Aime Cesaire, Return to My Native Land, trans. John Berger and Anna Bostock (Baltimore, Maryland: Penguin Books, 1969), pp.56, 58.

involves a back to the sources movement in the literatures of Africans and Afro-Americans in the Diaspora. And it is through "the journey" that we romanticize our past and it is in the past that we pack and crowd the lodestars or our concept of utopia. Jacques Roumain celebrates a going back to Guinea in

> It is the slow road to Guinea
> Your fathers wait for you without impatience.

Lenrie Peters in "Home Coming" longs to go back where "Luxuriant weeds have grown where we led/The virgins to the water's edge"; Abioseh Nicol is urged in "Up-Country";

> Go up-country, they said
> To see the real Africa
> For whomsoever you may be,
> That is where you come from
> Go for the bush—inside the bush
> You will find your hidden heart
> Your mute ancestral spirit
> And so I went
> Dancing on my way.[12]

While Jean Price-Mars in Ainsi Parla l'oncle expresses nostalgia for his lost home in Africa along with that home's happy uncomplicated life where one was free to "drink blood out of human skulls (as Okonkwo definitely did in Achebe's *Things Fall Apart*), Senghor wants to "return to the Negritude of the past, the Negritude of the sources,"[13] part of which is a return to his infancy:

> I know that paradise is lost—I have not lost
> sight of the childhood garden where
> the birds are in flower
> That the harvest will follow the hard winter season.[14]

In fiction, Achebe who admits that he is "basically an ancestor worshipper" charms us by recreating and celebrating a past which is forever lost through the rude intrusion of colonialism, a past in

---

[12] Quoted by S. Okechukwu Mezu in "Poetry and Revolution in Modern Africa," *Black Academy Review*, (Spring, 1970), p.15.
[13] JanheinzJahn, *Neo-African Literature: A History of Black Writing* (New York: Grove Press, Inc., 1968), p.252.
[14] Cartey, *op. cit.*, p.298.

which

> The land of the living was not far removed from the domain of the ancestors. There was coming and going between them, especially at festivals and also when an old man died, because an old man was very close to the ancestors. A man's life from birth to death was a series of transition rites which brought him nearer and nearer to his ancestors.[15]

And Camara Laye, after nostalgically recreating his lost childhood in the "unspoilt" and Edenic Guinea which he left behind while in Paris (romanticizing and mystifying everything in the process), also reveals in his own version of ancestor worship which manifests itself in totemic myth, and hi, totemism is manifest in the "animal ancestor" his father worships in the form of the little black snake which Laye's father caresses before embarking on the job of smelting gold, and which speaks thus to him in dreams:

> Lo, I am the guiding spirit of thy race, and eveia as the guiding spirit of thy race that I am myself known to thee, as to the most worthy.[16]

But the most astonishing attempt in modern African fiction to create a new concept of utopian literature is Ali Mazrui's *The Trial of Christopher Okigbo*. Using the techniques of "the journey"—this time, from life to death—Mazrui creates an apocalyptic utopia at the end of history and calls it "After-Africa." And the utopian principle around which the novel is structured is that of Pan-Africanism: the continental unity which eludes Africa on this earth Mazrui's *Herebefore*), is automatically achieved in After-Africa which is his dream-vision of what an ideal, united, modern continental Africa would be like when all separatist tendencies (like the one that gave rise to the Nigeria-Biafra war) are completely eliminated, for "Death is an exercise in Pan-Africanism"—a phrase that is repeated *ad nauseam*.[17] In After-Africa, all the rights and privileges due our ancestors are fully restored to them by Mazrui. To effect this version of ancestor worship beyond the grave, Mazrui creates a

---

[15] Chinua Achebe, *Things Fall Apart* (New York: Fawcett Edition, 1966), p.115.
[16] See Charles E. Nnolim, "An African Literary Aesthetic: A Prolegomena," in Ba Shiru: Journal of African Languages and Literature, Vol.2 (1976), p.61.
[17] Nnolim, "African Utopia and Ali Mazrui's *The Trial of Christopher Okigbo*," p.3.

gerontocary—government by the aged, the elders—for it is the elders on whom devolves high moral authority, high prestige, and all the elevated influence worthy of them in the Here-before. As Salisha explains to Hamisi:

> Those who had lived long in the Herebefore continued to have a margin of mystique in this world which followed. The elders of Africa, having died old, retained the credentials for extra consideration in the existence which followed.[18]

And so it is the elders who sit in final judgement over Christopher Okigbo and every other dead African arriving in After-Africa. To complete his picture of a return to the good old days beyond the grave, Mazrui propounds his theory of "social collectivism" through the mouth of Apolo-Gyamfi:

> Much of Africa's art was a collective experience. The legends, the folksongs, of folktales, the proverbs, the trance of primeval dance, were all shared moments of being (p.77).

Finally, initiation rites are revived in Mazrui's *After-Africa* when one passes from the status of being merely deceased to the status of immortal, and from the status of immortal to the status of Elder. When Hamisi seems not to understand the reason for the revival of rites de passage rituals in *After-Africa*, Salisha explains:

> Much of African life in the Herebefore assumed the validity of rites de passage. The move from one stage of life to another involved a legitimizing initiation. Sometimes it was circumcision, and sometimes alternative modes of ceremonial admission into a new stage of existence. From generation to generation, from one status to another, Africa had its way of opening the gates...Death itself in many of our societies, you will remember, was one more ceremonial transition...Death was not an interruption but a continuation (p.37).

II

As Mazrui rejoices at the final reunion of Africans beyond the grave where they would have no choice but to observe our ancestral customs neglected in the Herebefore owing to the civilizing process,

---

[18] Ali Mazrui, *The Trial of Christopher Okigbo* (London: Heinemann, 1971), p.38.

Achebe laments the break-up here on earth, of the age-old customs which held us together before the colonial intrusion. And in literary criticism, a group of erudite but angry young men had castigated all those creative artists of African origin who in their bid to appear modern had abandoned the authors of "Toward the Decolonization of African Literature" for a *retoux aux sources,* elicited an equally spirited response from Soyinka (one of the victims of the attack) who charged them with "Neo-Tarzanism" in modern African criticism.[19] The implications to this study of this critical endeavour is obvious: writers and critics of African and Afro-American origins-those who are the bearers of African utopianism-are, in the main, backward-looking while we have earlier established that their counterparts in Europe and the West are, in the main, forward looking. For the African, therefore, there is no reaching after the unattainable, no straining after a heaven of the future (man-made or through Divine intervention); rather, there are nostalgic, wistful backward glances at the glories of the past. There seems to be nothing racial about this. Nor does it seems to be a matter of intelligence. It is rather a question of world view. The Negritude movement, in the final analysis, is the black man's identification of his affinity to the earth, as Africans seem to regard themselves as the inheritors of the earth. Cesaire had pleaded that Negritude should

> Bind me without remorse
> bind me with your vast arms of luminous clay
> bind my black vibration to the very navel of the world

while Senghor rejoices that "Here I am restored to earth."[20] And those who have not forgotten Caliban with the African and Prospero with the European (c.f. O. Mannon's *Prospero and Caliban: the Psychology of Colonization*) will always remember Caliban protesting: "This island is mine!" Furthermore, when Cesaire claims that for him peoples of Africa are "truly the eldest sons of the world," and goes on to rejoice about

> those who invented neither gunpowder nor compass
> those who tamed neither electricity nor steam
> those who explored neither seas nor sky

---

[19] See *Okike,* VII (1975), and *Transition,* No.48 (1975).
[20] See Cartey, *op. cit.*, pp.286, 298.

but without whom the earth would not be the earth.²¹

The conclusion to be drawn is that in a universe where *progress* involves taming the sea and conquering space, the African is content with the status quo, with living in the past. One is thus quickly reminded of David Rubadiri's criticism of the Negritude movement when he says:

> I think that Negritude is dangerous...because its final result is to press down the creative spirit, to tie it, sometimes so tight that a work of art becomes meaningless.²²

To come finally to the point, if as Paul Tillich asserts, for a culture which has no utopia the present is inhibiting, the future holds no promise and the danger is very much there, along with the danger of falling back on its past, the implications for Africa are disturbing. Since we now recognize that utopian literature, when it is futuristic and forward-looking has made inventions possible, what happens to Africa where no anticipatory utopia has been identified to open up possibilities for man? Does this situation find her, as this study has earlier suggested, a society for whom lack of anticipatory invectiveness has meant a "stagnant, sterile present" where "not only individual but cultural realization of human possibilities are inhibited and remain unfulfilled?" The answer is not far to seek. We live in an age where "transfer of technology" is on everybody's lips, but we continue to send our best engineers and technologist to train in the effete factories in London when common sense dictates that they train in Japan whose innovative technology and technique of adapting other people's methods to suit her environment without destroying her culture, is the wonder of modern technological age. Since we do not project problems in the future and start to think of solving them now, it has not occurred to policy makers in various African governments to embark on massive exposure of our engineers and technologists to the wonders of Japan so that they may learn how Japan maintains and enviably buoyant economy while it imports 100 per cent of its oil and 90 per cent of its steel

---

²¹ Cesaire, *op. cit.*, p.74.
²² David Rubadiri, "Why African Literature," *Transition* (Kampala), Vol.4, No.15 (1964), p.41.

requirement: how Japan has succeeded in beating the West as its own game.

If an African architect or engineer is asked to write an essay on "African Architecture," he would likely wax lyrical on the great pyramids at Gizeh or the lighthouse at Alexandria. He would go back to the past. Any wonder that in an era when Europe and the West worry about conservation and how to preserve the environment, none of us bothers about what would happen to our beautiful rivers in the year 3000 or what happens to our wild life and our environment.

Since a people's world-view is reflected, for the most, in its concept of utopia in literature, and since utopian literature seems, in part, to be a reflection of and blue-print for that people's strategies for coping with the problems of the present and the future, a people without a forward-looking utopia is one without any concept of its future destiny. Here is where Azania comes in. Azania is a land literally flowing with the proverbial milk and honey, and with its mines literally scintillating with gold and diamonds. But in spite of the fact that these black people of South Africa are brutalized, alienated and exiled in their own country by a hostile white race, there is no sustained, prophetic-imaginative literature emanating from the South African peoples in exile, projecting into the future a time of final re-union or return of her scattered peoples to their promised land, to a new Jerusalem. There is much in their literatures about their painful exile, about their Exodus and Babylonian captivity but without a triumphant crossing of the Rea Sea as a prelude to an apocalyptic return in history (after the last white man must have been imaginatively driven into the sea), or through peace (by a *Deus ex machina* accomplished by divine intervention in historical time) Thus, a people like those of Azania who have no utopian blueprint imaginatively projected, or a coherent course of action realistically mapped out, may never, like the Israelites, achieve that moment of a final triumphant return and re-union which we associated with the legend of the Israelites.

In sum, Africans are a people who seem to be content to be facing all sorts of challenging futures without any organized or coherent blueprint (imaginative or practical) for solving the problems posed by the future. It is the disturbing conclusion that this study has no way of evading.

4

Politics in the West African novel*

To begin with, man, according to Aristotle, is a political animal, and no one need be surprised that the novel which is the one genre of literature manifestly originated and promoted by the bourgeois class would naturally gravitate into the realm of politics which normally deals with the day-to-day management of public affairs. The formalist may talk of "the poem *per se*," of beauty being its own excuse for being, of a poem (or novel for that matter) not existing to reach or even to please but to exist and be beautiful, but the discerning reader knows that art is propaganda where the writer is the persuasive purveyor of truth even if, in higher art, the end-result is an aesthetic experience. In the main, though, most literary periods are influenced by political events which, some assert, have become the major determinant of norms in the periodization of literary history. Political events seem to be the sole determinant of literary history: periods like "Commonwealth", "Restoration" are used for English literature; "Colonial" and "Revolutionary" in American literature; and "pre-independence" and "post-independence" periods in African literature.

But beyond lending mere appellations to literary periods, politics enters literature through the latter's affective powers, through what we normally term, the pragmatic theory of art for, directed always toward the audience, the pragmatic theory looks at art as an end, since very writer wants to change the perceptions of his audience, to give that audience a new way of looking at an

---

* First published in Kuka (1989), 20-34

experience. In the affective or pragmatic theory of art, we use the adage:

> Some wish to change men's minds;
> Others wish to change the world men live in.

The political novel in West Africa seems to adhere to Frantz Fanon's "fighting phase" (third phase) of colonial and post colonial literature, when "the native...turns himself into an awakener of the people; hence comes a fighting literature, and a national literature."[1] The West African novel is, from its inception, an exercise in politically creative commitment in prose. I define, therefore, in the broadest terms as political, any novel in which the author's concerns with public themes and public welfare are pre-dominant; especially any themes that extend beyond the concerns of the individual self and embrace the collective destiny of nations or the masses. Politics enters the novel at those times when the fate or destiny of peoples or classes are locked in the death throes of survival, when continuity in a people's way of life is threatened; when alien forces by way of military forces or colonial invasion endanger a people's future or make that future uncertain; and, in our body politic, when the vultures of corruption descend to devour a people's cherished ethical, religious or moral values.

In the light of the above, the West African novel was born in response to colonial invasion and its abuses which threatened our collective security as a people; it has since then been sustained by reaction to our collective disenchantment with political independence; and it will further thrive by protests to abuses inherent in the inequities engendered by the kind of society we have chosen to operate—inequities that have often erupted into open class or ethnic warfare. In the end, this study will posit that what unites our writers of the political novel is utopia—their single-minded quest for a just and egalitarian society free from oppression and exploitation by both external and internal masters.

According to Joseph Jourbert (in *Pensees*)

> Force and right are the governors of this world;

---

[1] Frantz Fanon, *The Wretched of the Earth*, translated by Constance Farrington (London: McGibbon and Kee, 1965), p.179.

force till right is ready.

The goal toward which our political novelists tend is that golden era when right will be ready, cushioned, of course, by economic abundance and the absence of want. West African novelists who are politically attuned are therefore in quest of that epoch in our lifetime or in not-so-distant a future when (now that we have achieved political independence) bribery and corruption will be wiped out from our body politic; for that time when intellectuals will take over political control which they have hitherto left in the hands of illiterate politicians and the military; for that time when politics is played here, as in Europe and the West, according to the rules of the game. If we must begin from the beginning, I must assert that the informing spirit of the political novel in West Africa is, in the main, the question of identity—the question of who we are, and what our position is among the community of nations. Respect for our identity is the motivating force behind Hamidou Kane's *The Ambiguous Adventure*, Achebe's *Things Fall Apart* and *Arrow of God*, Camara Laye's *The African Child*, and Armah's *Two Thousand Seasons* and *The Healers*. To just glance over our shoulders and look at poetry and criticism, the question of identity is behind all the ink spilled on the Negritude movement and in literary criticism, it is manifestly behind the spirit which informs the aims and the goals of the writers of *Toward the Decolonization of African Literature*. Professor Ernest Emenonyu had this in mind, also, when he attacked Lindfors for asserting that Ekwensi "obtained his stimulation from third rate American movies and fourth rate British and American paper-back novels", preferring himself that "no literary godfathers" outside Africa be found for African writers; urging in the same tone that "if none other, African themselves will recognize when a writer succeeds in portraying this authentic picture of the African and his setting."[2] All these amount to what we call "cultural nationalism" in our literatures, and "cultural nationalism" makes a political statement or at least assumes a definite political posture. If we are forced to generalize, we may assert that the preoccupation of most of our earliest novelists was with the matter of identity.

---

[2] See Ernest Emenyonu, "African Literature: What Does It Takes to be its Critic?" African Literature Today, No.5 (1973), pp.5, 7.

When the gag was removed from the mouths of West African writers through independence, they embarked on a systematic denunciation of the colonial regime Mongo Beti's *Ville Crueelle and The Poor Christ of Bomba* began what may be termed the West African "protest" novel. Ferdinand Oyono's *Une Vie de Boy*, Ousmane Soce's Mirages de Paris, Bernard Dadie's *Climbie*, Sembene Ousmane's *O Pays, Mon Beau Peuple*, and Olympe Bhely-Quenum's *Un Piege Sans Fin*—each draws, through sarcasm, sinister images of cruel, dishonest, debauched, and ridiculous colonial masters who use violent and cruel police officers and bloodthirsty prison administrators to humiliate and often kill innocent Africans.

In Anglophone West Africa, the politically attuned novelist revealed in very bad light the subversion of post-independence hopes and promises by those who were banked upon to redress the wrongs inflicted by the colonial masters. "Seek ye first the political kingdom" was the battle cry by Nkrumah who asked for the opportunity to be given Africans "to govern or misgovern themselves". Disenchantment ensued unfortunately when the "political kingdom" was achieved and the rulers including Nkrumah, set out on a path a misgoverning themselves. In novels by T. M. Aluko (*One Man, One Matchet*); Achebe (*A Man of the People*); Munonye (*A Wreath for the Maidens*); Armah (*The Beautyful Ones Are Not Yet Born*)—all made subtle and overt suggestions as they expressed their disenchantment with our failure to successfully operate a party-system democracy; as they pointed out in disgust the circumambient presence of bribery and corruption in our body-politic; as they expressed the hope that political salvation might lie in the involvement of the intellectuals in party politics.

It should be re-stated that political novels are written during periods dominated by intense political activity and major struggles, especially in times of war or major revolutions or struggles for independence; in times of great patriotic fervour; and from the desire to reach and speak for large masses of people. We may add that literature and politics are hardly separate and separable in the sense that political developments could determine the course of literature and in certain times, literary activities have been known to influence political developments. In France, for example, Emile Zola's *J'accuse* and Andre Gide's *Voyage au Congo* were inspired by the Dreyfus episode and the Congo question respectively. They, in turn, helped to determine the outcome of these two issues: the one leading to the release of Captain Dreyfus, and the other leading to the termination of King Leopold's hold on the Congo.[3] In the United States of America, the civil war embarked upon by President Lincoln to emancipate the slaves was supposedly triggered off by Harriet Beecher Stowe's Uncle Tom's Cabin, so that when the author was introduced to Lincoln after the war he quipped: "Are you the little woman who started this war"?

The desire to speak for the masses, and to free them from political and economic strangulation has led to another brand of the political novel in West Africa championed by avowed socialist and Marxist-oriented writers. Their main aim is to achieve the Marxist utopia—equality of the classes—by imbuing the oppressed populace, if possible, with enough revolutionary fervour to rise up and effect a social revolution. In Nigeria, we have Festus Iyayi (*Violence, The Contract*); Kole Omotoso (*The Edifice, The Combact, Sacrifice*); Femi Osofisan (*Kolera Kole*); Bode Sowande (*Our Man and the President*); Sonata Olumhense (*No Second Chance*). In the Ivory Coast and Senegal, *Dadie's Climbie* and Ousmane Sembene's *God's Bits of Wood* and *Le Docker Noir* carry forward the struggle of African trade unionists to effect, if possible, the dictatorship of the proletariat and achieve the political-cum-socialist utopia advocated by Karl Marx.

Although not noticed by many, West African female writers have embarked upon the writing of novels with the lodestars of political implication. Their works are, in the main, radical in orientation and feminist in contemporary literary parlance, and the feminist posture they have assumed makes a strong political statement. Read Nwapa's *Efuru*, and you cannot miss the aggressive and fierce independence of the heroine; and read Idu and you find a debased man like Amarajeme who has no inner resources, who constantly borrows money from his wife and who, when his wife deserts him hanged himself with a rope from the thatched roof of his hut. Nwapa's rambunctious "daughter" Buchi Emecheta carries the feminist trend rather too far in *Second Class Citizen*, but the

---

[3] See Raymond Okafor, "Politics and Literature in the Ivory Coast", *Kiabara*, Vol. II (1979), p.166.

technique is the same adopted by Nwapa, especially in *One is Enough*. What these women and their followers elsewhere in West Africa (Aminata Sow Fall and Mariama Ba) do specifically is to fight sexism and male chauvinism in our literatures by debasing the image of the man and elevating that of the woman, and by creating women who are fiercely independent, who are capable of economic self-sufficiency, and who are "not anybody's appendage".

The aim is to present a "corrected" image of the female (normally debased, helpless, dependent, a prostitute, a concubine, in the hands of male writers). Mariama Ba in *So Long a Letter* carries on her own feminist, private warfare (supported by Aminata Sow Fall) against the practice of polygamy in Moslem West African counties. Polygamy she urges, places educated women in a second class role, breaks hearts, breaks families, and sometimes places the hapless men she creates, in very untenable and debasing positions.

I have hinted earlier that political novels emerge also in times of war, and the Nigerian civil war gave rise to a large harvest of war novels each determined to make a strong political statement. I have in an earlier publication[4] adduced the following reasons why the ex-Biafrans wrote war novels:

1. Self-exculpation: to demonstrate that Biafrans had this ugly war imposed on victimized, blameless, oppressed Igbos by blood-thirsty and hate-filled Nigerians.
2. To put the historical records straight and record a memorable if traumatic experience in the political life of Nigeria and for the benefit of posterity.
3. For propaganda purposes: to score a diplomatic point by pointing out to the international community the real and hidden issues involved in the war and to prick the conscience of the allies on the "wrong" side of the conflict by subtle hints to them about the course of action they should have taken had they known the "facts".
4. To propagate the impression that while the shooting war is over, peace had not been won and that the struggle continues, especially the struggle for full reintegration into the mainstream of Nigerian life.

---

[4] Charles E. Nnolim, "Trends in the Nigerian Novel", *Matatu*, Vol. 2 (January, 1987), pp. 7-22

5. To recapture the Biafran manhood lost in the battlefield and substitute the power of the pen for the impotence of the Biafran soldiers armed with sticks and light weapons against Nigerian superior firepower, and in the process to highlight the pyrrhic nature of the Nigerian victory which was an overkill: the giant who jubilates for crushing a baby.
6. To depict the sufferings and the agonies, the dislocations and brutalities experienced by civilians during the conflict and to highlight the greed and corruption of officials in high places who have cashed in on the tribulation of the populace as opportunities for self-enrichment.
7. To demonstrate to outsiders the true state of affairs within Biafra by showing that all was not well within, that the Biafran army was at war with itself and was at times experiencing a civil war within a civil war – the army against itself and the civilians against the armed forces, and that at certain points during the war, the ideal that was Biafra was subverted from within leading mass disenchantment.
8. On a higher artistic level, to re-order reality and experience made chaotic by the war situation.

Those interested in reading the Nigerian war novel will find the following authors and titles useful:

1. Victor Uzoma Nwankwo: *The Road to Udima*, 1969
2. John Munonye: *A Wreath for the Maidens*, 1973
3. I. N. C. Aniebo: *The Anonymity of Sacrifice*, 1974
4. Flora Nwapa: *Never Again*, 1975
5. Eddie Iroh: *Forty-eight Guns for the General*, 1976, *Toads of War*,
   1979, and *The Sirens in the Night*, 1982.
6. Cyprian Ekwensi: *Survive the Peace*, 1976, and *Divided We Stand*,
   1980.
7. Ossie Anekwe: *Come Thunder*, 1984
8. Isidore Okpewho: *The Last Duty*, 1976
9. Andrew Ekwuru: *Songs of Steel*, 1979

By way of summary let me re-state that the West African political novel started with a search for identity and moved on to protest colonial abuses. After that, despair and a sense of failure crept in at the corners as the writers saw no end to the fiasco in both economic and political matters in our body-politic which have continued to deteriorate as the years rolled by. The female writers see no end to their plight as they take on in futility, a liberationist, feminist stance. Achebe's last novel, *The Anthills of the Savannah* shows even a deeper despair as the military dictatorship has gone berserk by continually eliminating themselves, especially as they military, after marginalizing the intellectuals on whom earlier writers have banked upon for our salvation in the realm of politics, started to kill off those intellectuals in the cabinets. The West African political novel wears a very unhappy face as the utopia sought for—political stability and economic self sufficiency—seems to be a mirage, a chimera.

5

The Nigerian tradition in the novel*

Many a critic might feel that it is much too early to speak of the Nigerian tradition in literature or of the Nigerian tradition in the novel. Perhaps it is, given the short span of the emergence of our written literatures on the world scene. But African fiction, including Nigerian, has been the subject of intense critical analysis in recent times, and we can no longer hide under the pretext that an attempt at deciphering trends is till premature.

By "tradition" I mean in this study the literary conventions and habits of expression used by the Nigerian novelist in the practice of his art, plus the observable narrative technique employed by the Nigerian novelist to highlight the Nigerian world-view in literature and by the Nigerian tradition in the novel, I mean that tradition which takes its roots from our oral literature and is given ballast by our folkways. Since, by "tradition" we normally mean a body of beliefs, customs, sayings, literary conventions and devices and habits of expressions handed down to a writer from the past—by the Nigerian tradition in the novel I further mean the tradition that respects, copies from, makes use of, and owes allegiance to our folk literature and creatively makes use of our local proverbs, legends, folk tale, local myths, *et cetera*, in giving expression to our national culture. I go even further to mean that tradition in which the voice of immemorial community, vestiges of primordial ritual and ceremony, and a judicious blending of our folk culture form the bedrock and the building-block of the novel's literary expression and narrative technique. I do not mean by "tradition" a "period" in the Nigerian novel, for we are all still sharing a simultaneous

* First published in Commonwealth Novel in English, vol. ii, No. 2 (1983), pp. 22-40

existence with both our novelists and our novels. The idea of "periods" in our literature will be left to our progeny. Nevertheless, this study tries to play a searching light on the essential line of development which seems to have emerged or is emerging in the brief span of the Nigerian novel—the main observable currents and constants as contradistinguished from the accidental or the peripheral. Furthermore, I do not mean by "tradition" what our novelists have borrowed from Europe or the West. I rather mean, what our novelists have made our own, different from any other, in spite of the circumambient presence of Europe and the West in all our literary endeavours. My over-all aim is to stress what is indigenous in our novels.

Having made the above observations, I must hasten to add that conformity to the tenets of this "tradition" would be the ideal rather than the norm, and that the Nigerian novel thrives on the protean nature of its variety rather than on strict adherence to a procrustean straight jacket called its "tradition". But to go to the novelists proper, the reader must be cautioned that we cannot deal with all Nigerian novelists in a short study such as this. We shall, therefore, confine ourselves only to those novelists who are either important historically or have established a tradition or have brought about some technical innovation to the art of the Nigerian novel. If we start chronologically we must necessarily mention Amos Tutuola, but only in passing, since his fiction provides the only a curious phenomenon in the history of the Nigerian novel. But before we tackle Tutuola, we must look again at the novel genre in its history and its meaning.

The major concerns of the novel, as literature of the bourgeois class, are with the problems of everyday living, the problems of human relationships, close attention to the realities of the bourgeois, the life of business and commercialism, the problem of life in modern cities, increasing class mobility, and the acquisition of money and material possession in a competitive world. Now, Tutuola's fictional world is a far cry from these novelistic conventions. While the tradition of the novel is the tradition of realism in literature, the use of traits drawn from the common idiom of life, the world of Tutuola's *The Palm Drinkard* and *My Life in the Bush of Ghosts* belongs to the fictional world of the bush and the jungle, of fantasy and the superstitious. Margaret Laurence writes in *Long Drums and Cannons* that Tutuola's forests are "the forests of the mind where the individual meets and grapples with the creatures of his own imagination."[1] Tutuola experiments with ethnic Yoruba myths which he has built up into his own private mythopoeia. We read Tutuola once and we have had it. It does, indeed, take perseverance to finish any one of his dream tales. We read Tutuola through as duty and not for our own literary enlightenment and edification for, in the Nigerian novel, Tutuola leads to a literary cul-de-sac. After one book by Tutuola, one has had enough, for Tutuola is not a novelist in the conventional sense, since a novelist usually deals with ordinary men and women projected on a realistic literary canvas. Tutuola, as I have said, leads to a literary cul-de-sac for there is no writer on the Nigerian scene today who imitates or copies him.

Furthermore, Tutuola fails us in his inability to make creative use of his private myths to describe real life situations. In the final analysis, therefore, Tutuola's use of Yoruba mythopoeia is novelistically still-born, for Tutuola is frozen at the level of the Tale and he has failed to elevate his creative talents to the level of the Novel whose province is the human predicament. But in the final analysis, to Tutuola will go the credit of being the first Nigerian to experiment (though unsuccessfully) with the novel form. Also, we shall always give him the credit of being the first Nigerian to "Africanize" the English language and domesticate it for local use in fiction. Moreover, we must admit that Tutuola's works have strong roots in our folk tradition, in our myths. He is the inaugurator of what approximates the Gothic tradition in our fiction, but he is not a novelist who deals with the problems of ordinary men and women with whom the reader vicariously identifies. Rather, Tutuola's forte is the tale, and when the history of our literatures come to be written, Tutuola will be classified and identified with other tellers of the classical tale—story writers 'like Edgar Allan Poe and Nathaniel Hawthorne. He will, therefore, not be forgotten for, as Eustace Palmer says: "His place in African letters is assured because he represents the transition from an oral to a written literature."[2]

We pass on to Cyprian Ekwensi. He is a writer over whom we might slightly disagree. He is a writer who owes a lot to the Onitsha Market pamphlet literature. And this literature owes a lot to the

---

[1] Margaret Laurence, *Long Drums and Cannons* (London, Macmillan, 1968), p.147.
[2] Eustace Palmer, *The Growth of the African Novel* (London, Heinemann, 1979), p.34.

tradition of the Italian novella. The novella gives the impression of dealing with life directly and paints scenes from the ordinary realistic view of life. Bourgeois literature, from the novella to the novel is representational in its realism and reportorial in its style as opposed to the fantasy of romance literature which is non-representational (i.e. not drawn from the common idiom of life). Onitsha Market pamphlet literature, as Emmanuel Obiechina has demonstrated, is literature for the masses and is paralleled to the novella of Boccaccio's Decameron.[3] Like the novella, it tells stories about the common people and supplies us virtually with the stylistic traits we find in Ekwensi's canon.

If we must, therefore, talk of the origins of Nigeria's first real novel—*People of the City*, 1954, by Cyprian Ekwensi—we must trace the roots of this novel to the Onitsha Market pamphlet literature. Ekwensi is therefore Nigeria's first real novelist. He is, in his own right, a literary pioneer whose main contribution to the Nigerian novel is that he is Nigeria's Daniel Defoe chronicling life in our cities. Ekwensi is Nigeria's novelist of the city heavily indebted to the Onitsha Market pamphlet literatures and suffering from its disability—in Ekwensi, we see the sad omission of cultural assertion or cultural nationalism. In him there is no attempt to correct the distorted impression of the African as enthroned in Joyce Cary and other Western writers who revelled in depicting the African as a noble savage or the disoriented African. He owes his literary debts to the pulp literature of the Western world, to writers like Edgar Wallace. No native proverb, no folk tradition, no Igbo myths and legends, no masked spirits, no wrestling in the traditional *Ilo* ever found space in Ekwensi's pages. But what he does with his characters is unique in the history of the novel in Nigeria. The individualism of his characters concerns him very much. Their development and existence in a wicked world concerns him. The judgments they make and the consequences of that judgment (most often ruinous) concern him He is a chronicler of men's inner lives, their inadequacies, their defeats, either because they refuse to fight or because they refuse to face themselves—their inner selves. He is excited by the prostitute, the crooked politician, the money-grabber, the sex maniac. His characters are mainly sinners, fallen men and women fighting to establish their identities in a terribly wicked and

---

[3] Emmanuel Obiechina, *An African Popular Literature* (London, Cambridge University Press, 1973), p.10.

vengeful world. All the unhappiness of his characters stems from one vital fault: they cannot stay quietly in one room but must be embroiled in action, not in the village but in the teeming city where they feel compelled to immerse themselves in the ecstasies of life. What energizes Ekwensi's characters, the compelling principle in their lives is money, sex, and power. Ekwensi is the first Nigerian novelist and he might be credited with establishing the picaresque tradition in our literature—the tradition of the migrant from the village to the city and from place to place within the city. But his picaro are not tongues in the classic sense. They do not come from the lowest stratum of society. They are not rogues as such, although only a thin line separates some of their rascality from criminality. Some are indeed criminals.

In style, Ekwensi has nothing enviable to pass on to posterity: forced didacticism, weakness in character delineation, untidiness in plotting, loose structure, lack of distance between author and his subject matter, and melodramatic endings are the observable aspects of his style. There is nothing to emulate in these. If the Nigerian novel had followed in the footsteps of Ekwensi, it would have been a sad thing indeed. In sum, Cyprian Ekwensi's novels bear a certain brittle quality because he starts most often with a framed idea, with an abstract truth which illustrates an idea about life, and then he forces his story to fit his ideas. His novels thus bear certain well-defined affinities with those of the pioneer early eighth century English writers like John Bunyan and Jonathan Swift—pioneers in the development of the English novel. Cyprian Ekwensi usually begins with a moral vision: "the city has a corrupting influence" or "the wages of sin are death" and then proceeds to tell his story to fit his moral philosophy. Ekwensi is thus a writer of what Arnold Kettle calls "the moral fable" not because he is more concerned with morals than other Nigerian writers but because his central moral discovery seems to have been made before he starts writing his novel."[4]

We pass on to Achebe. While Cyprian Ekwensi wrote for the semi-literate masses to whom he preached, and while he owes his literary origins to pulp fiction and chap-books, Achebe wrote for a more sophisticated, more educated audience and owes his literary debts to the great masters of the English novel—to Joseph Conrad,

---

[4] Arnold Kettle, *An Introduction to the English Novel* (New York, Harper and Row, 1968), p.40ff.

as some critics have asserted. Achebe is the inaugurator of the great tradition of the Nigerian novel. He is concerned with structure and form. He is very original, technically, and he has turned his genius to high-lighting the dignity in our folkways and our oral heritage. He is first and foremost concerned with cultural assertion and is a pioneer in what has come to be called cultural nationalism in Nigerian literature—in his stressing the innate dignity of the Nigerian—especially the Igbo man—and in his concern with the rehabilitation of the image of the black man already distorted by European writers.

Achebe is a pioneer in more ways than one. His novels set in traditional Igbo society—*Things Fall Apart* and *Arrow of God* have come to be regarded as the archetypal African novel. The archetypal African novel, according to Charles Larson, in *The Emergence of African Fiction* is one which describes the impact of the coming of Europeans on African societies and the disintegration of such African societies as a result.[5] Ngugi wa Thiongo's *Weep Not Child* and *The River Between* are such novels. In Nigeria, there grew up a crop of novelists whom we must call the literary sons of Achebe—John Munonye in *The Only Son*, T.M. Aluko in *One Man, One Wife*, Onuora Nzekwu in *Blade Among The Boys*—these are almost blind imitators of Achebe, and may be forgotten in the literary history of our country since what they have tried to do was done much better by Chinua Achebe.

Achebe is also a pioneer in another kind of novel—the situational novel, again to borrow Charles Larson's terminology. The situational novel exists to present a group-felt experience, so that whatever happens to the hero or character in the novel, the final result is felt by all the people involved in the story. The individual thus becomes identified with the community and acts as that society's consciousness. For example, what happens to Okonkwo, in *Things Fall Apart*, echoes what happens to Umuofia as a community. In *Arrow of God*, the voice of the community is clearly heard, and Ezeulu mirrors that community He is the collective consciousness of Umuaro and his own disintegration in the end mirrors the disintegration of Umuaro as a community. The voice of the community is clearly heard in Elechi Amadi's *The Concubine* and *The Great Ponds*, in Onuora Nzekwu 's *Wand of Noble Wood*,

---

5 Charles Larson, *The Emergence of African Fiction* (Bloomington, Indiana: Indiana University Press, 1971), p.117.

and in Flora Nwapa's *Efuru*. No Nigerian writer weaves our proverbs, our myths, our legends, our rituals, and our ceremonies into his narratives as much as Achebe, and none mirrors his society as imaginatively as Achebe. Achebe has thus established a great tradition in the Nigerian novel—the tradition of cultural nationalism, the tradition of ancestor worship, the tradition of great restraint and the art of the unsaid, the tradition of delightful turns of the proverb, the tradition of architectonic and definite concerns with form within the novel.

In sum, when all things are considered, we must all hark back to Achebe for what is great in the tradition of the Nigerian novel, that tradition which, in addition to embodying the best in the art of the story and the best technique in the form of the novel, promotes our awareness of what is really great and dignified in our culture, salted with the lilt of our local proverbs, the charm of our folkways, the respect of our ancestors, the beauty in our tradition—in sum the rehabilitation of the dignity of the black man bruised and damaged by the colonial master.

Flora Nwapa is important in the history of the Nigerian novel. But like Tutuola to be important, historically, is not synonymous with belonging to the great tradition in the Nigerian novel. Her importance derives from the fact that she is the most important female novelist in our society. Flora Nwapa is a novelist with a mission—to redeem the disparaged and debased image of women in our literatures—women debased by male writers like Cyprian Ekwensi and Chinua Achebe. She is out to present a "corrected" view of the female image in our literatures, to show them as capable of personal and economic independence, of dignified comportment. Nwapa, as a novelist, is a feminist at war with the male writer's image of the Nigerian Woman. She is out to fight sexism and male chauvinism in our literatures.

Nwapa's women are secure. They know their roles both in marriage and in society and they fulfil them adequately. But they are rather rebellious, rather fiercely independent. In *Efuru*, the character of Efuru is the embodiment of ideal womanhood in the Nigerian novel. She is beautiful, elegant, respectful, independent, rich (by all local standards). Idu, in *Idu* is the ideal wife, the perfect woman, the hospitable neighbour.
No woman in Nwapa's novels is a parasite that depends on men for sustenance. Only in Nwapa's novels can we see a well-to-do woman

who lends money to a man who is perennially indigent. When Efuru's husband deserts her and elopes with another woman, there was no hand-wringing. She bears it stoically, with admirable dignity. And when the second husband falsely accuses her of adultery, she deserts him and returns to her father's house and finds fulfilment outside life with a man.

In Idu, on the other hand, it is the man who has no inner resources to fall back upon, who "hanged himself from the thatched roof of his hut" when his wife deserts him. To bring out this contrast is part of Nwapa's mission in her novels. In *Things Fall Apart*, while it is taken for granted that Okonkwo has "justifiable anger" when he beat his youngest wife for not preparing his lunch in time, in Idu, wife-beating is severely frowned upon.

Flora Nwapa is also important in another respect: she is the novelist of the traditional woman's point of view, the chronicler of their gossips and endless chatter ("You know women's conversation never ends," *Idu*, p.97). We return to Nwapa for the traditional woman's preoccupation with the importance of children in an African marriage. Only in Nwapa do we fully glimpse the agonies attendant on a childless marriage for the Nigerian wife. Childlessness in Ojiugo's marriage with Amarajeme leads to her desertion of the latter for the more virile Obukodi. And Amarajeme's suicide by hanging comes as a consequence of that desertion. The raison d'etre for all marriages in. Nwapa's novels can be glimpsed in the following passages in *Idu*: "What we are all praying for is children. What else do we want if we have children?"[6]

Munonye is not a minor novelist by any stretch of the imagination. But he is not so important. We read Munonye for the story, for his interest in family relationships. Yes, Munonye is the novelist of family love and pride in family ancestry. Not for him the great issues affecting the nation, nor for him questions about who gets a share of the national cake, but of boys and girls growing up in the family, of mothers and fathers anxiously watching their children grow up and fall in love. His is always a miniature canvas in which a few families are sketched and their allegiances, rivalries, marriages, and quarrels occupy centre stage. In *The Only Son* it is the sensitive relationship between a troubled widow and an only son (who proves a disappointment) which engages us. In Obi, it is the childlessness of the marriage between Joe and Anna and the temptations which

[6] Flora Nwapa, *Idu* (London, Heinemann, 1969), p.150.

beset them as a young Christian family which engage the reader Munonye is the novelist of happy marriage and happy family life within the nuclear household. *Bridge to a Wedding* is the best realized example of Munonye's technique. In it, there is a great interaction among the members of Kafo's family, and there is great humour spiced with sly digs and harmless name-calling among the children. The entire family is at peace with itself, with Anna always singing or humming the Ave Maria, with her husband always pulling her legs and teasing her with one or the other of his practical jokes.

Family relationships are the central driving force in Munonye's novels—their loves, their secrets, their anger, their anxious separations and ecstatic reunions. They call each other pet names, endearing names, funny names. They give and take in marriage and thus build bridges that cut across towns and villages. In *The Oil Man of Obange*, it is indeed excessive love and concern for the welfare of one's children that land Jerry in disaster. But in spite of all this, Jerry was happy in his marriage with his equally doting wife, Marcellina.

As for Elechi Amadi, we go to him for exciting narrative. More than this, we go to him for plots with adequately motivated conflicts, with strong interplays of one force against another. He is strongest in depicting two strongly realized characters in sharp conflict, in rivalry, in fights. No one will forget the clash between Madume and Emenike in *The Concubine* or between Olumba and Wago the Leopard Killer in *The Great Ponds*. The plot of well-defined conflict is the legacy of Elechi Amadi—conflicts that involve larger communities in inter-village or inter-town conflicts and wars. Furthermore, Amadi's philosophic pessimism must go down in the annals of the Nigerian novel as most reminiscent of the Greek tragic mode. In Amadi's tragic vision, man is a mere toy in the hands of jealous and angry gods. But while in Greek tragedy there is a tragic flaw in the character of the hero—a fault or miscalculation which detonates the fatal explosives that the Fates had laid on the path of the tragic hero (for example, Oedipus triggers the explosion of those fateful explosives through his pride and stubbornness), in Amadi, a perfectly virtuous and faultless individual comes to a cruel and tragic end and no amount of expiatory sacrifice or life of moral uprightness is enough to change his or her destiny once the character is *fey* or fated to die. In *The Concubine*, neither the exemplary Emenike nor the devoted Ekwueme nor even the near-perfect Ihuoma is spared the avenging wrath of the powerful sea-god which was taken it upon itself to possess and jealously guard Ihuoma. Amadi's tragic vision thus appears fragile because it is a vision of life devoid of the moral conflict which the tragic flaw in a character triggers in the character's collision course with his destiny.

The Nigeria-Biafra war has introduced another literary dimension into our novels. There is now a crop of war novels each of which gives an insight into the internecine conflict. Nearly all of these novels just give a nodding concession to fictionality. Most are bland, reportorial, journalistic, with no message, no lessons to impart, and no thematic concerns to espouse. The titles merely show their topicality: *The Anonymity of Sacrifice*, by I.N.C. Aniebo; *Survive the Peace*, by Cyprian Ekwensi; *A Wreath for the Maidens*, by John Munonye; *Forty-Eight Guns for the General*, by Eddie Iroh, and *The Last Duty* by Isidore Okpewho. Okpewho's is significant because his novel is written from the non-Biafran vantage-point. None of these novels has gone beyond the reportorial present to embrace cosmic implications or lessons drawn from the war. None has been able to sketch for us a lost generation—people hurt physically and psychologically by the war—people who have lost their values and their bearings as a consequence of the war-experience. The Nigeria war novel is yet to be written.

But Gabriel Okara and Wole Soyinka in their own contributions to the novel genre in Nigeria displayed fresh insights that show great artistic vision. Both Okara's *The Voice* and Soyinka's *The Interpreters* are novels about post-independence Nigeria. The convoluted tale which both novelists tell in their own unique way is about the plight of the artist and the intellectual in post-independence Nigeria, in a Nigeria where no one dares be different, in a country too busy with Second and Third Development Plans to take note of the intellectual or the artist.

Okara's *The Voice* is the story of the intellectual as rebel. The hero's quest—trying to find from people whether any one of them has got "it" alienates a lot of people—in fact, the entire community, and threatens Chief Izongo to whom Okolo's voice is "like the voice of a mosquito which had driven even sleep out of their eyes." Chief Izongo is a demagogue and is power hungry and shows this by trying to maintain the status quo and his personal privileges by intimidating the people into believing that he knows better what is good for them. Okolo's obsessive quest, asking everyone if he has got "it" threatens everyone because he is asking them if they are satisfied with the way they are governed, with the quality of their lives and whether they have indeed allowed Chief Izongo "to buy the insides of all the people." He goes so far as to tell Abadi who has got his M.A. and Ph.D. but not "it", why this is so.[7]

Okolo is a rebel against the powers that be, against the rulers and politicians and the populace who have accepted "the shadow-devouring trinity of gold, iron, concrete." People like Chief Izongo continue to rule because ordinary people don't want to upset their lives by questioning and resisting the status quo. To Okolo, the worst enemies of society are those who say like the messenger: "As for me ... if the world turns this way, I take it. Any way the world turns I take it with my hands. I like sleep ... so I do not think," and like the elder who thinks nothing can be done when he says: "If they do anything I agree, since they do not take yam out of my mouth." These are people who have not got "it". They are the "think-nothing people" who are "like logs in the river" and "float and go whither the current commands."

Now, Okara's *The Voice* (1964) mirrors the predicament of the intellectual in post-independence Nigeria. Society has no place for him. He is a nuisance. What happens to Okolo, Okara implies, will happen to any intellectual who does not take his time For the people of Sologa bundled Okolo and Tuere and exiled them in a floating canoe, with their limbs tied up, and they inevitably drowned in a whirlpool. So, *The Voice* is a prophetic novel that opens up new directions in the novel tradition in Nigeria. It is a voice crying in the wilderness about the way society treats its intellectuals. Our society, Okara implies, is not yet ready to accommodate questioning gadflies, independent-minded intellectuals and free-thinkers who try to jar us out of our complacency. We are too busy acquiring material wealth and adulating our rulers to question the method by which we are governed. The drowning of Okolo and Tuere by society is symptomatic of the social ostracism our intellectuals suffer at the hands of the powers that be.

After Okara, Soyinka next engages our attention. He follows in the tradition of Okara, but while Okara deals with the ostracism of

---

7 Gabriel Okara, *The Voice* (London, Heinemann, 1969). This and other quotations are taken from this edition.

the intellectual, Soyinka deals with the ostracism and alienation and demoralization of the artist in a society too busy, too utilitarian, too committed to the teething problems of an emergent nation to take notice. All of Soyinka's interpreters—Kola, Sekoni—are artistis who, for the most part, have their artistic intentions thwarted by public servants.

Soyinka's interpreters and Okara's Okolo act as the conscience of the nation, the only ones who dare raise their voices against the authority. And neither Okara nor Soyinka falls back on his past, on tradition.

Both mirror the immediate present and deal with individuals who have refused to be an appendage to the government in power. This, in itself, is an advancement from the likes of Onuora Nzekwu and Elechi Amadi who make a ritual of our traditions in their writings.

In Soyinka and Okara the isolated intellectual or artist now occupies centre stage. Satire and social commentary dominate these novels, especially Soyinka's.

The ancestry of Soyinka's *The Interpreters* runs through Voltaire and Rabelais to Lucian. The satiric thrust is at hypocrisy in all its forms, and characters are usually the mouthpieces of ideas they espouse. Since the emphasis is on ideas, the author relies heavily on a free display of intellectual gymnastics, overwhelming his targets with an avalanche of his own or his characters' jargon. The organizing principle in Soyinka's *The Interpreters* is not around any novelistic form known to modern practitioners but in dissection, in analysis, in erudite discussion of the issues under attack. *The Interpreters* belongs to a genre of prose writing known as contes *philosophiques or romans philosophiques* in which dialogue and raillery at society's ills is the organizing principle and central subject matter.

Soyinka's satire is Horatian rather than Juvenalian—the intention is to ridicule, to highlight through gentle and broadly sympathetic laughter, the foibles and the failures and the ills in our society. But Soyinka's genius is often in danger of being obscured by the cobwebby tangles of language which give expression to ideas so finely imagined.

Soyinka's mouthpieces, his interpreters, use organized parties and social get-together to declaim against the callousness, the debasement of standards in Nigerian society, the injustice, the hypocrisy, the social snobbery, the nepotism, the mediocrity of civil servants, the corruption of our officials in high places, and the aimlessness of our intellectuals, including the "interpreters", themselves.

In the long run, we will long remember Soyinka for his erudite prose and for extending the frontiers of the English language in our literatures. He is the most literary of our prose writers, the James Joyce of our literary artists. And if we take the *Season of Anomy* into consideration along with *The Interpreters*, we shall remember him for boldly weaving both foreign and local myths into the fabric of his narrative, for making creative use of both classical and Hebraic mythology.

A general commentary on the predicament and place of the Nigerian novelist is in order here. The Nigerian novelist is a brave soul writing in a foreign tongue and copying a tradition the roots of which he hardly understands. For example, some Nigerian novelists are not fully exposed to the many genres of the novel form. They have not experimented with the romantic novel, the bildungsroman, the gothic novel, the novel of ideas, the epistolary novel, science fiction, the utopian novel, the stream of consciousness novel, and the futuristic novel.

The one distinguishing mark of the Nigerian novelist is his timidity. He is not adventurous. He is not daring. He is afraid of exploring new frontiers of fiction. That is why he works on a very small canvas.

That is why after Achebe pre-empted them by making use of our oral tradition and exploiting the implications of culture-conflict, almost every other novelist got mired in that method and became nothing more than a mawkish imitator. I have mentioned the smallness of the canvas of the Nigerian novelist. He is parochial in his concerns and limited in his vision. His is always one small corner of the world, and most often it is his immediate past. This contrasts with modern trends in the European novel. Being heirs to a race of people that see themselves as world conquerors, the European novelist writes with the universe as his canvas. His outlook is global. He is forward-looking and projects himself imaginatively into writing futuristic literature. Read Orwell's 1984, More's *Utopia*, Bellamy's *Looking Backward* and you see what a mind a fertile imagination can do. By writing science fiction, the European novelist has made it possible for man to land on the moon, because he has earlier on, imaginatively landed man there.

So, the Nigerian novelist should come out of his shell and be more imaginatively enterprising. He should study Ali Mazrui's *The Trial of Christopher Okigbo* and learn a few lessons from the author's intellectual and imaginative courage. The Nigerian novelist can help shape Nigeria's future by imaginative projection. What kind of society would Nigeria have in the year 2080? How would her citizens intermix? Would they then be real citizen of a free Nigerian or would state of origin be the criterion? What kind of shifting political alliances would we have then? Could we hear, in fiction, the voice of a model Nigerian in 2080?

An important aspect of the Nigerian novel must be mentioned here since it has become the proverbial pebble in the Nigerian novelist's shoe—the problem of language as a medium of communication. Here, the Nigerian writer is still unsure of his touch. Should he write in what has come to be called *the vernacular style* where Achebe has excelled? In this style English language is grafted on to the speech patterns of local speakers, with a heavy sprinkling of the local proverb. This style is best seen in *Things Fall Apart* and *Arrow of God*. Cyprian Ekwensi distinguishes him-self in the use of *Pidgin English* which is the standard mode of communication among the masses of urban dwellers in West Africa. This fits perfectly with his city novels. He fumbles his way through *People of the City*, his earliest novel, until he perfects this style in *Jagua Nana*. In any case, we expect to find in one novel by a Nigerian, what we call *Standard English* (which is used when an author speaks in his own voice or in the voice of an educated character in the novel, but which is not purely the English of the English man) inter-mixed with *been-to English* (which is the language of the sophisticated elite among the characters)—a style which is used with a devastatingly comic and satiric effect in Soyinka's *The Interpreters*. We also expect to find in that very same novel *Pidgin English* and the *vernacular style*, in addition to a few native or vernacular words and phrases thrown in for good measure but possibly explained in the glossary in the form of a "dictionary of strange words." The problem of language as a medium of communication is still very much with the Nigerian novelist and solution to this problem will, it seems, continue to elude the Nigerian writer for some time to come.

Finally, we must not lose sight of the constraints under which the Nigerian novelist works. First, and foremost, he writes in a foreign language and this severely limits him in the use of idiomatic expressions. Secondly, the Nigerian novelist must work for a living while he practices his art: There are not art academies, no literary grants, no fellowships, no chairs in the universities for writers in residence, no writers' journals devoted exclusively to interviews with well-known writers or to tips from great practitioners on the practice of their art. We are, unfortunately, still in a country of philistines too busy with survival of the nation to worry about the fate of her artists. We live in a country that is yet not ready for her artists. If this persists for long, the future of our Nigerian novelists will be a bleak one indeed.

Prolegomena to a definition of the African aesthetic in literature*

I must first call attention to the key words in my study. "Prolegomena" simply means "prefatory remarks". My audience, therefore, must be warned that the study which follows is not definitive by any means but merely suggestive: it just draws attention to a study that needs to be made. I must also caution my audience from the beginning that by the nature of my study, what follows are sheer gropings into polemics rather than any attempts to grapple with particularities and minutiae.

No critic in the past, that I am aware of, has tried to give African literature a sense of its generic uniqueness or a clear sense of its formal conventions or a clear definition of its aesthetic. When, therefore, it comes to literary criticism, one must admit that African literature has had no systematic attention paid to it by any great critic with the synthesizing mind of an Aristotle. The reason is simple: African literature is very new on the world scene (thirty or forty years old) as far as literatures go; it exists in mixed forms (oral, written in vernacular, written in foreign languages); it has suffered from its inception from the stigma of inferiority branded on it by former colonial masters; it has had many extra-literary pressures placed against it, especially from missionaries and from publishers; and finally, it embraces a thousand and one genres that have to be re-defined individually, in their African context.

---

* First appeared in BA SHIRU, Vol.7, No.2 (1976), pp.56-74

One other preliminary chore: what does this study mean by "African Aesthetic?" For the purposes of this study I mean a system of isolating and evaluating the literary works of African peoples; a system that reflects the special characteristics and the dynamic imperatives of the African experience as reflected in its literature. I also mean here, by "Aesthetic" not "the branch of philosophy dealing with the beautiful", but rather, with the theories and unspoken imperatives that govern the literary creations of modern African writers—imperatives that could be pinpointed as certain constants that are decipherable as recognizable features of African literature. My meaning, also, subsumes this: attempting to decipher the well-spring of the African writer's inspiration—what it is that 'kicks him in the stomach,' as it were, and following this, what it is that emerges when the finished work fulfils the artist's intention. In other words, I intend to approach the phrase "African Aesthetic" as the way modern African creative writers view and express their universe and the result of what they have viewed and so expressed. What then follows, what I have termed my mere gropings into polemics, are attempts to identify the categories into which the finished literary works of African writers seem to fall, generally.

The first question that comes to mind is one that requires an awesome answer. The question is this: what is it about Africa that makes it so unique an entity that it demands a definition of its own aesthetic? It is an awesome question because "Africa" is an ill-defined world that often excludes Africa North of the Sahara but includes Africa South of the Zambezi; or conversely it often includes Africa South of the Sahara but excludes apartheid South Africa (depending on intentions). In each case, those involved are peoples different from one another in culture, history, geographical location, language, et cetera, as the Zulu from the Tuareg, and the Watusi from the Igbo. Add to this the difference in climates, the discordance in political ideologies, the factionalism in religious persuasions, the diversity in historical influences, and you have a continent as hard to categorize as any on the face of the earth. But for the purposes of this chapter, "Africa" simply means Africa South of the Sahara.

To begin with, to be able to define the African aesthetic in literature, a glance at a society in the dim past—the Greeks, whose aesthetic principles in art are well-defined—would help a little. When we talk of classical Greece, we are reminded at once of Greek art. The Greek artist tended to ignore the emotional, subjective feelings of the artist himself. The emphasis was on something outside the artist's mind—the thing he was trying to imitate or re-create. Objectivity was the aim and the hallmark of Greek art, for this artist was judged by the skill with which he imitated nature successfully, and *imitation* meant 'copying' the essential and persisting forms in nature.

In the Greek artist's attempt to fulfil or complete nature, a harmonious design bent toward a logical, well-rounded and logically finished totality was the aim. Hence, the Greek aesthetic was concerned with form, with completeness of outline, and with subduing the part to the whole. One easily sees this in the emphasis on the total figure rather than on colour in their painting. Thus, in a society that placed much value on rounded forms and ideal figures, the all-rounded individual was the ideal hero.

With the above in mind, let me list headings under which what might coalesce in the future as signpost for discussion. Of the African aesthetic in literature (after the sound and the fury of the present have long become dim echoes in the past) might be organized:

i.   Oral literature and the folk tradition
ii. Cultural nationalism and the Negritude movement
iii. Ancestor worship
iv. Literature of colonial experience
v.   Politically committed literature
vi. The literature of Apartheid
vii. The problem of language in African literature.

The above, by no means, exhausts the list, but for the purposes of this study they will serve as signposts under which one could argue one's case, although it must be admitted that at this time certain trends on the African literary scene are still too much in a state of flux to be identified with any amount of certainty.

Traditional African Art and Folk and Oral Tradition

We are all by now victims of a cliché about traditional African art being communal (since it invariably expressed tribal values and emphasized clan solidarity); that it was functional and utilitarian;

that it always served a religious and social purpose, and that invariably it was executed on the prompting or desire for worship and in the service of ritual. Traditional European art, on the 'other hand, was said to be individualistic, egoistic, striving after abstract beauty. But these statements must be taken for what they are worth—generalizations. I am not convinced that pop art, even though European, is individualistic and egoistic. Pop art serves a mass culture, and I am not so sure it strives after pure beauty. And who is so blind to the social, political, and ritual importance of the celebrated works of Euripides and Aristophanes, and of Virgil, Horace, and Juvenal—all of classical antiquity—and of Byron, Shelley, Voltaire, Rabelais, to speak of modems.

One, therefore, is bound to dismiss these case-hardened platitudes on the communal function of traditional African art, and when they are repeated by intellectuals who pride themselves on being the new arbiters of taste in matters relating to African literature, one is bound to resent them. In a recent publication, Chinweizu, Madubuike, and Onwuchekwa Jemie tell us:

> The artist in the traditional African milieu spoke for and to his community. His imagery, themes, symbolism, and forms were drawn from a communally accessible pool. He was heard. He made sense. and again: For the function of the artist in Africa, in keeping with our traditions and needs, demands that the writer, as a public voice, assume a responsibility to reflect public concerns in his writings, and not preoccupy himself with his puny ego. Because in Africa we recognize that art is in the public domain, a sense of social commitment is mandatory for the artist.[1]

Now, these are barefaced platitudes and since the troika speak with dead seriousness, one is bound to conclude the troika are uninformed, for the present study will demonstrate that African literary artists are the most committed in the twentieth century. Secondly, the stand taken by the troika is downright insulting to our artists who are, in fact, the best prepared practitioners of their craft in all art history: they are the most travelled; they have been exposed to comparative literatures of the world; they have, on the average,

---

[1] Chinweizu, et al., "Towards the Decolonization of African Literature, *Okike*, Vol. III (June, 1975), 74, 78-79.

stayed in school longer than any literary artists of any other epoch or continent we care to compare them with. And to pretend for one moment that no traditional African artist spoke to himself and practised a privatist mysticism is to display a puerile naïveté that flies in the face of historical facts. One wonders whether the troika are blind to the existence of secret societies and secret cults in pre-colonial Africa. Was there no art that ministered to these secret cults and served the cabal? Would not that art indulge in privatist mysticism since only the initiated knew what it spoke about? And what of the masked faces that preponderate in African art? Were not masks worn by only the initiated? The oracles in pre-colonial Africa, also, spoke in cryptic language, and the art that decorated their shrines which were guarded vigilantly by a few select priestly class, surely spoke to only the initiated. Cabalistic societies in pre-colonial Africa, produced esoteric art works and some of the songs they sang in their gatherings were not the common property of the populace, for they were certainly arcane.

Generalizations, therefore, will not do. I am more willing to be convinced by Isidore Okpewho who admits that traditional African art did in many instances aspire to the beautiful, that it often existed for its own appeal to the eye, and that many a time it had no known ritual origin or societally inspired functional value. And according to Okpewho, "the urge to create beauty will remain an integral impulse whatever the level" the African artist may be involved in.[2]

Some old African art did aspire to the beautiful. Art for art's sake (a phrase that seems to frighten certain African aesthetes, Chinweizu *et al.*, surely among them) does not necessarily mean extreme individualism, '*me* against everyone else'; it rather implies, even when it strains after pure beauty, '*me* in relation to my community' not '*me* divorced from my society'. Art for art's sake is not a prerogative of the mind of Europe. African artists did create for sweet beauty's sake; they spoke a private language of their own; they expressed their individuality in their artefacts. It seems that because of our recent colonial experience and our collective efforts to fight off the undignifying experiences of colonialism, we tend to forget that the society that produced Ife bronze heads had no collective enemy to fight off. They had no ideological battles to declaim against. They were relaxed. They could afford to speak in

---

[2] Isidore Okpewho, "The Aesthetic of Old African Art," *Okike*, VIII (July 1975), 39.

cryptic language, yes, to themselves!

What I intend to do in this study, of course, is to re-spell out certain functions of our folkways that our writers and critics might do well to take a second look at. To whatever society (secret or communal) that our traditional folkways and oral tradition appealed they did have the appreciation of the beautiful in mind—beauty surprised at its own arrival—in addition to performing the following functions:

i. impart practical wisdom
ii. provide some didactic purpose by teaching lessons in prudence, generosity, patience, wisdom, and common sense
iii. point to a moral through songs, sayings, legends, myths, proverbs
iv. make people—especially younger members of the society—aware of
   their ethos, their cultural heritage, tribal history, mores, laws.

African folkways and the oral tradition dealt with man's dilemma in his existential being and tried to grapple with man's dilemma and adventures in life as Tutuola's *A Palm Wine Drinkard* makes clear. Furthermore, our folkways posed one important question: How does each generation handle the human dilemma as opposed to generations before it: i.e. realistically, or obliquely, i.e. romantically? The aim of our folkways was then to utilize its many conventions in order to instruct, to amuse, to warn each generation on how to handle the human situation through songs, song-tales, riddles, beast fables, parables, riddles, jokes, proverbs, anecdotes, legends, fables, epics, myths, folktales, and short stories.

Our ancestors indulged in *riddles* to test one's knowledge of wise sayings. They made use of jokes to release tension through laughter, to make a point, and to avoid direct confrontations. Proverbs (accepted as truths ascertained through experience) were used to offer instruction on how to avoid pitfalls in life. Proverbs were also employed to instruct, advise, warn, guide. And the importance of proverbs in our folkways is seen in the way the oral performer made repeated use of them through the *adage*, a more succinct compression of the proverb; the maxim, which contained more practical advice than the proverb, etc. The parable was used to expand the proverb and to teach, guide, and allow universal application to certain truths. *Myths* preponderated in our folkways because, in the absence of scientific inquiry and proofs, some explanations had to be found for the sources of the great forces in nature (e.g., life and death, the nature of the heavenly bodies, the struggle between good and evil, the origin of the seasons, and so on). Myths were also used to show the ways of the gods with men. Fables were told in order to guide through allegory, by holding up man's self-delusions for his own personal examination. Another aim of the fable was to point out a moral and impart the wisdom of the tribe. Along with fables, *folk tales* were told to draw attention to the doings and the plight of the little people of the society and how the gods rewarded them for their honesty or punished those who were greedy or overambitious. Finally, *legends* and *epics* were historical accounts about people who really lived in the dim past. The epic hero (usually the founder of the tribe who successfully battled with spirits for seven days and seven nights) was romanticized and celebrated and often deified as super human. The idea was to instil pride in the origins of the tribe.

In traditional African literature, the oral performer spoke in prose and verse and song. He usually told of happenings in the land of spirits—a land that could be reached after crossing seven expansive seas and grassy woodlands, away from all human habitation. Usually one travelled with protective unguents rubbed all over one's body. The oral tale invariably ended in a moral, a fact that has misled critics like Charles Larson (see *The Emergence of African Fiction*), into forcing all modern African novels into a procrustean folklorist straight jacket.

As I shall argue later, what we call 'cultural nationalism' in African literature is quite misdirected. Cultural nationalism should concentrate on enriching and reviving our folkways rather than assuming its present defensive posture. The richer our literatures are in our folk tradition the more authentically African they would ring.

Ancestor worship

The belief that the living and the dead belong to the same category of beings and are in constant communion with one another has been expressed often enough in modem African literature as to form part of its aesthetic. It is called ancestor worship. We find this in Birago Diop's poem "Souffles" with its refrain of "the dead are not dead"; we find this in Tutuola's *The Palm Wine Drinkard*, where the hero goes off in search of his own palm wine tapper in the land of the dead; and Chinua Achebe admitted in an interview with Lewis Nkosi:

> I think I'm basically an ancestor worshipper... Not in the same sense as my grandfather would probably do it, you know, pouring palm wine on the floor for the ancestors...With me it takes the form of celebration and I feel a certain compulsion to do this.[3]

And in *Things Fall Apart* Achebe tells us:

> The land of the living was not far removed from the domain of the ancestors. There was coming and going between them, especially at festivals and also when an old man died, because an old man was very close to the ancestors. A man's life from birth to death was a series of transition rites which brought him nearer and nearer to his ancestors (p.115, Fawcett edition).

In the *Dark Child*, Laye Camara's ancestor worship manifests itself in totemic myth, and totemism is manifest in the "animal-ancestor" his father worships. The little black snake would speak thus to Camara's father in a dream:

> Lo, I am the guiding spirit of thy race, and it is even as the guiding spirit of they race that I make myself known to thee, as to the most worthy. Therefore forbear to look with fear upon me, and beware that thou dost not reject me, for behold, I bring thee good fortune.

And when, at last, Camara's father decides to reveal his special relationship with the snake to his son, he admits:

> My name is on everyone's tongue, and it is I who have authority over all the blacksmiths in the five cantons. If these things are so, it is by virtue of this snake alone, who is the guiding spirit of our race. It is to this snake I owe everything: it is surprised, when I awake, to see this or that person waiting for me outside my workshop: I already know that he will be there ...Everything is transmitted to me in the course of the night, together with an

---

[3] *Africa Report* (July, 1964), p.20.

> account of all the work I shall have to perform, so that from the start, without having to cast about in my mind, I know how to repair whatever is brought to me. These things have established my renown as a craftsman. But all this—let it never be forgotten—I owe to the snake, I owe it to the guiding spirit of our race.[4]

In Camara, therefore, ancestor worship subsumes a higher pantheism through the omnipotence of the word and the transforming power of fire, as his father, guided by the little black snake, smelts gold, Camara wonders:

> On these occasions was he not invoking the genies of fire and gold, of fire and wind, of wind blown by the blast-pipes of the forge, of fire born of wind, of gold married to fire? Was it not their assistance, their friendship, their espousal that he besought? Yes. Almost certainly he was invoking these genies, all of whom are equally indispensable for smelting gold.[5]

Nationalism and the literature of colonial experience

As was mentioned earlier, as far as literature was concerned, artistic nationalism should be apolitical and should only be a nationalism that celebrates and revitalizes African oral tradition and its folkways. Such nationalism, therefore, should shun all the "isms" of modern political, economic, social, and ideological struggles. It should rather concentrate on weaving artistically into African creative literature the logic of our traditional legal system, the soundness of our healing ways, the meaning of our ritual, the beauty in our traditional art. But it should be a nationalism that is not *heard* but *overheard*: it should be handled with sophistication and dignity. No screaming, no noise, no sabre-rattling, no bravado. When Stephen Dedalus, in Joyce's *A Portrait of the Artist as a Young Man*, says at the very end: "I go to experience for the millionth time the reality of experience and to forge in the smithy of my soul, the uncreated conscience of my race", I think he was headed in the right direction toward cultural nationalism. Only an alert, sensitive intelligence can be trusted to give valency to our time-honoured institutions and to husband the artistic heritage of our ancestors.

---

[4] Laye Camara, *The Dark Child* (New York: Farrar, Straus and Girouz) 1970, pp.25-26.
[5] Ibid., p.35.

But we live in a real world and whatever was said about the apolitical nature of literature must be qualified. Capitalism, communism, socialism, democracy, militarism, colonialism—alien words and concepts that have recently infiltrated African political and social systems—these can no longer be completely ignored in our literary expression. But in literature we must never allow them to take over and overrun our artistic expression. For the purposes of creative expression, the African writer must be prepared not only to accept but to accommodate the nationalist implications of the new alien ways in our midst, if only to help him transcend their disquieting influence on his creative temperament through *understanding* them. The writer must possess at all times the highest measure of social consciousness.

By marrying the old folkways to the new colonialist-infiltrated ways of modern African life, the artist should be able to re-channel life's emphasis in order to create new myths out of new experiences. For example, the African in the modern city in torn between the old and the new: How does he cope with the dilemma? How would he weld the old ways with the new ethos without sacrificing his dignity and his values? The nationalist-minded writer must be able to grapple with this, not in the simplistic manner of Ekwensi (the ways of the city are always wicked) but rather, in the manner of Achebe in *No Longer at Ease* and of Soyinka in *The Interpreters*.

That is, a changed and changing African world should have sensitive writers that are able to adjust to its ever-changing societies. And here is the crux of the matter: the writer must be able to make a change of direction in his artistic vision when the life and the world he has always known seem to abandon him or seem to be ahead of him by constantly changing before his eyes. On this note, I might add that Achebe and Ngugi are in danger of suffering an eclipse in their artistic future, for it seems to me that each has exhausted his creative quarry. For Achebe, the nationalist African writer par excellence, his peak was reached in *Arrow of God*. His imaginative quarry was the break-up of the old ways because of the intrusion of colonial, alien forces. Ripples of his insights into the consequences of this clash of cultures are only felt in *No Longer at Ease*. The rest is anti-climax.

For Ngugi, the Mau Mau uprising and the Emergency in Kenya of pre-independence is the well-spring of his creative vision. He groped his way from *Weep Not, Child* through *The River Between* before writing *A Grain of Wheat* where the clarity of his vision is most vivid and most clearly articulated. Unless he and Achebe can demonstrate that their artistic vision has not ossified and case-hardened like those bronze statues of Ife, both suffer the danger of being written off as artists who are only able to produce what Charles Larson has called the African "archetypal novel"[6]— one which describes the coming of the white man and the initial disintegration of traditional African society as a consequence of that.

Taine had suggested in *History of English Literature* (1864) that a literary work is a transcript of contemporary manners, a manifestation of a certain kind of mind, and that we could recover from the monuments of literature a knowledge of the manner in which men thought and felt at a particular epoch in history. The French man, Taine, had suggested (and the English had scoffed at the idea) that the distinguishing mark between the early literatures of Great Britain and that of France was that the former was the literature of a defeated people while the latter was the literature of a conquering people. Well, I am an African, but I will say this, no matter how many skies fall: the major distinguishing mark of African literature of the twentieth century is that it is a literature displaying the mentality of a colonized people. It began in reaction to colonialism; it has thrived in reaction to colonialism One might add an aside here: Defoe's *Robinson Crusoe* and Shakespeare's *The Tempest* could be said to be the beginnings of the literature of a colonializing people—culminating later in Kipling's poetry, e.g. "The White Man's Burden."

Any study of the African aesthetic in literature, therefore, must recognize the fact that the well-spring of African writers' creative force in literature arose from one inherent, though unstated premise; to expose the enemy—the colonialist masters—from without (see Achebe's *Things Fall Apart*, Oyono's *Une Vie de Boy*, Ngugi's novels). This premise has since moved forward to subsume another unstated premise (a very healthy growth): to expose the enemy from within (see Achebe's *A Man of the People* and Armah's *The Beautyful Ones Are Not Yet Born*).

To go back a little in history, it must be remembered that the very first literary works of black Africans began in protest against slavery. Phyllis Wheatley had wished in her poem that others back in

---

[6] Charles Larson, *The Emergence of African Fiction* (Bloomington, Indiana: 1972), p.28.

Africa "may never feel tyrannic sway"—that of slavery, and Gustavus Vassa had strained to establish the torture of what it meant being a slave, as he nostalgically reminisced over the vibrancy of the life he was snatched away from back in Africa. More recently, African poets like the Congolese Tchicaya U'Tamsi, Guinea's David Diop, Togolese R.E.G. Armattoe, and the Angolan poet Agostinho Neto—all made their mark on the literary scene by way of poetry that is inspired by a concerted denunciation of colonial abuses. The cry for revenge, the sarcasm, the biting irony—all are anti-colonial in spirit. In *Neuf Poetes Camerounais*, Philombe writes a poignantly telling anti-colonial poem: "Civilization":

> They found me in the healthy shade of my bamboo hut
> they found me
> dressed in *obom* and animal skins
> with my palavers
> and my torrential laughter with my tomtoms
> my gris gris
> and my gods
> What a pity!
> Let's civilize him
>
> Then they showered my head with their wordy books
> then they bedecked my body
> with their own gris gris then they inoculated me
> in my blood
> my bright transparent blood
> with avarice and alcoholism
> and prostitution
> and incest
> and fratricidal politics
> Hurrah!
> behold me now, a civilized man!

Although the above is laughter-provoking, there is nothing funny in David Diop's poem, "The Time of Martyrdom":

> The white man killed my father
> My father was proud
> The white man raped my mother
> My mother was beautiful
> The white man beat my brother under the highway sun My brother
> was strong
> The white man turned towards me

His hands red with black blood
And in the voice of the Master:
Hey boy! bring me a whiskey, a napkin, some water!

In prose fiction, one of the earliest novels dealing with the theme of colonialism is Rene Maran's *Batouala* (1921). In condemning the crimes of colonialism, Maran addresses the imperialists in the most caustic terms:

> Rabindranath Tagore...told you what you are! You build your kingdom on corpses. Whatever you wish, whatever you do, is steeped in lies...Whatever you touch you devour.

Achebe's *Things Fall Apart* is a much more subtle, yet poignant attack on the disruptive effect of colonialism on an unsuspecting African society:

> Does the white man understand our custom about land? How can he when he does not even speak our tongue? But he says that our customs are bad; and our own brothers who have taken up his religion also say that our customs are bad. How do you think we can fight when our own brothers have turned against us? The white man is very clever. He came quietly and peaceably with his religion. We were amused at his foolishness and allowed him to stay. Now he has won our brothers, and our clan can no longer act like one. *He has put a knife on the things that held us together and we have fallen apart* (my italics).

In Ngugi's *A Grain of Wheat*, the brutality of the British colonizer is recorded in all its stark shock during the Emergency in Kenya. Mugo tells Mumbi:

> When I was young I saw the white man, I did not know who he was or where he came from. Now I know the Nzungu is not a man-- always remember that—he is a devil—devil...I saw a man whose manhood was broken with pincers. He came out of the screening office and fell down and he cried: to know I will not touch my wife again, oh God, can I ever look at her in the eyes after this? For me I only looked into an abyss and deep inside I only saw a darkness I

could not penetrate?[7]

In Achebe's *Things Fall Apart* and *Arrow of God*, the District Commissioner is the villain, the agent that sunders the cohesiveness of the tribe. In Oyono's *Une Vie de Boy* the villains again are the colonial masters who are transformed into Mephistopheles figures while Madam Decazy becomes a Circe figure and the siren that brings confusion into the society. The sole sufferers of their loose living and the wickedness of their lives becomes the houseboy, the poor African boy, Joseph Toundi, whom the author transforms into an innocent scapegoat who bears the "Black Man's Burden'.

Here, too, must be mentioned a body of African literature colonially inspired but much more vituperative. It is literature from apartheid South Africa. While Achebe and Oyono can afford to be subtle, while they and others are even relaxed enough to laugh at the wicked and wily ways of the colonial master, there is nothing subtle or funny about literature coming from Black South Africa. No justice can be done to this body of literature that, ironically, was given impetus by a white man from South Africa—Alan Paton—in a searing pamphlet entitled "The People Wept." Also, in *Cry the Beloved Country*, Paton makes it clear that apartheid is born of fear—fear of whites that the millions of native blacks will engulf them. Because of this fear, he says, there exists in South Africa today a perversion of human relationships. And it is this fear that is the central theme in his novel:

> A sadness falls upon them all... Sadness and fear and hate, how they well up in the heart and mind, whenever one opens the pages of these messengers of doom. Cry for the broken tribe, for the law and custom that is gone...Cry, the beloved country, these things are not yet an end. The sun pours down on the earth, on the lovely land that man cannot enjoy. He only knows the fear of his heart.[8]

It is this fear which brings about the dehumanization of the African, which is the source of the inhuman laws and inhuman living conditions controlled by a set of rules that Nadine Gordimer is concerned with the *The Late Bourgeois World*. It is these conditions

---

[7] James Ngugi, *A Grain of Wheat* (London: Heinemann, 1971), p.207.
[8] Alan Paton, *Cry, the Beloved Country* (New York: Scribner's 1948), pp.73-74.

that preclude any obvious attempts by individuals to establish warmth and love and close relationships across racial lines. These perversions of human relationships make the South African diaspora pregnant with frightening implications.

Nationalism and the negritude aesthetic in African literature

The Negritude aesthetic is the *locus classicus* of what has been described as 'cultural nationalism' in African literature.

> Cultural nationalism, or that aspect of it called literary nationalism, is so fundamentally universal a phenomenon in unequal social situations such as that engendered by colonialism that its inevitability (in the African literary scene) hardly deserves an argument.[9]

The cultural significance of Negritude, Obiechina asserts:

> can best be seen from the background of the usual pattern of cultural nativism which characterizes the struggles of every colonized or oppressed people to re-establish and raise the status of their devalued culture. In accordance with this pattern, cultural assertion may take the form of their extolling - the virtues of specific aspects of their indigenous culture their debunking some specific aspects of the culture of the colonizing or dominant group, or both forms. Thus, Negritude as a typical nativistic movement repudiates certain intrinsic values of European civilization such as its machine technology, its extreme materialism, its contractual determination of social relationships, and its slavish adherence to scientific planning of every detail of life...
>
> The anti-westernism of the Negritude ideology is important only in so far as by devaluing the Western culture the African culture will once more find its pristine dignity. Just as European colonialism by postulating the superiority of its attendant culture undermined the African culture, so, by a natural process of reversal, the African culture will regain his (sic) lost dignity by the destruction of colonialism and through an undermining of the superiority complex

---

[9] Emmanuel Obiechina, "Cultural Nationalism in Modern African Creative Literature", *African Literature Today*, I (1968), 25-26,

of the European culture.[10]

These are important statements on the Negritude aesthetic, although my study disagrees with Obiechina in one important detail: I do not agree, as my concluding statement will demonstrate, that the anti-westernism of the Negritude ideology is important *only in so far as by devaluing the western culture* the African culture will once more find *its pristine dignity* (my italics). The importance of the Negritude aesthetic is more fundamental and more valuable than Obiechina would have us believe.

To repeat here all the known clichés of the Negritude aesthetic would add little to scholarship. A well-articulated African aesthetic, however, must re-emphasize and restate some key points. The Negritude aesthetic tried to kill three birds with one stone: it was at once a revolt against Europe, a search for identity, and a celebration of our Africanness. As a revolt, it began in the Caribbean with the castigation of white society and white values. It was a revolt against assimilation, against white supremacy, against economic exploitation by the West. It subsumes all the known ambivalences one notices in African aesthetic in literature: nationalism anti-colonially inspired literature, primitivism. In it we see Caliban rebelling (this time, successfully?) against Prospero. The idea was to place Negritude in the path of Blanchitude and reduce the latter to ashes. Leon Damas in *Pigments,* Cesaire in *Cahier d'un retour au pays natal,* Jean Price-Mars in *Ainsi parla l'oncle*—all revelled in passionate vituperation and vehement denunciation of Blanchitude by asserting their Negritude. Theirs began as the Negritude of rejection, of anti-assimilation—what Senghor later called anti-racial racism.

But Senghor's brand of Negritude began the Negritude of reconciliation and understanding, thus tempering a movement that was getting out of hand at the hands of Caribbean writers. In *Postface to Ethiopiques* Senghor, who is married to a Frenchwoman, pleads for a crossbreeding between African and European cultures. This crossbreeding, he argues, is inevitable for a richer world culture, for it would hopefully produce "Eurafrica"—a marriage of black and white civilizations that would produce a "concert where Europe is the conductor and Africa the drummer." If for nothing

---

[10] Ibid., pp.27-28.

else, this crossbreeding of cultures would, hopefully, help Prospero learn a thing or two from Caliban, in the optimistic hope that Caliban's liberation would help Prospero turn from a tyrant to a more humane person: the marriage of cultures thus would help humanize Europe.

The second important phase of Negritude is its search for identity - what Jean-Paul Sartre calls the black's attempt to reconquer his "existential unity as a Negro." This search involved a return by the black to his ancestral values, an Orphic descent into the underworld of his soul, a search for a unity of being among all blacks of African origin, a longing to return to African cultural roots and a seeking after Africa's lost pride in its past.

This search for identity inevitably led to the third and most enduring aspect of Negritude. It became a celebration. The Negritude poets loved to revel in the exoticism of their blackness. They pointed out the anlage of the African creative process: that as a basic creative principle the emphasis was more on the vibrations of the word than the word itself, and the insistence on rhythm as a basic creative principle of Negro poetry. This is what Janheinz Jahn identified as *Nommo* or the creative power of the word by which the Black artist weaves a spell by the magic omnipotence of the word or the incantatory magic factor in the poetry of all black peoples which transmutes the poem into something imbued with magic (see Neo-African Literature). What emerges from this posture is that the rhythm, the music, the lyricism, the gaiety that characterize the poetry of all writers of African origin reveal a richer, more relaxed, more natural approach to life by all black people. This has also become a permanent feature of the African aesthetic in literature.

Unfortunately, this celebration did degenerate into what is called primitivism, which Leon Damas articulated in:

Give me back my black dolls my black dolls my black dolls black

And Cesaire in:

Hurray for those who have never invented anything for those who have never explored anything for those who have never tamed anything.

But from whatever angle we view Negritude what matters to me is what this study considers as its most enduring contribution to the African aesthetic in literature. I locate the centre of this contribution in Negritude's concern with the rehabilitation of the black man; in its stressing the innate dignity of the African personality; in its turning for inspiration in art and letters to African folk culture which, it insisted, was still a reservoir of the rhythm and lyricism of its poetry; in its insistence on the "felt" quality of the poetry of all African art of all African peoples; and most importantly, in its encouragement of the study and appreciation of our African heritage. Here, then, is where I strongly disagree with Obiechina.

The Negritude movement, granted, had its weaknesses—weaknesses inherent in the extremity of its posture as committed literature. But although the extremes of Negritude are seen in the writings of Caribbean and Francophone Africans, one must not overlook the writings of Anglophone Africans who, by the subtlety of their works, have expressed the African personality in a more dignified, quieter fashion. In essence, they are *negritudistes* also, for they share as much concern for a cultural rebirth of Africa as their Francophone counterparts, not in overt ideological aggressiveness but by the content of their art, in their treatment of themes authentically African, and in their portrayal of African traditional ways of life. Achebe's *Things Fall Apart* and *Arrow of God*, Soyinka's *A Dance of the Forests*, J. P. Clark's *Song of a Goat*, T.M. Aluko's *One Man, One Wife*, all vividly portray the richness of traditional African culture and, in so doing, they all portray in a most healthy way, the authentic African personality.

The Negritude ideology has veered from the extreme of rejection to the extreme of celebration. The Anglophone writers, I predict, having provided the needed balance, will be trusted to lead us to a much needed Negritude of the fourth phase: a Negritude of honest soul-searching of self-criticism, even of self-abasement, if only to show that the peoples of the African race are not just music and dance and rhythm and loose walking (if they were only these and nothing else, they are nothing!), but are people capable of objectivity, capable of intellectuality, capable of hate-blended prejudices.

The use of language and the African aesthetic in literature

When it comes to the use of language in African literature, the African creative writer's problem parallels that of his European counterpart during the Renaissance: both were confronted with the proper use of language (whether vernacular or foreign) in which to express oneself. Both the English and French writers of the Renaissance and their African counterparts in this century were the victims of a monumental hoax which forced both to suffer from an inferiority complex about their vernacular. In Renaissance Europe, a popular humanist theory insisted that "modern" dialects were the language of plebeians who spoke "vulgar" languages. In the belief that the ancients had used superior languages, Greek and Latin, Francis Bacon, not trusting the survival of the English tongue, had most of his works translated into Latin, and Roger Ascham complained in Toxophilus (1545), which was grudgingly written in English, that "to have written this book either in Latin or Greek...had been much easier." Mulcaster, another English contemporary of Ascham, began a campaign for other English writers to use the English language because English was "the joyful title of our liberty and freedom, the Latin tongue remembering us of our thraldom"—a passage that every African literary artist should paste on his typewriter. Du Bellay in his *Defence et illustration de langue francaise* (1549), appealing to the nationalistic sentiments of his fellow Frenchmen, had argued that French people were as good as the Romans or any other people, ancient or modern, and that it was the patriotic duty of every Frenchman to write in French and thus enrich it with his learning—another wade mecum that is urged on our African writers.

The African writer of today who churns out masterpieces in a foreign language must be reminded of two things. First, one must draw his attention to Dante and Petrarch and Boccaccio. What made Dante a world famous writer who takes his stand by the immortals, are not his writings in Latin, e.g. *De Vulgari Eloquentia* but *The Divine Comedy* written in his 'vulgar' Florentine. Boccaccio's *Decameron* and Petrarch's sonnets—all were written in the vulgar tongue, even though these writers were highly educated in Greek and Latin. By lending the weight of their authority to the vernacular, these writers brought authority and dignity to bear on their native Italian and thus catapulted it into a language worthy of world recognition. This is a healthy nationalism in the use of language in literary expression.

The other thing the African writer must bear in mind is that throughout literary history no writer has been proved great who insists on talking to his own people through an interpreter—via a foreign tongue. The African writer must understand that the only way to internationalize African languages will be to write in them, thus lending their authority and prestige to these languages.

To assume a language, one critic has remarked, is to assume a world. The African writer who writes in a foreign tongue must understand that yelling curses back at Prospero in Prospero's own tongue is half the story and a misguided idea at that. According to George Lamming:

> Provided there is no extraordinary departure which explodes all of Prospero's premises, then Caliban and his future now belong to Prospero...Prospero lives in the absolute certainly that Language, which is his gift to Caliban, is the very prison in which Caliban's achievements will be realized and restricted.[11]

The tragedy of our era is that our African writers not only imprison themselves in the language of their masters but physically imprison themselves in the very land of their enslavers for the paltry glitter of the enslaver's money. Prospero, of course, very cunning and self-effacing, laughs up his sleeves, confident that whatever the African achieves in the way of literary art would only be derivative, and as long as it remains in Prospero's language, it would continue to show the latter's continuing stranglehold.

An important difference then is that while the English or French writer during the Renaissance recognized his imprisonment and thraldom as he wrote in a foreign language and did something about it, the African writer recognizes his bondage in the language of the colonial master but not only does nothing about it but incomprehensibly hugs it more tightly to his breast.

Although Senghor laments, like his European counterpart during the Renaissance, being forced to write in the language of the

---

[11] George Lamming, *The Pleasures of Exile* (London: 1960), p.109.

former colonial master: "Do you feel," he laments, "my suffering and despair, which is beyond compare, to be forced to express in French this heart which comes from Senegal?"[12] Leon Damas welcomes the opportunity French affords him to hurl back insults at the colonial master in the only language he could understand—his own. In a speech at Brazzaville (1954), Damas said:

> The miracle which results in the fusion of our intimate poetry with a language—of completely different origin...is...that the Negro poet finds the right to break with tiresome syntax and can hurl the words of France into a delirious torrent which belongs to the African race alone.

One is not so sure of the wisdom of this posture. In any case, it points out the ambivalences existing in the African writer's perception of the use of a European tongue in his creative expression.

Whatever, of course, is the historical or sociological or even economic (there is the question of audience and the pocket book, you know) imperatives that force African writers to write in a foreign language, the very practice has created one certain desideratum: lack of sublimity (in the Longinean sense) in our writings. I mean here, what Longinus calls excellence of language, nobility of diction, grandeur of thought expressed in lofty language, that spark in language that leaps from the soul of the great writer to the soul of the reader enough to send the latter into ripples of transport. Sublimity will continue to elude the African writer who writes in a foreign tongue no matter what pretences or masks he puts on.

On yes, we shall always praise Achebe for cleverly adapting English to the "speech patterns" of the Igbo. But he himself will admit that whatever Igbo proverb he transliterates into English falls several decibels short of the ŕclat of the original. Writing in alien tongues over which the African writer cannot claim complete mastery, torn between European and one's native speech concepts, unsure of one's audience (or, more accurately, aiming at an alien one), the African writer is inherently handicapped as an artist. Great ideas he may have, inspired insights he may possess, but inspired language and nobility of diction—this last has eluded the African

---

[12] Leopold Senghor in Anthologie de la nouvelle poesie negre et malagache.

writer's repertoire of chameleon-like attributes.

But the core of the problem is etched in a thorny dilemma: the African writer plods along in a foreign tongue over which he has no complete mastery; and he performs worse in his own mother tongue! The colonial master took care of that, too, forcing him in his impressionable years at school to despise his own mother tongue not only through benign neglect of it but also by imposing fines or corporal punishment on anyone who used the mother tongue on the school premises and in some cases during high school, in the dormitory. Never, therefore, having cultivated his own mother tongue and worse, knowing he would have practically no audience if he ever attempted to write in it (with what gaucherie one can only imagine!), the African writer chooses the better of two very bad alternatives: he writes in the language of his enslaver. And seeing what a poor job he does of it, he moves to Europe to be nearer his slave master and master his language some more! Taking all these into consideration, the problem of language in African literature will for a long time be enveloped in a thick fog and resolution of the problem has a very bleak future.

But in spite of everything, we do have vernacular literature in Africa. Thomas Mofolo wrote *Chaka* in his native Sesotho, and some vernacular literature exists in scattered instances in Yoruba and Igbo. But as long as there is no natural or adopted lingua franca in Africa, and so long as the OAU insists on recognizing only three languages—English, French, and Arabic—in its deliberative procedure, so long will our writers eschew the vernacular for lack of audience.

But now comes the crucial question in my study: how does the use of language shape the African aesthetic in literature? The answer lies in the observable turns and twists of language which the African writer has evolved in order to cope with the multi-varied experiences of the modern African Diaspora. In the English language we find the following:

Standard English: used when author speaks in his own voice or in the voice of an educated character in his work
Pidgin English: the spoken language of the masses or urban dwellers in West Africa.
Been-to English: the language of the sophisticated elite who have studied overseas. Often this is affected and stilted. In Soyinka's

The Interpreters this is carried to extremes by one of the characters who pronounces "morals" as "merals" (with Soyinka's double entendre clearly embedded in its implications!)

The Vernacular Style: Here the English language is adapted or grafted on to speech patterns of local speakers, often with a heavy sprinkling of the local proverb. Achebe is the master of the vernacular style.

Vernacular Language: Here we have works written in one of Africa's several tribal languages, as in Mofolo's *Chaka*, written in Sesotho, and as in *Omenuko* by Peter Nwana, written in Igbo.

It seems that this is the pattern into which language-use in African literature will fall in the foreseeable future.

Conclusions and summary statements on the African aesthetic in literature

We must first and foremost admit that African literature is still too new on the world scene for certain literary trends to become recognizable. To expect ossification and to make case-hardened statements about the 'tradition' of African literature is to ignore this fact.

One admission this study has forced me to make is that African literature as it stands today is maggot-ridden to the core: it is flawed by the very nature of its concerns, for it is, in the main, *litterature engagee*, and committed literature has a way of dying a natural death—certain to be dulled and dimmed by the fog of time when the issues it fought over are no longer current. Secondly, its authors have a staggering problem with the use of the appropriate language. If what happened to works written in Latin and Greek by English and French writers during the Renaissance are any indication, death awaits much of what we produce today in foreign tongue. Thirdly, it is socio-anthropologically rooted, which makes our literature hold interest by matters peripheral to literature. When the curiosities excited by our custom become common-place knowledge, much of our current literature will face an eclipse. Fourthly, and very importantly, there is a clear and present danger that those entrusted with the husbanding of Africa's artistic heritage are on the point of selling Africa once again for a mess of pottage: all our known literary artists are domiciled either in Europe or in the United States. We know that any artist worthy of his noble mission must be in constant touch with his society, with his sources, with his roots, for these are the truest and best sources of his artistic inspiration. An artist divorced from his society and his language for too long will soon begin speaking in strange voices. And it is bad enough that our artists write in foreign tongues (a fact that already separates them from the masses of our people). The tendency and fact of being domiciled abroad is the greatest threat to the independence and undiluted autonomy of African art and of our African artists. No tree thrives by being grafted on to the branches of another. "Bring yourselves home!" one cannot help screaming at our literary artists. Only by so doing can African literature be brought home to its roots. And our artists must be reminded that the survival of our cultures and our folkways depends on artists who are in continuous touch with them, who are constantly nourished by their culture, and who keep enriching themselves by deepening knowledge of their heritage. The alternative would be for those who are far removed from their sources to begin shouting loftly platitudes from Sorbonne or Oxford or Harvard at uncomprehending Africans.

As Achebe might tell us, when Mother cow chews cud, the young cow watches her mouth. Our beginning artists need models. How can they take, as it were, the talisman from the lips of our celebrated writers who do not live among their people and with whom they never had the opportunity to share a pinch of snuff or a calabash of palm wine? To live away from one's culture, our artists must be told in no uncertain terms, is to court artistic suicide.

Now, in looking hard at the constants in the African aesthetic in literature, several things stand out. First, since aesthetics deal with the ugly and beautiful, the first question is: how does the African writer deal with the ugly and beautiful in literature? The answer is not far to seek. Since much of African literature is of anti-colonial inspiration, the African writer identifies the ugly with the villain—the white colonial master.

That is, while the exploited, brutalized, and unsophisticated masses of the African people are depicted as the good people, the white colonial master is shown as the embodiment of cunning, vileness, and wicked deeds. In Oyono's *Une Vie de Boy*, the black boy, Toundi, is the embodiment of innocence. He is the victim while his masters, all of whom are white, are devil figures. In

Achebe, the District Commissioner is the evil agent that helps break up the tribe, while in Ngugi, the British and their agents—collaborators and those who have broken their oaths—are the devil figures while native Kenyan patriots and the masses of displaced people are the collective, innocent victims The 'black man's burden' is now the white man.

Even in works where Africans are seen as evil people who oppress their poorer masses, these evil people are almost in all cases the agents of departed whites. In the parlance of post-independence terminology, they are neo-colonialist stooges. We see such corrupt politicians in Achebe's *A Man of the People* and in Armah's *The Beautyful Ones Are Not Yet Born*.

The result is that the African aesthetic in literature, without shouting the slogan "Black is beautiful", has invaded and successfully overturned the sacred cow of the European aesthetic—that white is good and black is evil. In the African aesthetic, white is evil and black is good. In Grabbe's *Duke Theodore of Gothland*, the following dialogue confirms this. Berdoa, a black character sings the praise of his African mistress:

Berdoa: Never, Ella, shall I forget thee, thou purest of African women; how noble was her heart! How woolly was her hair! Two feet-long her bosom. And oh, she was so black, as black as innocence (my underscoring)
Gustav: What? Is innocence black?
Berdoa: Well, we Negroes have a different taste from yours: for us, the beautiful is black, but the devils are all white. (my underscoring)

Senghor and Camara have also extolled the beauty of black women to the consternation, I am sure, of the mind of Europe. This overturning of the set aesthetic symbols of Europe by African writers must be viewed as an important accomplishment of the Negritude movement.

Another important conclusion that this study leads one to make about the African aesthetic in literature is the smallness of the canvas of the African writer, vis-a-vis his European counterpart. The African writer is provincial, even parochial in his concerns while the European writer writes with the whole world as his canvas for he belongs to a race of people that see themselves as world conquerors. While, therefore, the European writer's outlook is global, the African artist writes like one backed into a corner, looking, not for a way to escape, but how to defend his diminished territory. The African writer writes with a defeatist mentality. He is defensive. He is the most apologetic, the most denunciatory, the writer with the least sang-froid in the entire world. This mentality is one that will for a long time deny the African writer sophistication, sureness of touch, elegance of diction, sublimity of language, the echo of a great mind, for the African writer protests to the point of inelegance. He is the most restive, the most fractious, the most splenetic writer in the world, in this century.

The outcome of all this is that while the European writer of the present century is forward-looking, while he projects himself into the future, while he thinks positively and writes futuristic literature, the African writer is both inward and backward-looking busy as he is defending the dignity of his people, affirming the beauty in his women, and decrying the inhumanity of past injustices by former colonial masters. Unless this trend is reversed, posterity will look back on our literature and judge us as the most insecure, the most narcissistic, and the most defensive group of men and women that lived in the twentieth century. Posterity then, in making a comparative study of literatures, will easily see the literature of our former colonial masters as that of a minority people with a majority complex, and ours as that of a majority people with a minority complex. They may find it hard to understand.

Finally, one must point out the 'evolutionary aesthetic progress' of modern African literature as a trend that differs markedly faith the traditional African aesthetic. Traditional African art was not marked by the phenomenon of rapid changes in its aesthetic conception. The society was relaxed.

Rapid changes in social thinking were rare and artistic execution followed very established patterns perfected over several centuries. That is, in the absence of rapid societal changes, 'artistic movements' were either very slow or downright static in traditional African societies. On the contrary, the European aesthetic in art and letters has been marked by rapid changes and sudden fluctuations that reflected the instabilities of their societies. Changes of government (almost unknown in traditional African societies), constant cataclysmic wars involving changes in dynasties, the rise and fall of empires, social and economic revolutions—these things made Europeans view the world as chaotic so that their art not only reflected these changes but also tried, in each era, to be the means of restoring order to a chaotic universe. On the African literary scene we do have already in one generation what has been identified as pre-independence and post-independence literature. If the African writer follows the European beacon his direction will be unpredictable for many years to come.

One more word: a disquieting aspect of African literature is that it has a marked tendency to be more visceral than cerebral. The result has been that *la litterature engagee* has given birth to 'committed criticism'. This has, in turn, given birth to what Solomon Iyasere has called a case of misplaced hostility,[13] especially when an expatriate sees artistic blind spots in our literature. Committed literature and its attendant committed criticism, one hopes, will disappear when we have outlived the insecurities of the present era and settled down to create works that aspire to the beautiful.

---

[13] Solomon Iyasere, "African Critics on African Literature: A Study in Misplaced Hostility," *African Literature Today*, VII (1975), 20-27.

7

A house divided: feminism in African literature*

Ever since that suffragette, Mary Wollstonecraft Godwin, published her controversial *Vindication of the Rights of Women* [1792] in England, in which she hammered on "the tyranny of men" (until the woman she fought for won the right to vote in 1928), the relationship between men and women took on a more exciting turn. Things never quite remained the same for men and women on both the political and literary fronts. On the political front, the first Women's Rights Convention which met in Seneca Falls, New York [1848] was led by Lucretia Mott and Elizabeth Stanton who urged that the American constitution should be amended to read: "We hold these truths to be self-evident, that *all men and women* are created equal." Since then, what most men refer to (with sneer-blended amusement) as "feminism" or "the women liberation movement" has indeed not advanced very far from the Mott/Stanton submission, in spite of the barrels of ink spilt on the issue, whether we listen to The National Organisation for Women in the U.S. (NOW), which organized a much published demonstration at Springfield, Illinois, in 1976 (to urge the Illinois legislature to ratify the Equal Rights Amendment in the American Constitution), or to its adventitious "daughter" in Nigeria termed Women In Nigeria (WIN).

In the feminist movement, politics and ideology collapse and

---

* First published in *Feminism in African Literature*, ed. Helen Chukwuma, Enugu, New Generation Books (1994, 248-261).

merge, even when both its politics and its ideology take what may be termed at times "freak forms", to sneering male chauvinists—from bra burning in the United States (contemptuously referred to as a protest by women "not to be seen with any visible means of support"), to demonstrations with placards (by housewives and company secretaries) reading, ironically, "we shall no longer be dictated to)"; from "streaking" stark naked by undergraduate girls, to "alternative life-styles" whereby a man and a woman share room and bed with no legal ties or bonds; from demands by women for use of sex-neutral words (whereby even God is to be addressed unisexual terms as "S/HE", to denouncing child-bearing and pregnancy as a punishment inflicted on the female sex by God and men. Any wonder that unconvinced and influential psychologists like Freud and Jung insist that women who go to such lengths are abnormal and suffering from either a "castration complex" or worse, "penis envy".

Feminism, as a movement and ideology urges, in simple terms, recognition of the claims of women for equal rights with men— legal, political, economic, social, marital, *et cetera*. Its tenets are more individualistic than communal and thus places more premium on individual self-fulfilment than achieving, in the African context, the collective needs of the community This is where, as will be pointed out in the conclusion, many doubt whether it does not subvert the African philosophy of thought, whether this is not a chink in its armour. But be that as it may the concept of feminism both at the local and international levels has a worm that squirms at its core and is maggot-ridden by its human condition, because the dilemma of the feminist is the dilemma of the proverbial chichidodo which hates excreta with all its soul but thrives on maggots that breed inside faeces. The dilemma is this: woman hates or at least, confronts man, her vaunted oppressor, but needs love; and the love she needs for emotional fulfilment can only be provided by "enemy" man. So, even a genius in her own right. Simone de Beauvoir had to take on Jean Paul Sartre, as life-long companion, in a sort of "alternative life-style" arrangement. And, as Ramatoulaye *(Une Si Longue Lettre)* will agree, when a woman has the love of her man and he hers, she has everything; and where she does not, it doesn't matter what else she has. Any feminist then who is "normal" and well-adjusted in human and societal contexts, loves to be imprisoned in the love of a man, needs the emotional cushions which only a loving man can provide, either through marriage or a liaison..

On another level, in a world that is unfortunately (for the rabid feminist) patriarchal in the main, every responsible normal woman needs a stable home as base, and a home (not a house) is the normal dwelling place of man as the head; even the most uncompromising feminist traces her origins, her genealogy from the male line, hence the last name or surname of every female is patronymic. In burying her name through patronymy—Simone de Beauvoir, Betty Friedan, Elaine Showalter, Mariama Ba, Flora Nwapa, Buchi Emecheta, Omolara Ogundipe-Leslie, Chikwenye Ogunyemi—all surrender themselves to the male, to patronymy for identity, all the fight for total equality still remains in the realm of shadow-boxing. So, since home and family always involve the male as head, the house of a spinster may be a love-nest but it is still shackled with the adventitious connotation of a transit-camp, of a halfway house, for the concept of family in the sociological sense is male-oriented, is patriarchally circumscribed. If, then, the ultimate aim of feminism is total equality with man, the movement should start to fight for change from these fundamentals. And there is yet another dilemma: men are the children of women, and in fighting men, feminists seem to expend inordinate energies in a demeaning fight with their children—children they have carried and suckled. Men are wiser and more dignified; they do not expend their energies fighting their mothers.

II

With the dilemma enumerated above, we come to the next stage of this study: feminism in the African literary scene. The contours of the feminist literary landscape in Africa, in general, and Nigeria in particular, present a panorama of undulating topography. It is a house divided against itself and at present looks discomfortingly like the leaning Tower of Pisa. With a house so divided, there is little wonder the brood is scattered leaving the activists clucking like hens after a swoop from a menacing kite. A close observer would quickly notice that the feminist house in African literature is divided into so many camps, the most identifiable of which are a) the feminists; b) womanists and accommodationists; c) accommodationists; d) reactionaries and middle-of-the-roaders; and e) gynandrists.

Feminists

These fall into two main groups—critics and writers, the critics are led by Chikwenye Ogunyemi and Omolara Ogundipe-Leslie, with supporting voices from Juliet Okonkwo, Helen Chukwuma, and Rose Acholonu.[1] This is an embarassed group that have become panicky, trying to rally and whip into line their fellow writers that deny their involvement with the feminist movement in their public utterances, urging these writers [by sometimes putting words into their mouths] to present a common front, in order to stop those male writers they indelicately call "phallic critics" from putting sand into their feminist garri. These female critics, in addition to demanding total equality with men, add sassy, if saucy and intransigent and rebellious attitude to the feminist ideology.

The second group—Mariama Ba, Flora Nwapa, Buchi Emecheta, Tess Onwueme [as writers], and Ama Ata Aidoo [as writer/critic], are Janus-faced: most of them write feminist tracts in their creative output but deny involvement in the feminist movement in their public utterances.

Womanists/Accommodationists

These are mainly creative writers — Flora Nwapa, Mariama Ba, Ifeoma Okoye, Zaynab Alkali, Helen Ovbiagele. In her "Poetics"[2] on feminism, Chikwenye Ogunyemi [acerbic, erudite, disturbingly incisive and critically acute] defines "womanism thus:

> "Womanism is black-centred, it is accommodationist. It believes in the freedom and independence of woman, like feminism [but] unlike radical feminism, it wants meaningful union between black women

---

[1] See, especially, Chikwenye Ogunyemi: "Woman and Nigerian Literature", in *Perspectives on Nigerian Literature*, VoL I (Lagos: Guardian Books Nigeria Limited, 1988); Omolara Ogundipe-Leslie, "The Female Writer and Commitment", in *Association of Nigerian Authors Review* (1985); Rose Acholonu: "The Female predicament in Our Folk and Written Tradition", an unpublished paper presented at the Fifth Ibadan Literature Conference, 1980

[2] See above

and black men and black children, and will see to it that men will change from their sexist stand...This ideological position explains why women writers do not end their plots with feminist victories."[3]

And Marie Umeh adds that in a womanist novel, "whereas feminist plots end with the separation of the man and woman... womanist novels are committed to the survival and unity of males and females."[4]

Accommodationists

Again, these are all creative writers who are not really out to preach total equality with men. While they advocate some measure of equality, they concede a leadership role to the man and do not contest his headship of the family In their works, they stress as womanists do, the unity of man and woman in spite of bickering, misunderstandings, and the jostling for power. Reconciliation, not separation; convergence, not divergence; love. not hatred; affection, not mere passion; a pooling together of resources, not a scattering; a building together, not destruction of the latent love between the sexes; an establishment of the family under patriarchy, not advocacy for a new arrangement—these form the focus of their own ideological praxis. In accommodation, there is no question of the male's authority and hegemony in the family under a loving, mutually respectful relationship. The champions of this sub-ideology are Ifeoma Okoye, Zaynab Alkali, Helen Ovbiagele, and [equivocally and qualifiedly] Manama Ba.

Reactionaries and Middle-of-the-Roaders

These, again, are writers who either prefer to "stand and wait" [Mabel Segun, Adaora Ulasi] or, having found their voice, prefer to use it in declaiming against the feminist tendencies of their fellow women while at the same time singing the praises of their husbands

---

[3] Ibid, p.5.
[4] Marie Umeh, "Ifeoma Okoye", in *Perspectives on Nigerian Literature*, Vol. II [Lagos: Guardian Books Nigeria Limited, 1988], p.265.

for having planted, nurtured, and raised them with tender loving care in what other feminists would regard as embarrassing self-abasement [Catherine Acholonu in a dedicatory note]. Others like Zulu Sofola and Rebecca Njau are unashamedly reactionary: for forging iron handcuffs to bind fellow women to steel shackles of patriarchal traditions in her major plays, and Rebecca Njau for afflicting her heroine with madness in her major work.

Gynandrists

This is a term struggling still to find legitimacy among feminists themselves, like the term, *Gynacritics*. These are male writers praised by feminists for belonging to the feminist camp or championing the feminist cause. These are male writers, also who are said to cast African women in a good and noble image - Isidore Okpewho, Ousmane Sembene, Ngugi wa Thiong'o, and Elechi Amadi. The Gynacritics would be the equivalent of male gynaecologists who in the practice of medicine see to the health and welfare of women. In literary criticism they are muted to be Ernest Emenyonu and Femi Ojo Ade, to mention but a few.

Having sketched the various groups above, some fleshing out will be in order. To begin from the beginning, we shall first examine the works of Africa's pioneer female' writer, Flora Nwapa who saw it as her duty to present a different image of the African woman from that previously presented by male writers. As the pioneer female African writer, to Flora Nwapa goes the credit of blazing the feminist trail. She definitely saw it as her duty to redeem and correct the disparaged and debased image of African women as depicted by sexist male writers like Achebe and Ekwensi—women created helpless, dependent, brutalized, disparaged, either concubines or prostitutes [destined, in Ogunyemi's words "to carry *foofoo* and soup to men dealing with important 'matters'"].[5] But her first steps into feminism were tentative and faltering. While in *Efuru* and *Idu* she creates super women, she builds into them those traps that will never free women from dependence on patriarchy: they want marriage; they want children; they have sloppy sentimentalism that

---

[5] Ogunyemi, *op. cit.*, p.66.

binds them "in love" to their husbands; they are barren most often in a child-hungry society. Efuru is rich but the curse of Uhamiri which Nwapa afflicted her with, denies her happiness, and Idu is near-perfect but she is tied by maudlin sentimentalism to Adiewere whom she "followed" to the grave carrying a pregnancy. Superior in character, industry, wealth, and beauty, Nwapa's heroines may be; debased, poor, irresponsible, and improvident their male counterparts may be depicted, but Nwapa never frees her fellow female heroines from those "traps" marital, biological, cultural, psychological—that bind them with iron hoops to patriarchy. What with the following statement in Idu which keeps echoing in her other works: "what we are praying for, is children; what else do we want if we have children? And with the following in *One Is Enough* where her feminism reaches its high water mark:

> A woman's ambition was marriage, a home that she could call her own, a man she could love and cherish and children to crown the marriage.

What, then, we call Flora Nwapa's feminism consists in this: she allows complete separation of male and female, as she encourages rebellious, separatist, independent tendencies in her heroines, and in her lack of commitment to the survival and unity of men and women brought together in marriage. Her womanism, then, consists in her denying her heroines complete emotional independence from their men, in her unquestioning apportionment of culpability for infertility to most of her heroines forcing them to consult various medicine-men for cure or leaving the marital home in frustration. In one voice, she says in *Women Are Different* that "marriage is not the only way", but in another, she subverts this stance by depicting th childless, old maid, Rose, with a bleak and lonely future when the question is asked: "but Rose, what had she"? showing thus, that for women, childlessness and spinsterhood are neither a satisfactory nor an enviable way of life.

Nwapa's daughters never quite freed themselves from her janusfaced, confusion-ridden feminist ideology as all seem to be condemned to follow this erratic, con-fused course. Buchi Emecheta first comes to mind; Buchi, who throws all lady-like decorum to the winds and carries personal grudge to the point of nausea. Because her husband burnt the manuscript of her first novel she paints the pictures of her victimized women in the titles of her works. Wicked men have kept forlorn woman *In the Ditch* (1972); made her a *Second Class Citizen* [1974]; a woman whose worth is measured by *The Bride Price* [1976]; or just merely *The Slave Girl* [1977]; ironically experiencing *The Joys of Motherhood* [1979]; and made to bear *The Double Yoke* [1981]. Each title thus reflects just one more phase in the brutalized plight of women in the hands of the "enemy" man. On those titles alone, it could be quickly deduced what women suffer in the hands of man—as slaves to culture, tradition, patriarchy. In technique, where Flora Nwapa merely renders the men of no consequence to allow her superior women to occupy centre stage, Buchi Emecheta proceeds to paint grotesque, repulsive pictures of them. In *Second Class Citizen,* Francis is wife beater, a never-do-well in his studies, while Nnaife *[The Joys of Motherhood]* in addition to his repulsive and ugly mien, is assigned the unmanly profession of "houseboy" in an expatriate's home where he does nothing but cook, sweep, wash for a living.

And yet, while cursing all African men for "treating women the way they do" *[In the Ditch],* one senses the same confusion, the same fuzziness of vision that smudges Nwapa's feminist ideology. Except in *Second Class Citizen* which is autobiographical, all her heroines succumb pitiably to the system they fight so hard to overcome, for Emecheta is not charitable enough to allow them the same success and freedom she allows Adah/Emecheta in *Second Class Citizen.* Akunna dies in *The Bride Price* because she flouts tradition. Ojebeta quite, disconcertedly, in *The Slave Girl* adheres strictly to tradition. Thus, woman loses in Emecheta whether she conforms or rebels. Even motherhood which is the ideal reached after by Nnu Ego in *The Joys of Mother-hood* is no insurance or guarantee against unhappiness since that "joy" is a question mark because: "If you don't have children, the longing for them will kill you, and if you do, the worrying over them will kill you." Where then lies relief in Emecheta? In one voice, Nnu Ego laments: "God, when will you create a woman who will be fulfilled in herself, a full human being, not anybody's appendage", but in another, she roundly condemns her co-wife, Adaku, as a prostitute for successfully making a clean break with marriage and establishing herself independently. As we have seen, the same "traps" which bind Nwapa's heroines to man, to tradition, equally bind Emecheta's protagonists. But, All said and done, Buchi Emecheta is a feminist in her insistence that there is no unity betweens the oppressor, man, and the oppressed victim, woman; in effecting a complete break between man and woman; in insisting on recriminations and acrimony, not reconciliation; divorce, not unity; hatred, not love.

Mariama Ba comes to us as a womanist at heart but a feminist in ideology, for the feminist path she treads is strewn with ambivalence. As a womanist, she tells us through her persona, Ramatoulaye Fall, of her belief in "the inevitable and necessary complementarity of man and woman," of her belief that "life is an eternal compromise". But she is a woman pushed to the wall and on the path of vendetta through her persona, Ramatoulaye. Since *Une Si Longue Lettre* which is an anti-polygamy tract was likely to fall on deaf ers, Mariama Ba is forced to assume a feminist stance since compromise on the issue of polygamy in a Moslem country seems impossible. Having painted Modou Fall and Mawdo Ba as devils incarnate in her reputation-wrecking letter for abandoning monogamy [for Ramatoulaye/Mariama believe firmly in marriage—their womanism], she raises her feminist placard:

> We have a right, just as you [Daouda Dieng/men] have, to education, which we ought to be able to pursue to the furthest limits of our intellectual capacities. We have a right to equal well-paid employment, to equal opportunities. The right to vote is an important weapon.

Her feminism further consists in advocating for divorce where the woman could not bear to compromise like Ramatoulaye, in her praising Aissatou Ba for having the courage to effect a divorce with Mawdo Ba, in advocating a bloody end to philandering by husbands in *Un Chant Ecarlate*, in her allowing her daughters unusual freedom in a Moslem country to wear trousers, smoke cigarette publicly, and entertain male guests privately in their rooms.

Back to Nigeria, the younger crop of feminist writers' give their older mentors cause to worry and leave the likes of Ogunyemi and Omolara Ogundipe-Leslie speechless, either by their unco-ordinated vision or in their back-tracking from the envisaged feminist utopia. Tess Onwueme first comes to mind: in her efforts to keep the feminist flame burning, she creates impetuous, rebellious teenage women who are uncertain whither they are headed, guilty as hell with incest and scandal, searching heedlessly for "a hen too soon". In *A Hen Too Soon* and *The Broken Calabash*, the rebellion and iconoclasm of Gladys and Ona, respectively, seem pointless, for their path of incest and scandal points to no respectable road for others to follow. Since these women go unpunished, they leave us flat and with the nagging question whether we have reached a point where the feminist ideology must be allowed to destroy our ethical, traditional, and moral order. Onwueme's concept of feminism is thus dangerously frozen at the level of adolescent, unprincipled level, and if pursued further, it will destroy society such as we know it, since no mechanism of poetic justice is inbuilt to deal with these breakers of convention.

After Onwueme, the rest is anti-climax, as Ifeoma Okoye, Zaynab Alkali, and Helen Ovbiagele hold out the olive branch and invite the men in, after some initial turbulence, some misunderstanding. These are the accommodationists whose technique it seems, is first to push their women and their male counterparts to the brink, point to the abyss by occasioning separation, allow them miss each other, and then pull them back to themselves for the sake of themselves, letting them pick up the pieces in soft moments of confession, regrets, and forgiveness. This new trend, championed by Ifeoma Okoye *[Behind the Clouds]*, sung by Zaynab Alkali *[The Stillborn]*, and celebrated by Helen Ovbiagele *[Evbu, My Love]*, may look like the stuffing of sand into the feminist garri-sack, by women themselves, but it seems the only sensible ideological solution to the feminist imbroglio: after all, with so many sisters cosily fraternizing with so many of their sexist brothers; with a house so divided; with so many feminists simultaneously chasing with the hounds and running with the deer, the accommodationist path seems to be the only logical one to take. Woman needs solidarity with man for self-fulfilment, and man needs solidarity with woman for self-fulfilment—for there is need for that "inevitable and necessary complementarity of man and woman" about which Mariama Ba makes so much.

If rabid feminists watch with dismay this seemingly retrogressive trend among their younger writers: with Zaynab Alkali allowing Li's dreams to remain a stillbirth [after Nwapa's Amaka, Emecheta's Ada and Mariama Ba's Aissatou had successfully taken the plunge], they will be further dumbfounded by the further surrender to patriarchy and traditionalism by Nana Ai [in Alkali's

The Virtuous Woman]—Nana whom the author further physically handicapped and made "virtuous" because she only treads the conservative path. What might prove worrisome to the feminist cause in Ifeoma Okoye and Alkali is the atavistic recrudescence of Nwapa/Idu syndrome, the maudlin over-sentimentalism which reties Ije and Dozie *[Behind the Clouds]* and Li and Habu Adams *[The Stillborn]*, a subversion of the fight which earlier feminists seem to have won. And for Alkali, especially, the reconciliation of Li and the crippled Habu Adams is the proverbial case of the winged termite that finally fell for the toad after first flying to the high heavens.

The feminist cause suffers further travail and subversion at the hands of the group I call sheer reactionaries and fencesitters—a group led by Zulu Sofola, Catherine Acholonu, Mabel Segun, Adaora Ulasi, and Rebecca Njau. Enough comments have been made about the first two. Mabel Segun and Adaora Ulasi would rather not be bothered. Rebecca Njau and Bessie Head afflict their heroines with madness. It seems that those who are not reactionary or silent, are unkind to themselves and thus do damage to their cause.

III

If the female writers live in a house divided, their counterparts who are critics are much more united in a single-minded effort to carry the fight to the court of the male writers who are their *bête-noir*, their enemy, the agent of their disparaged position, their oppressors. This might be a case of misplaced hostility, for the debasement of the female image is as old as the Bible and the Koran, and has other origins in pre-historic literature and mythology. The image of Eve, [the Bible], Helen of Troy, Circe, and the wicked sirens of mythology luring men to their deaths [classical literature]—all predate Nigerian writers. With the above in mind, there may be no need for the female critics to single out Nigerian male writers for special vilification. Be that as it may, speaking almost with one voice, the feminist critics: Chikwenye Ogunyemi, Ama Ata Aidoo, Omolara OgundipeLeslie, Juliet Okonkwo, Helen Chukwuma, Virginia Ola, Rose Acholonu—all are single-mindedly dedicated to the enhancement of the female image in our literatures. What delights the feminist Aristotle, Ogunyemi, is the unity of intent demonstrated by her fellow critics in academic garb. When she is tired of abusing male writers and critics. she hears kudos and encomiums on her "daughters" who have not spared the male writers and critics. She further gloats over the fact that Omolara Ogundipe-Leslie has spiritedly attacked p'Bitek and Soyinka for their sexist depiction of women in their works. She calls on Virginia Ola, Juliet Okonkwo, Rose Acholonu, and others to close ranks and get their act together.[6] On her part, Rose Acholonu protests against "the consistent brutalization of the female which continues to demean the female image in our literature", and urges the women to rise up and do something because, "the liberation of the female image lies in the hands of the female."[7]

And what irks Ama Ata Aidoo about Achebe and Soyinka is their cavalier attitude to NA omen in their works. Achebe is blamed for allowing Okonkwo to beat his women while his other wives "hover around, whimpering, 'Okonkwo it's enough....'"; and Soyinka is excoriated for creating merely "nimble-footed, wicked-witted women whose roles are only to serve men."[8] But in spite of the above, -like her fellow creative writers [Nwapa, Alkali, Ifeoma Okoye] she denies she is a feminist or at best, she is ambivalent about it:

> "Feminism. You know how we all feel about that embarrassing Western philosophy? The destroyer of homes. Imported mainly from America to ruin nice African women."

Then she quickly adds:

> "I shall not protest if you call me a feminist. But I am not a feminist because I write about women...No writer, female or male, is a feminist just by writing about women. Unless a particular writer commits his or her energies actively to exposing the sexist tragedy of women's history; protesting the on-going degradation of women; celebrating their physical and intellectual capabilities, and above all, unfolding a revolutionary vision of the role of women tomorrow, as

---

[6] Ogunyemi, *op. cit.*

[7] Rose Acholonu, *op. cit.*, pp.3, 13.

[8] Ama Ata Aidoo, "Unwelcome Pals and Deccorative Slaves: the Woman as Writer in Modern Africa," in Afa: Journal of Creative Writing, 1982, pp. 40, 41 Ama Ata Aidoo, "Unwelcome Pals and Decorative Slaves: The Woman as Writer in Modern Africa," in *Afa: Journal of Creative Writing*, 1982, pp.40, 41.

dreamers, thinkers, and doers, they cannot be described as feminist writers."⁹

So, whither African feminism? The answer is enveloped in mists and fogs. The confusion pointed out earlier, among the writers, will seem "to continue unabated, especially now that 'the younger generation of writers have come to realize the incompleteness of woman without man. But from a more philosophical angle, feminism which is western in orientation and individualistic in its goal if made the ultimate good sought after by our women, will eventually destroy the communal nature which is the mainstay of African societies. Meantime, is the conflict of expectations engendered by the clash of feminism with traditional values not the heroines created by Rebecca. Njau and Bessie Head? Is that conflict not the cause of exile in Mariama Ba's work 'where' Aissatou had to leave for New York; and for Emecheta's protagonist in *In the Ditch*. With so many African female writers unsure of the future of feminism and of their rebellious female characters whom they most often destroy or make mad, one could predict a bleak future for the movement.

But all is not lost. The African woman, through the efforts of the female writers and critics is now much more aware of her identity and is determined not only to assert her separate personhood, but also to break away from the encircling shackles imposed by men and tradition, even if, sometimes not so successfully. In the above is the nub of the "gains" made by feminism in African literatures.

---

⁹ *Ibid.* If Aidoo, as writer, seems ambivalent about her position in the feminist camp [like others], Omolara Ogunidpe-Leslie [more critic than writer] is consistent in both her poetry and criticism. In "Africa of the Seventies" and "To a 'Jane Austen' Class at Ibadan University", she strains to admonish fellow women to struggle and ensure that they are not left behind my men in humanity's efforts to change society [see *Sew the Old Days and Other Poems,* Ibadan, Evans Brothers, 1985]. Catherine Acholonu, in a truly ambivalent posture, publicly denies and disowns feminism but, hiding under the mythic/allegorical umbrella in her play, *The Trail of the Beautiful Ones*, makes feminist pronouncements through the mermaids:
The days are gone when we suffocate ourselves under the sea for fear of recognition. These days it is they, these others [the male folk] who have to hide away from us, we are in control.

8

Achebe's tragic heroes*

The challenge which this study poses is not as simple as it seems on the surface. After seventeen years of Achebe studies, what could any critic say that has not been said?

What new facts would the critic unearth that are not contained in *Critical Perspectives on Chinua Achebe*, edited by Inns and Lindfors? The challenge of this essay, therefore, is to try to avoid, as far as humanly possible, a rehash of previous criticism on Achebe and to make use of some critical parallax, in order to view different angles of the same subject matter from, as it were, different observation posts.

A study of Achebe's "tragic heroes" gives the facile impression that Achebe writes "tragedies". For the rabid Aristotelian, only in dramatic works proper, can a critic speak of tragedy in the classical sense of the term. I would, therefore, shift my premise a little by asserting that taken in total, Achebe's philosophic pessimism wears almost in all cases, a tragic face. Achebe's novels belong in the literature of the tragic vision. In a typical Achebe novel, the hero who finds himself in an untenable, often extreme situation, is at the same time a man of uncompromising will, who eventually pays full price for what he wants and for the course of action he has chosen to pursue. On close examination Achebe's handling of his characters bears certain identifiable affinities with the classical concept of tragedy. Tragic events must have significance that transcends the immediate consequences of the events just witnessed. They must

---

* First published in *Wahlverwandtschaften: Elective Affinities* (Bayreuth Boomerang Press, 1993), pp. 87-96.

have a universal human validity that goes to our understanding of the ultimate meaning of life and grapples with many questions about life. And what we expect in a classical tragedy is a sense of dignity because the hero is out of the ordinary, for tragedy is man's encounter with that great and ultimate meaning which the transcendent world embodies. In classical tragedy, man casts himself athwart the purposes of the world which, in the final analysis, is beyond himself. But it is a confrontation of ill-matched powers, and man is bound to lose, but after that loss, there is an adjustment which the immutable world demands before things come once again to normalcy.

The question has often been asked whether there is a concept of African tragedy different from the classical or European conception. Critics of African literature argue that there are certain demonstrable aspects that mark out African tragedy from the European, the major ones being its communal and religious nature—what happens to the individual or the culture-hero involves whole communities and clans. An Okonkwo or an Ezeulu becomes such a culture hero. The very title of *Things Fall Apart* underlines this African conception of the tragic. Achebe thus becomes a pioneer in African fiction of this peculiar view of tragedy, while the European view generally marks out the individual as its quarry for the tragic. Charles Larson in *The Emergence of African Fiction* hints obliquely at this view of African life when he talks of the situational novel of which Achebe is a pioneer—the kind of novel which exists to present a group-felt experience so that whatever happens to the hero or protagonist, the final result is felt by all people involved in the story. The individual thus becomes identified with the community and acts as that society's consciousness. For example, what happens to Okonkwo in *Things Fall Apart* echoes what happens to Umuofia as a community In *Arrow of God,* Ezeulu represents the collective consciousness of Umuaro as a community, and his disintegration in the end mirrors the disintegration of Umuaro as a community.

With the above in mind, a few observations about Achebe's "tragic heroes" are pertinent before we proceed further. In Achebe's canon, man is a shaper of his own destiny, and man's downfall stems, not from the blind operations of inscrutable destiny or fate (as in the Greek example) but from man's decisions and deliberate actions. Achebe's philosophic pessimism thus differs markedly from

Elechi Amadi's own philosophic bent. In Elechi Amadi's tragic vision, man is a mere toy at the hands of jealous and angry gods—a perfectly virtuous and faultless individual, like Ihuoma or Emenike or Ekwueme undergoes cruel agonies or suffering or death, and no expiatory sacrifice or life of moral uprightness is enough to change his or her destiny once he is marked out for suffering or death. Amadi's tragic vision thus bears a certain brittle quality because his is a vision of life devoid of the moral conflict which the tragic flaw in a character triggers, in that character's collision course with his destiny.[1] Rather, in Achebe, man is not a mere toy at the hands of the gods and is not caught in a tragic web from which he cannot extricate himself if he so wills. For him, tragedy is associated with the great crises in human endeavours, and man rises or falls by steering the mazy and harassed course inherent in human choices. In *Things Fall Apart* and *Arrow of God*, neither Okonkwo's nor Ezeulu's hands are tied by the course of events. Had Okonkwo allowed himself to benefit from the experience of exile and been mellowed by the advancement of age, he would have lived to a ripe old age in a changed and changing Umuofia. And had Ezeulu followed his better judgement and listened to the plea of the ten envoys sent by Umuaro to persuade him to eat those two extra yams at their own collective peril, his end and that of Umuaro might have been different.

So, one of the qualities which distinguishes Achebe's tragic hero is that of the uncompromising spirit which makes him an unyielding personality. No fate or destiny ties his hands to a predetermined end. In great tragic action, the tragic hero always pays full price for what he wants in life, and we value heroic action according to its cost to the protagonist. Thus, Okonkwo and Ezeulu display a richer heroism in their great confrontation with the forces of change which they could not cope with, than happens in many other novels of culture conflict coming from Africa. A true hero falls as far as he has risen—the greater the height the more resounding the fall, and no tragic hero worth his salt ever chooses the golden mean in times of crisis. Neither Oedipus nor King Lear, nor even Ezeulu ever stopped to listen to those voices which called for caution and reflection, voices which, if listened to, would have ensured

---

[1] See Charles E. Nnolim, "The Nigerian Tradition in the Novel," *Commonwealth Novel in English*, Vol.II, No.2 (1983), p.32.

longevity for the hero. In sum, Achebe's vision of unresolved contradictions, for his protagonists always find themselves in an existentialist dilemma where they are forced to make their own decisions by which they stand or fall. In highlighting the existentialist problems facing his protagonists, Achebe usually subordinates ethical and moral issues to the existential. And the existentialist dilemma in Achebe's tragic vision often revolves around the Sophoclean view that a man must bear the full consequences for his actions, and pay the full price for his frailties.

Achebe's fictional world is generally one of conflicts and misunderstandings, of inter-clan clashes, of culture conflicts and the attendant disintegration of traditional values of petty jealousies and bickerings among co-wives, of jungle justice and unnecessary violence. There are no happy marriages in Achebe, no soft and romantic moments between husbands and their wives, no intimate family counsels involving a father, his wife and children as is often exquisitely depicted in Munonye. No major protagonist in Achebe ever dies quietly and peacefully on his bed. He either commits suicide (Okonkwo) or goes insane (Ezeulu) or gets blown up in an air raid (Gladys in "Girls at War"), or escapes in a fisherman's boat under whips of panic (Chief Nanga) or ends shamefully in jail (Obi Okonkwo). There is no major protagonist in Achebe who doesn't curse his son and none that takes kindly to change with grace. The mythic pattern, therefore, which informs Achebe's tragic vision is the myth of the triumph of error over reason, of the triumph of conflict and dissolution over peace and unity, of the defeat of the culture- hero by the demon within. His, therefore, is a tragic vision which accretes around the myths of sunset and darkness (for the hero and his culture), the myth of the fall not ascent, of defeat not victory, of despair not hope.

As a respected pioneer in African literature Achebe's philosophic pessimism has imbued African literature with a general sense of loss, enough to be part of its aesthetic, so that our fiction, our poetry and our drama are imbued with this circum-ambient sense of loss—the loss of our heroes, the loss of our culture and values, the loss of our religion, the loss of our land, the loss of our dignity as human beings, the loss of Confidence in ourselves, the moral loss among our youth who have unresistingly succumbed to the allure of Europe, the loss of our language, and finally, the loss of that unity which was our bulwark against foreign invasion. The theme of *Things Fall Apart* thus becomes the archetypal theme of almost all subsequent literary output by the African in this century. Two passages from *Things Fall Apart* are significant; both lament a loss which became a clarion call to almost all African writers who seem to have re-echoed in one literary form or the other Achebe's original vision. As Okonkwo on return from exile saw that the clan "had undergone such profound change during his exile that it was barely recognizable,"

> Okonkwo was deeply grieved. And it was not just a personal grief. He mourned for the clan, which he saw breaking up and falling apart, and he mourned for the warlike men of Umuofia, who had so unaccountably become soft like women (p.163).[2]

The above lament is re-echoed more profoundly in a similar one:

> Does the white man understand our custom about land? How can he when he does not even speak our tongue. But he says that our customs are bad; and our brothers who have taken up his religion also say that our customs are bad. How do you think we can fight when our own brothers have turned against us. The white man is very clever. He came quietly and peacefully with his religion. We were amused at his foolishness and allowed him to stay. Now he has won our brothers, and our clan can no longer act like one. He had put a knife on the things that held us together and we have fallen apart.[3]

Now, what subsequent African writer hasn't echoed these passages in different contexts and under different theme clusters—Ngugi? Cheikh Hamidou Kane? Oyono? Ousmane Sembene? Mongo Beti? Peter Abrahams? Alex La Guma?—to restrict ourselves to fiction. What else is missing in the themes of these writers: loss of land, custom, morality, language, religion, clan unity? African literature after Achebe has become one long landslide of lachrymal lament!

---

[2] Chinua Achebe, *Things Fall Apart* (London: Heinemann, 1958), p.183. Subsequent references will be from this edition.
[3] Ibid., p.158.

II

Now, to the novels proper. Okonkwo as a "tragic hero" first catches our attention. At the heart of his "strength" squirms the worm that eats into his downfall, for the trajectory of his tragic fall traces an arc, linear in its track, that leads to his down-fall. Okonkwo is a man literally killed by too much action for he has no time to think; he only realizes thought in action. He champions no particular philosophy of life, his life seems not to be ruled by idealisms, only practicalities, and reflection on abstract principles about life seems to be his personal aversion. And it is this unreflecting re-course to violent action that is Okonkwo's tragic flaw and it later proves his undoing. As a man of few words (he was a stammerer) he does not engage in reasoned dialogue, nor does he have the time to inquire into the whys and consequences of things. So, when Ekwefi, his second wife whom he seems to love most among his three wives, murmured about his gun that never even killed a rat, he shot at her and missed; when one of the wives failed to cook his midday meal, he beat her up unminding that it was the week of peace; when Ikemefuna ran to him for protection crying he was about to be killed by one of the men in the convoy, he cut him down with his matchet, and when court messengers came to ask the village elders to disperse, he also cut one of them down, triggering off events that led to the break-up of the clan and his own suicide. He thus unreflectingly decided to fight his own separate battle and realized to his own dismay (a soft of anagnorisis) that his clan was not ready to embark on a war against the formidable forces of the commissioner. His suicide thus becomes tragically a sort of "separate peace" with himself. Okonkwo's tragedy stands out like a sore finger if one remembers the republican nature of his people— for Igbos traditionally rule themselves through dialogue and consensus. "Let us go and whisper" is the traditional Igbo method of arriving at a consensus. In sum, what leads Okonkwo to his downfall is inherent in the flaw of character which dictates that he act rather than reflect. So, he fails to heed the Igbo saying which advises that it is from the compound of the coward from which the living view the ruins of the brave man's former household. Fear of being found weak; fear that he might be found to resemble his useless father, Unoka; an exaggerated notion of his manhood; lack of respect for the customs of the land (breaking the Week of Peace); the disappointment over Nwoye as a son unworthy of him; the disappointment by the clan which fails him (he thinks) as Nwoye has failed him—all these led to he fall of Okonkwo.

Now, to Ezeulu of *Arrow of God* of whom we have said little.[4] If for Okonkwo, power is snatched from the jaws of danger and from the exaggerated assertion of one's manhood, for Ezeulu, power reposes in pride and in dignified and stubborn resistance to influences or advice from outside himself. Ezeulu's tragic flaw emanates from his own rhetoric and the refusal to taste the medicine of his own prescriptions. Here is a man who sings, *ad nauseam,* that a man must dance the dance prevalent in his time, that "the world is like a mask dancing: if you want to see it well, you do not stand in, one place," but refuses to dance to the tune of the times when ten elders urged him to eat the two sacred yams because of changed circumstances. The confusion that followed swept Ezeulu from power and disintegrated Umuaro. Ezeulu, one must assert, is not a mere toy at the hands of the gods, and there is neither a primordial curse on his head nor a pre-ordained tragic end. Ezeulu is a better realized tragic figure than Okonkwo. He is faced with that Sophoclean dilemma which confronted Oedipus: the dilemma of a man who wants to flee from his destiny in the opposite direction and collides head-on with it.

Ezeulu's tragic flaw is hybris and this, true to the Greek tenet, brought about his downfall. Achebe's tragic heroes are men too rigid in their ways while the flood of change, too dangerously close by already, sweeps them in the process. Okonkwo, Ezeulu, Chief Nanga, each does not seem to read the hand-writing on the wall: for Okonkwo and Ezeulu, the white man's religion and civilization became the thing bigger than *nte* that got caught in *nte's* trap—there is no resistance to that change, and stubborn resistance cost both their position in society and their societies never became the same again. For Chief Nanga, change came suddenly in the form of military rule because he and his fellow politicians had overplayed their hands, not knowing they had outlived their own usefulness and overstayed their welcome.

Ezeulu's tragic flaw is overweening pride and blindness to the

---

[4] *Arrow of God* (New York: Double Day/Anchor Books, 1969), pp.3-4. All quotations are from this edition.

realities of the brittle quality of the power he and his god, Ulu, hold in Umuaro. His inability to reconcile himself to the tenuous nature of his power is the source of his downfall. His own exaggerated notion of his position and his resentment over and even refusal to face the fragile nature of his power are revealed in the following passage:

> It was true that he named the day for the feast of the pumpkin leaves and for the New Yam Feast, but he did not choose the day. He was merely the watchman. His power was no more than the power of a child over a goat that was said to be his. As long as the goat was alive it was his...But the day it was slaughtered he would know who the real owner was. No! the Chief priest of Ulu was more than that, must be more than that. If he should refuse to name the day there would be no festival—no planting and no reaping. But could he refuse? No chief priest had ever refused. So it could not be done. He would not dare (pp.3-4)

Ezeulu, it seems, is as blind and stubborn as Sophocles' Oedipus and this gives cosmic dimension to his character. Akuebue had opined in a conversation with Ogbuefi Ofoka that Ezeulu "is a proud man and the most stubborn person you know is only his messenger" (pp. 242-243).

I have said elsewhere[5] that Ezeulu fails himself and Umuaro because he chooses to be blind to the limitations of his powers. The very fact that he bristles on realizing the *TRUE* nature of the fragility of his powers ("Take aware that word dare ...Yes I say take it away. No man in Umuaro can stand up and say that I dare not. The woman who will bear the man who will say it has not yet been born", p.4), helps to trigger his own downfall and reveals to us that Ezeulu, in the final analysis, is not a very adroit politician. The delegation of ten elders sent to him to urge him to roast and eat t,he two yams reminded Ezeulu that Ulu was not a nature go (like the Earth-goddess or Amadiora, god of thunder and lightning) but god over Umuaro by *convention* and *compromise,* and could only retain its power over Umuaro by dancing the dance prevalent in their time. Ezeulu also ignored, to his peril, Nwaka's words that unless Ezeulu trod carefully, what happened at Aninta might happen at Umuaro:

---

[5] See Charles E. Nnolim, "Technique and Meaning in Achebe's Arrow of God," *Kiabara*, Vol. 3, No. 2 (Harmattan, 1980).

And we have all heard how the people of Aninta dealt with their deity when he failed them; did they not carry him to the boundary between them and their neighbours and set him on fire (p.31)

Ulu as a god might be capricious and might have killed Ezeulu for mere sport as others might like to interpret, for there are those who insist that Ezeulu's tragic end stems from the enigmatic relationship between an inscrutable god and a power-seeking votary. But I like to insist that Ezeulu as a "tragic hero" comes to a bad end because of his own blindness to reality, his own exaggerated concept of his powers, his over-weening pride, his poor sense of history in fighting the fractious powers in Umuaro, his poor political instinct, his uncompromising personality (that enabled him to resist the offer of chieftaincy from Captain Winterbottom and the urge by elders to roast the two sacred yams in order to save Umuaro from starvation) and, finally, his refusal to adapt to the changing times. So much for Ezeulu.

If we adhere to Aristotle's observations about tragic characters in his *Poetics*, we may easily be spared the need to proceed further with Chief Nanga *(A Man of the People)* and Obi Okonkwo *(No Longer at Ease)*. Real tragic situations, Aristotle has argued, must awaken pity and fear in the audience. Good men, therefore, should not be shown sliding from prosperity to misery, for that disgusts us nor should evil men be seen passing from misery to prosperity for the same reasons, for pity is aroused by undeserved misfortune and fear by the plight of someone like ourselves. Therefore, a thoroughly corrupt man like Chief Nanga, passing from prosperity to exile (not even misery, for the coup did not touch his person) will not be the object of our study, for Nanga's wealth was acquired corruptly and no one need shed a tear for Chief Nanga, for abandoning a loot which never belonged to him in the first place.

On another point, Okonkwo and Ezeulu represent a constituency whose destiny was inseparable from theirs, so that the break-up of Okonkwo and Ezeulu echoes, in its sheer cosmic magnitude, the break-up of Igbo society of which they were the embodiment. The sense of tragic loss in each case was incalculable. Chief Nanga represents no constituency but his own purse so that his disappearance from the scene (by some *deus ex machina,* the coup d'état) calls for mass celebration rather than regret. Chief

Nanga, therefore, deserves no place among Achebe's "tragic heroes".

On the same low bench I shall sit Obi Okonkwo, that immature lad who persisted in practising the art of evasion until he got trapped in that which he most wanted to avoid. If, for Aristotle the tragic hero is a man, great and noble but not pre-eminently just or virtuous but whose misfortune is due not to vice or depravity but by some error of judgement or tragic flaw, where does one place Obi Okonkwo? Does his sorry end have the dimensions of tragic actions? Does he represent a constituency whose destiny is intertwined inextricably with his (our measure of the African sense of the tragic), and is he a man of great and noble mien, of high destiny. We regret that Obi Okonkwo ends in jail but we do not pity him. He possesses no courage or conviction (why not challenge an effete custom like the Osu system and marry Clara?); he is down-right immoral (helping procure abortion on his intended); he is manifestly corrupt (getting caught in the act of taking bribe); his idealism evaporates at the sight of temptation (even when he decided to eat a toad, he did not have the high-sense of eating a fat one - a low aim that earned him nothing but contempt from his people); he is insensitive (the way he abandoned Clara who nearly died after the abortion); and he is not his own man (he can neither face his parents and fellow Umuofians at Lagos over Clara nor face up to other problems, including financial, which nag his existence). He is the classic example that an untried virtue is no virtue at all. When Mr. Omo advises Obi on how to claim a certain amount of mileage "on actuality basis" to account for travel allowance granted him to visit Umuofia, the "anti-corruption" campaigner Obi quickly succumbs by claiming he spent his leave in the Cameroons. Obi has not lived to disprove to Mr. Green that "the African is corrupt through and through". Obi Okonkwo and Teacher Nanga do not, therefore, qualify to be numbered among Achebe's "tragic heroes".

Finally, Achebe's "tragic heroes"— Okonwo and Ezeuluare dignified personages who are too dignified to be corrupt, too stubborn and proud to accept or listen to wise counsel, too involved with their people's destiny and identity to be seen as separate entity, so that whatever affects them adversely equally himself the throbbing consciousness and destiny of his people. The sad end of Okonkwo and Ezeulu reflects the communal tragedy of Igbo society under relentless and inexorable pressures from the colonial intrusion.

9

Achebe's masked spirits: *culture's hum and buzz of social implications*

The novel as genre is remarked for its insistence on criticizing, expressing and ministering to the culture of its origin. Critics are agreed on the point that any good novel worth the name must not only insist upon but also prove its own cultural relevance. One calls to mind Henry James's most damaging criticism of the American novel (in his essay on the life of Hawthorne) no state; no sovereign, no court, no aristocracy; no country gentlemen; no palaces; no castles; no personages; no manors; no great universities; no cathedrals; no ivied ruins; no Epsom. In other words, he is telling us that the American novelist is inherently disadvantaged owing to the absence of those deep cultural roots which Europe boasts of but which are denied a society so new on the world scene as America.

If we are in agreement that cultural relevance is a must in a novel worth our appreciation, we are likely to agree also that part of the charm (I do not say all,) part of the pleasure we derive from Achebe's *Things Fall Part* and *Arrow of God* stems from what critics have come to call his ancestor worship - a concern of his which involves the celebration of all that is dignified and meaningful in Igbo culture at a point in history the society was losing grips on its own cultural cohesiveness. What crystallizes for the reader in the two novels mentioned above is a unique, achievement-oriented society with a well-defined, democratically entrenched means of social identification in which there is rank, not class—an arrangement which guarantees a classless society where, however, life is not aimless since there are more wives to acquire, more titles to take, higher and higher positions of social importance to aspire to; in short, an elitist society with a place for exalted status but with a refreshing absence of that root cause of social snobbery which is the unfortunate hallmark of all class-oriented societies.

In reading *Things Fall Apart* and *Arrow of God* one is immediately struck by Achebe's concern with and the importance of what he calls "the Masked Spirit," and often the Egwugwu in Igbo society. If, as Lionel Trilling tells us *(The Liberal Imagination)* "manners" are the things that for good or for bad draw the people of a culture together and that separate them from the people of another culture; and that "manners" are that part of a culture which is not art, or religion, or morals, or politics, it becomes much easier to perceive the importance of the masked spirit not only in Achebe but also in much of the novels written by Igbos. For, the masked spirit in traditional Igbo society was a vehicle of much more than manners - it was the repository of all that was held sacred, mythical, mysterious, magical and supernatural in Igbo culture. As will be demonstrated, it exercised social controls in a way that was not only unchallenged but unassailable. The masked spirit was sacrificed to *(Arrow of God);* it was the supreme judicial body and the supreme law enforcement agency *(Things Fall Apart);* it combined in a curious way the charm and attraction of spectator sports with all attendant youthful frivolities, with the weighty dignity and respect worthy of the ancestors who are believed to be moving inside them. If animism is the end-result of a superstitions bent in a society, the masked spirit is the supreme example of traditional Igbo belief that spirits (in this case those of departed ancestors) do walk the visible world. As we shall see in the course of this study, the masked spirit is the supreme disciplinarian, the supreme magician, the supreme judge, the sports hero, the respected policeman, so that, in a curious way, in the cult of the masked spirit is enthroned in Igbo society and culture all that partakes of the religion, the morals, the mores, the law, the judicial process, the politics of Igbo society in a way that makes it impossible to separate in its institution, manners from culture.

In the light of the foregoing I contend that if ancestor worship is Achebe's major contribution to the novel from Black Africa, the centre of that worship must be located in his portrayal of the importance of the masked spirit in his novels dealing with Igbo society. His portrayal of the importance of the masked spirits becomes the technique which compels him to discover, to develop, to define, to explore, to evaluate, to seriously attend to his subject matter which is the portrayal of all that are important, dignified, and sacred in Igbo culture at a point it was woefully beginning to disintegrate owing to the intrusion of colonialism's unappreciative agents. We must at this point remember Achebe's own words *(The Nigeria Magazine,* June 1964) in which he admits that he is a committed writer who feels it his duty to serve society, and who feels the major concern of African writers should be this:

> that African peoples did not hear of culture for the first time from Europeans; that their societies were not mindless but frequently had a philosophy of great depth and value and beauty, that they had poetry and, above all, they had dignity.

As must have become clear, the present study is not Achebe's portrayal of Igbo culture and society but on an aspect of that culture which deals with the cult of the masquerade, for, as I have hinted above the function of the masquerade (a term I prefer to use more frequently in this study for its simplicity) (1) in society is one aspect of cultural relativity Achebe's sensitivity to which reveals the depth of his insight. To those who wonder how a classless society such as that of the Igbos functioned, how it enforced its laws with no king, no police force, and no standing army, this study will be of singular interest. To buttress my points in cases where Achebe's novels are inadequate or in other functions of the masquerade his works ignored altogether, I crave the reader's indulgence to refer to Igbo novels that deal with this particular aspect.

Too much has been made of the importance of wrestling in the life of Igbo youth and manhood that the reader of Achebe's *Things Fall Apart* and Munonye's *The Only Son* is apt to come to erroneous conclusions. It is one of the unwitting ways literature can falsify reality. The fact is that, although wrestling played a large part in the traditional recreational endeavours of Igbo youth, it was, in fact, minor to masquerading. Although, the quality of Igbo manhood was tested in the wrestling arena, it was more so in the masquerade cult. Nothing in traditional Igbo manhood was more tempting, more intoxicating, more prideful, more dizzyingly heady than donning a mask and distinguishing oneself in it. Unlike wrestling (which like boxing one easily outgrows) to retain one's foothold in the masquerade cult, a young man must have been tested by those events which, as Joseph Conrad might put it *(Lord Jim),* show in the light of day the inner worth of a man, the edge of his temper, and the fibre of his stuff; tests that reveal the quality of his persistence and the secret truth of his pretences, not only to others but also to himself. Secondly, the masquerade cult was more at the core of Igbo educational process than wrestling, involving, as it did, a progressively deepening cult enjoyed only through a series of initiation rites. One needed no such initiation rites to participate in wrestling matches which, in any case, needed only brawn, not brain, while the masquerade cult was at the core of Igbo society with a quality of elitism in it.[1]

It was clearly there at the apex of Igbo achievement-oriented structure and only the most worthy had a place in it. This is clearly demonstrated with Achebe's characteristic restraint in *Things Fall Apart* where we are informed that the nine masked spirits *(egwugwu)* sat as judges in the family dispute between Uzowulu and Mgbafo. In his own words: "each of the nine *egwugwu* represented a village or clan. Their leader was called Evil Forest. Smoke poured out from his head." And then, "He (Evil Forest) took the first of the empty stools and the eight other *egwugwu* began to sit in order of seniority after him Okonkwo's wives, and perhaps other women as well, might have noticed the second *egwugwu* had the springy walk of Okonkwo." Here in one deft stroke Achebe informs us that Okonkwo's meteoric rise in society had placed him in the second highest position in the leadership hierarchy of the clan; that an aura

---

[1] There arises here the problem of terminology, there are, in Igboland, innumerable kinds and grades and even shades of the cult of the Mask. Some Masks appear only for ceremonial and judicial purposes and the elite drawn from older members of the society are eligible for initiation into its cult Lesser Masks are for more frivolous purposes such as dancing, racing young men, and singing during festivals, and these are donned by younger, initiated members of the society for heady display of youthful prowess. The term "masquerade" is meant here not to connote any of the pejorative meanings which the word calls up in Western minds: acting or living under false pretences. In this study it is used as a collective term to mean persons wearing masks for various cultural purposes. It must be emphasized, however, that both the ceremonial Mask and the more sportive, youthful variety are, to the uninitiated, referred to as "masked spirits" and unmasking either variety is regarded equally as a most heinous crime calling for swift retribution. The coming of Christianity has added a masking phenomenon unheard of in traditional Igbo society: mere children's masks donned by the uninitiated children of Christian parents.

of mystery and magic surrounds the masquerade cult (note the steady smoke pouring out of the head of Evil Forest); and that the *egwugwu* is the highest judicial body of the society. Nor must we forget that Okonkwo's major regret on his return from exile was his recognition that "he had lost his place among the nine masked spirits who administered justice in the clan."

What makes the masquerade cult such a giddy seducer of youth is the aura of mystery and magic surrounding the whole thing, plus the awe, power, and dignity with which the cult is encompassed. The secret of the cult is the most guarded, even today, in Igbo society. The point is that masked spirits have always been regarded as the visible, living reincarnation of departed ancestors and the symbol of the vital link which unites the individual with the community. Those moderns who still retain in lingering nostalgia over the destruction of all that were respectful and sacrosanct in Igbo culture look at the current diminished respect for the cult of the masquerade as the most painful aspect of that break-up which *Things Fall Apart* recreates so splendidly.

An interesting phenomenon is the respect with which Igbo writers (iconoclasts in other ways) treat the masquerade cult in their works. Achebe tells us in *Things Fall Apart* "No woman ever asked questions about the most powerful and the most secret cult in the clan;" that "the ancestral spirits were abroad;" that "when, as on that day (when they sat in judgment), nine of the greatest masked spirits in the clan came out together it was a terrifying spectacle;" that during the annual ceremony which was held in honour of the earth deity "the ancestors of the clan who had been committed to Mother Earth at their death emerged again as *egwugwu* through tiny antholes;" and that "one of the greatest crimes a man could commit was to unmask *an egwugwu* in public or to say ar do anything which might reduce its immortal prestige in the eyes of the "uninitiated".

These are assertions made in all reverence with none of that serio-comic tone with which a Chaucer might have approached such a subject. And in one of the rare exchanges between the immortals and humans the respect due the ancestors is preserved:

> Uzowulu's body I salute you." ...
> "Our father, my hand has touched the ground," he said.
> "Uzowulu's body, do you know me?" asked the Spirit.
> "How can I know you, Father? You are beyond our knowledge."

Those who are acquainted with John Munonve's *The Onlu Son* will recall that one of the worst instances of authorial intrusion in the narrative occurs when he, the author, comes out *in propria persona* to announce that "The Nigerian Society for Preservation of African Culture forbids that the names (` of two insignificant creatures which represent the sign' of the masquerade cult) be revealed." Then after a delightful scene in which school boys toy with the teacher's curiosity about the secret of the masquerade "leaf" (a big hoax which the boys were ready to parry indefinitely), Munonye informs us why the boys could not, even had they wanted, reveal the secret. After telling us how the boys winced and shrugged their shoulders in horror and dismay at the teacher's dangerously profane statement that "those things which you see are bad men, pagans in dirty masks and crests," he continues:

Such things must never be said with the mouth or heard with the ears. That was one more of the unforgettable laws learnt during initiation. "Will you with your mouth, you child, disclose a spirit?" the tall and terrible flagellant of a masquerade had asked while exploding its cane on the candidate's back. "Say, not even in the grave. "Then the masquerade picked up a double-edged knife and brushed it determinedly on a whetting stone..." I'll cleave your head into two unless you promise to tell me as soon as you've been taught that, what moves inside mask." No, never; not even in the grave? the candidate replied. Let the head go off instead.

Such is the terrible ordeal and secrecy demanded by the cult and Achebe and Munonye who speak like insiders bound by the code (I am almost certain they were initiated) could not, in honour divulge the secret nor speak disparagingly of it.

But Clement Agunwa, who belongs to a younger generation that was not forced to undergo initiation into the masquerade cult, did not hesitate to divulge the secret in a passage Munonye might never forgive After first going through the motions of mystifying' the masquerade ("It was, surely, the voice of the head- the masquerades who tear through the earth into the open through ant holes ") he demystifies it in *More Than Once:*

> What did he (Nweke) expect to see? A transparent creature wearing a masked head and perhaps dyed or crimson, chilly to touch. That was his vague idea of spirit. But what did he actually see really? Old

Nwafor Umeh with a piece of wooden rod in his mouth. Nweke actually caught him speaking through this mysterious rod.

It is time to take a closer look at the major functions of the masquerade as represented in works of Achebe and the other writers already mentioned. To the point already made that masked spirits formed the highest judicial body *Things Fall Apart* must be added at once that they also combined in their social functions the duty of police to maintain order, and the force of an army both to coerce and enforce the law in those instances when "the law of the land must be obeyed." Except in those occasions during a festival when the masquerades entertained crowds with dancing and with the frivolous chasing around of initiated young men in a test of endurance and speed in both long-distance and short-distance races, nothing about a masquerade is taken lightly except, perhaps, by Christians. But even the Christians fully paid the penalty for any indiscretions, as Enoch who unmasked the *egwugwu* in *Things Fall Apart* and his fellow church members found out to their utter dismay-both his compound and the church building to which he belonged were set on fire and completely razed to the ground.

To the masquerades, then, more than to the elders or any age group, belonged the unquestioned and incontrovertible authority for administering justice and enforcing the law. In fact, there are only two things in life the Igbo grow up to fear and dread the greatest; masquerades and poisonous snakes. In their sting, there is no appeal. To the masquerade cult belonged the dirty job which the normal daylight operation of things made impossible in society. It was the unspoken force that would have compelled Okonkwo to go into exile, assuming that such a powerful man tried to resist the inconvenience. The razing of Enoch's and the church compound to the ground by the *egwugwu* demonstrated the swift, ruthless, terrifying fashion in which masquerades exercised social controls.

A minor role played by the masquerade was that of the disciplinarian to recalcitrant boys as Clement Agunwa tells us in *More Than Once*. When Nweke carelessly threw down the child he was babysitting it was arranged that a masquerade discipline him:

'There is no festival, no burial. Why has this masquerade came (sic) up now? It must be to perform a disciplinary function. Somebody must have offended. Did anybody urinate in the spring? Or did anyone owe a debt which the masquerade has been asked to collect?

Again, here in one stroke Agunwa tells us many things about the function of the masquerade in society-disciplining a boy, burying the dead, celebrating a festival, collecting debt. Elsewhere in the same novel, when certain girls failed to take part in sweeping the village square it was the masquerades who would collect the fines. On this point, John Munonye informs us in another novel, *Obi*, the use of masquerades to enforce participation in village communal labour. Masquerades would be asked to do the usual thing, which was to loot the offenders' houses ..."

In *Things Fall Apart* when Ezeudu died we observe another important function of masked spirits in society-burying the dead lending solemnity and dignity to the occasion, especially when the dead is an important member of society. It is on such occasions, too, that magic is also added to the solemnity as we witness one of the ancestral spirits coming to the funeral "carrying a basket of water." Even before a person dies, the masquerade can be used to keep unwanted visitors away from the sick chamber. Munonye tells us in *Obi* that when Akueke was at death's door (knocked unconscious by Joe whose manhood she insulted): "a fat masquerade, hastily produced, kept watch at the entrance and sent away all visitors except those that were male and adult members of Udemezue's family."

If all this sounds lugubrious, one must cheer up with the reminder that the major function of the masquerade in society was, and still is, entertainment. This is its major function represented both in Achebe's *Arrow of God* and Munonye's *The Only Son*. The masquerade dance is always the high-point of every traditional Igbo festival; in fact, Christian festivals such as Christmas and Easter are graced with the presence of masquerades — a phenomenon that missionaries and teachers fought to no avail. In *Arrow of God*, it was during the *Akwu Nro* festival that Obika's age group brought out a new Mask — a fact the million ant-holes in Umuachala it would come through," while he heightens our suspense by filling the atmosphere with magic.

> An occasion such as this was often used by wicked men to try the potency of their magic or to match their power against that of

others. There were stories of Masks which had come out unprepared and transfixed to a spot for days or even felled to the ground.

He adds:

> If Otakagu age group chose to bring out a new Mask without first boiling themselves hard it was their fault.

Achebe had once described himself as an ancestor worshipper. I suggest that the reverence with which he represents the masked spirits in his novels is a conscious manifestation of that worship because, in the cult of the masquerade is the incarnation and embodiment of that aspect of Igbo culture in which the ancestors themselves mixed religion with leadership, justice, myth, manners magic. No important burial, no important festival, no serious judicial process, no communal labour was complete without in some way involving the masquerade. In the masquerade cult was the very source of spiritual vitality among Igbo youth—the very heartthrob of the continuity of the best in society's traditions—so that the cult derived its power from two formidable sources: the backing and solidarity of the community and the aura of magic and mystery surrounding it.

In criticism such as this, attention must also be paid to the structural and thematic use made by the author, on an aspect of his work so important as this study has tried to demonstrate. In *Things Fall Apart* masked spirits or the *egwugwu* are thematically important since the *egwugwu* are represented as the symbol of communal unity and the living embodiment of that vital link which exists between individuals and their departed ancestors. As Achebe points out on the appearance of masked spirits at Ezeudu's death:

> The land of the living was not far removed from the domain of the ancestors. There was coming and going between them, especially at festivals and also when an old man died, because an old man was very close to the ancestors.

The unmasking of the *egwugwu* by the Christian zealot Enoch (who wept louder than the bereaved) echoes in *Things Fall Apart* not only the collective breakup of the cohesiveness of the Clan after the intrusion of alien forces but also the powerlessness of the Clan against those alien forces which the District commissioner represents. In another, yet unexplored aspect, the *egwugwu's* brutal, retributive justice against Enoch and the church building to which he belonged parallels the "enlightened' but equally brutal retributive justice of the alien forces which wiped out Abame (for the killing of one white man on an iron horse) and imprisoned leaders of Umuofia (for the burning of Enoch's church)—all without due process of law.

In *Arrow of God* where Achebe informs us early in the book that a "spirit was expected to return from the depths of the earth and appear to men as a Mask," it is one of the wry irony of things that Obika dies immediately after donning a night Mask-literally going back to the ancestors with whom he had just communed. It is also ironic that early in the book it was Obika who had a terrifying apparition of Eru, whose grandiloquent title Ezeulu says is "the Magnificent, the one that gives wealth to those who find favour with him " Ezeulu had allayed Obika's feelings by painting a rosy picture of the luck that was likely to be his for seeing Eru because, he says, "When he (Eru) likes a man wealth flows like a river into his house; his yams grow big as human beings, his goats produce three and his hens hatch nines." As it turns out, Obika's apparition was a kiss of premature death. Those whom the gods love die young.

It is interesting how Achebe wove the Mask into the narrative of *Arrow of God* as evidenced in the following passages. The Corporal sent to arrest Ezeulu by the sick Winterbottom, having missed him, tells Ezeulu's people: "But we cannot come and go for nothing When a masked spirit visits you have to appease its footprints with presents. The white man is the masked spirits of today", or we can glance at the humorous passage where we are given a view of Nwaka's wives heavily decked with ivory anklets during a ceremony so that their walk was "like the walk of an Ijere Mask lifting and lowering each foot with weight ceremony" or we can recall the angry Ezeulu saluting Umuaro: It was the like the salute of enraged Mask", or we can see the astute Ezeulu sending Oduche to school to learn the secret of the white man's power, shrouding his message in a proverb: "The world is like a Mask dancing. If you wish to see it well you do not stand in one place", or we are made privy to the secret product of Edogo's carved Masks most of which "were for fierce aggressive spirits with horns and teeth the size of fingers", or we can be disappointed when having waited for so long we are told that "an Agaba (brought out by the Otakagu age group) was not a Mask of songs and dance. It stood for the power and aggressiveness of youth."

The point is made, that Achebe weaves the Mask into his narrative both in his use of proverbs and in his use of concrete detail so that just as it is a vehicle of meaning in *Things Fall Apart* it partakes of narrative texture in *Arrow of God*. If we interpret the unmasking of the *egwugwu* (which Achebe referred to as the "death of an ancestral spirit") as symbolizing the communal tragedy which overtook Igbo society in *Things Fall Apart,* could I suggest that the death of Obika (after donning a Mask) is interpretable as the "death of an ancestral spirit" in *Arrow of God* which is a personal tragedy. If this is entertained, may I conclude by suggesting that it is a touch of genius which enables Achebe to connect the "death of an ancestral spirit" with the collective and personal tragedies which bring to a close two of his best works in which tragedy is the end-result of cultural conflict and social change. As I see it Ezeulu's sanity does not crack by the mere fact of Obika's death (he is neither his favourite nor his eldest son) but by the realization that Obika's death literally with the Mask on, is an ominous warning to him who is versed in native lore and magic that the potency of Obika's magic is no longer effective, forecasting to him a larger, more cosmic erosion of those powers over Umuaro on which his own influence lay, evidenced in the mass conversion to Christianity which his own stubbornness had engendered.

10

The critic of African literature: the challenge of the 1980s

Contemporary African literature is literature in full motion, a literature that is still being born and enriched by the discovery of new writers and new talents. It is literature in movement—not just movement in one direction but in many directions at once. Furthermore, as things stand, the major problem for the sensitive critic is the awareness that African literature is not only in motion: it has just taken off; it is in full flight and there is no hint of arrival at any foreseeable destination.[1] And as trends in criticism inevitably follow new directions in art and letters, the first challenge the critic of African literature of the 1980s must face is to avoid repeating the critical methods and judgements of the past, for criticism is a judgment that is current, not a rehash of old judgments. This does not say that the critic should ignore the judgment or criticism of the past. In fact he cannot deliver judgment that has validity and currency if he does not arm himself with the judgments and evaluations of our literatures in the past twenty years.

On glancing through trends in criticism of African literature in the past twenty years, we see an early period dominated by expatriate critics who were more fascinated by the curiosities of the background culture enveloping our literatures than the literature qua literature itself. We would like to brush aside and forget, if we could, the era of criticism dominated by these expatriates who saw

See similar statements on American literature by J. C. La Driere in *Directions in Contemporary Criticism* (Milwaukee, Wisconsin, The Bruce Publishing Company, 1953).

our literary output as nothing more than "quaint books from Africa" containing "anthropological curiosities" that did nothing but reveal the "primitive social idiosyncrasies of Africa." We would like, if we could, to forget the "contributions" of Anne Tibble, Judith Gleason, Margaret Laurence, and the early Gerald Moore—for these were critics who shunned analysis and the search for total meaning in a work and embraced with the ardour of missionary zeal the dishing out of competent summaries and the revelling in unrestrained interest in ferreting out the ethnographic data revealed in the tale, without failing to attach to their comments the discovery of literary debts owed certain European masters.[2]

The next but important era of criticism of African literature produced what one may term "literary midwives"—practical critics whose main job was, it seems, to make hard reading easier for the layman, to be the mediator between the specialist and the layman, especially, the struggling undergraduate who must be led to understand the work and to get at its meaning. The works of these critics are immensely popular: G. Killam's *The Novels of Chinua Achebe*, 1969; Eustace Palmer's *An Introduction to the African Novel*, 1972 (later expanded to *The Growth of the African Novel*, 1979—the appellation "growth" is a misnomer since we see only an updating); Gerald Moore's *Seven African Writers*, 1962 (later expanded to *Twelve African Writers*). These were critics who by what seems a common consensus avoided establishing a theoretical basis for the works examined but, as was said earlier, to make reading easier for those who find it hard to understand a relatively difficult literary text.

The supreme achievement of these critics has been to elucidate for the reader who is pathetically eager to understand, what a literary text is saying and is pathologically incapable of such understanding without the help of summaries and background information. It is my opinion that all such criticism that aims solely at the altruistic notion of educating the uneducated minds at the lowest level possible is misdirected and limited in scope. But it is not useless as is borne out from the popularity of these efforts.

The study of single authors flowered through the efforts of two important publishing houses: Evans Brothers Limited, and

[2] See Anne Tibble: *African English Literature* (London, Owen, 1965); Judith Gleason: *Novels by West Africans in English and French* (Evanston: University of Illinois Press, 1965); Margaret Laurence: *Long Drums and Cannons* (London, Macmillan, 1968); Gerald Moore: *Seven African Writers* (London: Oxford University Press, 1962).

Heinemann Educational Books. Under their African Writers Series, each publishing house began a healthy trend that combined with varying merits, sound autobiographical background of each single author studied, with searching critical analysis of the author's works. Easily the best among the lot is Eldred Jones's *The Writing of Wole Soyinka* (Heinemann), followed by Emenyonu's *Cyprian Ekwensi* (Evans), Sunday Anozie's *Christopher Okigbo: Creative Rhetoric* (Evans), Robert Fraser's *The Novels of Ayi Kwei Armah* (Heinemann), G. A. Heron's *The Poetry of Okot p'Bitek* (Heinemann). Others include Gerald Moore's *Wole Soyinka* (Evans), Michael Wade's *Peter Abrahams* (Evans), and G. D. Killam's *The Novels and Plays of Ngugi Wa Thiong'o* (Heinemann)

At present, criticism of African literature is vigorously pursued and is dominated by what one might call "academic" critics (usually university men and women teaching and researching in institutions of higher learning). This cadre of critics with their preponderant use of technical terms seems clearly to address fellow academic critics and scholars of African literatures. Backed by sound academic preparation and grounded in solid theoretical knowledge of literature, these critics have produced by far the most thought-provoking critical essays on African literature to date. In their various efforts, they are aided by scholarly journals the best of which are *African Literature Today,* (edited by Eldred Jones), *Research in African Literatures* (edited by Lindfors), and, with uneven output, *The Commonwealth Journal of Literature* (edited by Alastair Niven). The current enthusiasm for analytic criticism on the pages of scholarly journals seems justified by results and by the uncanny ability of these critics to reveal delightful and intellectually satisfying insights into every imaginable aspect of our literatures. Here the Izevbayes, the Nnolims, the Emenyonus, the Iyaseres, the Ogunbas, the Lindfors (to mention but a few) have had field day. But these disparate efforts, no matter how brilliant, cannot create for us an aesthetic of African literature. And to arrive at an aesthetic of African literature (the subject of many conferences on African literature) is the major challenge of the 80's. And herein lies the major weakness, the major flaw of these brilliant critical essays: there is no unified focus. Furthermore, the unstated critical theory and poetics which inspire these efforts seem to borrow heavily from the poetics and literary theory of the West. And this looking back over our shoulders to get inspiration from Europe and the West, this lack of grounding in an established African literary theory is a desideratum, a situation which has inspired vigorous reaction by the authors of a recent book entitled: *Toward the Decolonization of African Literature* (Fourth Dimension Publishers, 1980). Sometimes I think we all deserve whatever pettifogging abuses the authors of this book heap on each one of us.

And since up to now we have not established or tried to establish any theory of African literature, we doubly deserve what we have got from another expatriate critic who has desperately tried to fill the void; I have in mind Charles Larson's *The Emergence of African*.[3] So, we naturally pause to examine that much-discussed, much-vilified, controversial work. As has just been said, it is a work that tries desperately to fill a void by trying to advance some theory of African fiction. And herein lie its fascination and its weakness. While I am in no way a champion of *The Emergence of African Fiction,* I hazard to say that it is a work in the "right" direction although grossly flawed in execution by its condescending dicta and by what Izevbaye calls the enthronement of "stereotypes as if they were facts".[4] But wherein lies its appeal; it is in its attempt to establish some theoretical framework for interpreting African fiction, in its brave effort to marry theory with analysis (an effort that has largely eluded Larson's African counterparts). To establish a theoretical framework and then proceed to apply analysis guided by this theoretical framework is the forte of Larson's methodology—a procedure that has been strenuously avoided by indigenous African critics. Charles Larson's work, of course, has given offence to many a reviewer largely because the signposts on which he hangs his categories—his "Africanisms", his "archetypal novels", his "situational" plot structures, his "Pamelas" - are wrongheaded and annoying to the sensitive African reader and critic. Very much quoted, very much in currency, Charles Larson's *The Emergence of African Fiction is* an attractive dish with caustic soda. Neither Nwoga, nor Obiechina, nor even the brilliant Eldred Jones has attempted, like Larson, to marry the synthesis of theory with analysis in any extended work. The only possible exception.

Anozie whose study of Okigbo advances a theoretical construct--structuralism—for analyzing Okigbo's "creative

---

[3] *Fiction* (Bloomington, Indiana: Indiana University Press, 1971)

[4] Dan Izevbaye: "The State of Criticism in African Literature," *African Literature Today*, No.7 (1975), p.4.

rhetoric" in his poetic canon. It is indeed an exception, but he goes overboard in forcing poetic analysis into a procrustean structuralist straight jacket that results in stilted and anaemic interpretation. In the long run, however, we all shall look back to Anozie as a pioneer in the African's attempt to marry theory with analysis and to provide the first efforts at "scientific" criticism of African literature.

Having said the above, one must mention Wole Soyinka's *Myth, Literature and the African World* as a pioneer in its kind for providing a theoretical framework detailing the ritual origins of Yoruba drama and the importance of the Pantheon of Yoruba gods, Sango, Ogun, and Obatala—in Yoruba world view. Now, this is another step in the right direction. To provide a mythic and archetypal framework for examining Yoruba drama reflects, in Soyinka's words a "positive apprehension" of African world view in drama, eliciting "the African self-apprehended world in myth and literature."[5] One regrets, of course, that Soyinka's work is limited by its ethnic bias and thus denies us a broader perspective for interpreting African drama in general.

In fiction, Ernest Emenyonu's *The Rise of the Igbo Novel* (London, Oxford University Press, 1978) next comes to mind. It is a seminal work that makes a modest contribution to criticism of fiction written by Igbos by establishing the oral base of the novels. But the ethnic bias is evident so that it suffers the same limitation as Soyinka's work. Its chief merit is the theoretical basis of its findings which, like Soyinka's, could be applied in larger contexts whenever the poetics of African fiction or drama comes to be studied. While Soyinka demonstrates the ritual basis of Yoruba drama, Emenyonu traces the influence of the oral tradition both in the vernacular novels written by Igbos and also those written by them in English. The ultimate importance of the works of both authors, the reason I regard them as seminal, is that the theoretical premises they have established will have influence in the study of African fiction and drama beyond each work's ethnic base. The limitations of Emenyonu's approach are not restricted to the ethnic bias already mentioned; the work lacks the dense erudition and condensed methodology of Soyinka's study. Emenyonu's fault, if a fault there

[5] Wole Soyinka: *Myth, Literature and the African World* (Cambridge: Cambridge University Press, 1976), pp.2-3.

[6] Matthew Arnold: "The Function of Criticism at the Present Time," in *Victorian Poetry and Poetics*, ed. W. E. Houghton and G. R. Stange (Boston: Houghton Mifflin Company, 1968), p.527.

be, stems from the audience in mind: while Soyinka addresses fellow critics and scholars, Emenyonu seems to have had an undergraduate audience in view.

Now, we must pause again to examine a new critical work on the literary scene mentioned earlier in this study. It is a brilliant much discussed book entitled: *Toward the Decolonization of African Literature* by Chinweizu, Onwuchekwa Jemie, and Ihechukwu Madubuike. Large parts of the book had earlier appeared in *Transition* (No.4, 1975), and in *Okike* (Nos. 6 and 7, 1974, 1975), as brilliant and hard-hitting commentary on the poetic and critical practices of our emergent literatures. It was then unavailable in one piece to a number of readers. But now that it has appeared and is fully fleshed out as a book, to read it is a must. Everything wrong with our poetry, our novels, and our criticism is ferreted out and catalogued, often with the most caustic comments. It is a much needed spoonful of medicine for all those errant writers in all genres of African literatures who have not *been* weaned from the literary breast of our former colonial masters. But in the end, with all its brilliance, *Toward the Decolonization of African Literature* leaves us empty. After devoting more than one hundred pages on Adrian Roscoe's wrong-headed *Mother Is Gold,* on Charles Larson's condescending *The Emergence of African Fiction,* and on excerpts from Izevbaye's critical essays, one began to expect a new direction, a positive turnabout to evaluative criticism, to some poetics or theory of African literature that should form a touchstone for these errant critics.

But no. The blood-letting continues. Every poem, every novel, every critical essay worth its salt, is examined by the troika and equally condemned. One must say it in their favour the no single critic, no group of critics are as diligent, as painstaking, and as forthright and incisive as the authors of the book under discussion. But here comes the hitch: *Toward the Decolonization of African Literature is an* unfortunate example of what happens when what is appropriately said in one medium is transferred to another without consideration of the requirements, of the demands of this other medium Let me explain: *Toward the Decolonization of African Literature* was a brilliant idea as an article or a series of hard-hitting articles. IF made, within the constraints of 15-20 pages of each appearance, a self-contained, tightly woven statement that satisfied the end of the medium (in this case a scholarly journal) through which it was expressed. But as a book, it is flawed to the core. For the audience at which it was aimed (fellow scholars and practising critics) it became a warmed-over, fly-specked soup. Moreover, one wonders at the wisdom of writing a whole book on entirely negative responses, on entirely defeatist principles. All things considered, *Toward the Decolonization of African Literature* is no more than a carefully sequenced and highly honed series of brilliant blackmail. All things considered, this approach is unacceptable. For what the authors finally achieved is the feeling in all of us that they went with bulldozers on a demolition campaign of our literary edifices with no plans for positive reconstruction. But having said this, it must be stressed that no one can ignore the validity of their posture and their conclusions: to shock us into an awareness of how deeply and pervasively we all have been bitten by the neo-colonial bug and how we all have depended on our former masters as our intellectual and emotional crutches. But the tiresome overkill is bothersome and is likely to continue in the planned volume two which we all imagine will concentrate on our dramatic practices. One wishes this were abandoned so that the troika might apply their brilliant minds and awesome intellect to developing the great job they started on the appendix of volume I entitled "What Is African Literature?" Here, they began to apply correctives. They began a theory of African literature. In this wise, one could say that *Toward the Decolonization of African Literature* is a book that began at the end.

The task facing the authors of *Toward the Decolonization of African Literature* is the task facing all of us in the 1980s; to build up carefully and painstakingly a poetics, a theory of African literature. We need a scholar or a group of scholars with the synthesizing mind of an Aristotle to build up for us a poetics of African literature whose uniqueness is no longer a tatter for debate, whose vital juices are fed with uniquely African orature so that by the time we have stepped into the 1990s, the nagging debate about an established African aesthetics literature has finally been settled. For the moment, we urgently need our own version of Northrop Frye to pen for us *The Anatomy of "African" Criticism;* we need our own I. A. Richards to write us *The Principles of "African" Criticism;* we need our own T. C. Pollock to write us *The Nature of "African" Literature;* we need our own Wellek and Warren to write us our own *Theory of "African" Literature.* As one can easily see, the word "African" has been inserted into each established title to domesticate it for us, to do for us what these Western critics have done for their own literatures. Only when a theory and poetics of African literature have been established would we stop interpreting our own literatures without leaning on the crutches of European world view. Only then would our literatures be completely decolonized.

To face the future, we must first congratulate ourselves for having come a long way from those times when expatriates with their inadequate tools claimed to have all the interpretive answers for our literatures. At the moment, we have arrived at a time of new self-confidence or at least of self-searching. We are now confident enough to see our own faults and criticize our own works. At the moment, we are proud of our academic critics whose approaches border on the scientific, who are interested in revealing the structural and thematic properties of the work, in more and more analytical processes, than their predecessors of ten years back. The academic critic daily demonstrates to us that reading African literature is serious business, that careful reading is important for understanding African literature, and that there is no more room in criticism of our literatures for the dilettante expatriate "expert".

Now that our critics are basking in the warmth and sunshine of a new self-confidence, we have no more choice now but to move steadily and inexorably toward sounder and sounder knowledge of the demands and rigours of criticism, and toward sounder methods and approaches. In other words, we are moving slowly but surely toward scientific criticism. Matthew Arnold had urged that criticism worth its salt should have the quality of *disinterestedness*, that obeys an instinct that prompts it

> to try to know the best that is known and thought in the world, irrespectively of practice, politics, and everything of the kind; and to value knowledge and thought as they approach this best, without the intrusion of any other considerations whatever..[6]

To be scientific in our criticism is to be careful of one's terms, using them as unequivocally as possible and restricting our statements to what is as verifiable as possible, while not hiding the means or the sources relied upon, in order to allow our assertions to be traceable for verification.

For the 1980s then, we expect our critics to be aware of, and alive to the shifting trends in our literatures. The authors of *Toward the Decolonization of African Literature* have insistently urged: that African literature and its criticism should not be divorced from the masses, that the language should be within the ken of the average reader, that the subject matter should deal with the everyday life and realities of the people, and that our literature should not divorce itself from the participatory nature of our earlier orature. This is sound advice and no African writer on the contemporary scene should ignore it. And of recent our best writers have started to produce works that clearly involve the masses. Ousmane Sembene's *Gods Bits of Wood* and Ngugi wa Thiong'o's *Petals of Blood* clearly are novels depicting the plight of the masses in con-temporary Africa. And since trends in criticism inevitably follow each new direction, each twist and turn of art and letters, the forecast for the 1980s is that our critics would have no choice but to embrace more and more what has come to be called the Marxist approach to criticism. As our writers move closer and closer to what we call "social art"—art that contemplates society—we expect art that is propagandist, art that tends toward proletarian concerns, and inevitably, art that has Marxist overtones. It gleans then that social relevance will also be the measuring stick of our criticism which must be sensitive to the affective nature of social art and the reduction of art to social engineering with the artist as an arch ideologue. Already, some of the more avant-garde among us have declared themselves Marxist critics—the Femi Osofisans, the Omolara Leslies, the Jeyifo Bioduns. I predict that in the 1980s we are poised to hear more and more from critics with the Marxist wand. The Marxist-sociological approach to criticism of African literature will be inevitable in the 1980s.

Another challenge facing critics of African literature in the 1980s is facing the neglected frontiers of our literary and critical endeavours. We all have, up to now, neglected the short story as a genre worthy of critical attention, even though there is already a respectable body of short stories written by our most celebrated writers and other budding writers. The silence of our critics in this regard is baffling. One wonders whether we are again waiting for expatriates to take the lead, or is it that the hobby-horse of our earlier critical orientation is absent in the short story—the absence of anthropological curiosities. Whatever the case may be, our critics must be reminded that the short story as a genre is still stillborn on the African literature scene. To deliver this baby, to ensure the healthy birth of the short story (through vigorous critical response) into the mainstream of the African literary scene is a major challenge facing critics of African literature in the 1980s.

One more thing: comparative literature (a truly fertile area for criticism) is still in its infancy on our literary scene, and there is yet no respectable body of criticism on this expanding genre. The University of Port Harcourt which prides itself on its comparative approach (it awards post-graduate degrees in comparative literature) is still too much in its infancy to produce a body of criticism to which we might turn for our enlightenment. The success of its experiment will depend on the quality of its staff and the quality of its post-graduate programme

Finally, one must again call attention to Soyinka's work on myth criticism which was limited to the ritual origins of Yoruba drama. We need more of myth criticism that would embrace other genres and other African cultures since Africa is acknowledged to be rich in mythology. To research deeply and scholarly into this mythology and to use it to inform the major concerns of our literatures is another task facing our critics in the 1980s.

We are done: it remains for me to end where I began. Contemporary African literature is in full motion; it is a literature that is still being born and enriched by the discovery of new writers and new talents, and is therefore in movement—not just movement in one direction but in many directions at once. To follow critically each strand of this movement, to inform it with evaluative and sound analytical and scientific criticism and to build around it a sound poetics and critical theory, are the major challenges facing critics of African literature in the 1980s.

Moral values in the Nigerian novel*

While Nigeria squirms and agonizes over the recent elections and the disgruntlements attendant on charges of "massive rigging" by supposedly "honourable" members of the society, and while the President's "Ethical Revolution" seems to be still-born, no one seems to know which way for Nigeria to turn to get back her moral and ethical bearings. Some members of the society still believe in a "coercive force", moral or military, as the last hope for Nigeria and Africa although a quick glance at these years of military regimes in the continent of Africa, is enough to discourage those in Nigeria and Ghana or Zaire or Chad or Sudan, that "coercive force" in the gabardine of the military is enough to bring moral salvation. In the face of despair which now grips all of us, I suggest a ray of hope in our literatures. Why literature as a possible moral corrective? Why not more church sermons and more "moral instructions" in our schools? I lodge my hope in our literatures because of the permanency of its nature and in the pervasive influence it has on the very young and on our youths. The literary voice, tiny and most often *overheard* rather than *heard,* etches itself on our psyche as permanent records to which one returns again and again by the very nature of its permanent existence. The moral that literature teaches is imparted in the form of the proverbial "spoonful of sugar that makes the medicine go down." Literature makes for interesting reading.

---

* First published in *The Role of Education in Contemporary Africa* (New York: Paragon Press, 1988), pp•21-29.

African oral literature by consensus is remarked by the moral code that it attaches at the end: "this little story teaches us that ..." seems to be present in almost every African fable, every fairytale, every folktale. The attachment of a moral or a philosophy of life to every tale is not the preserve of the African raconteur. Horace, the great Roman writer hands us two unforgettable dicta: I speak the truth, laughing *(ridentem dicere verum)*, he tells us, and insists further that the function of literature is to "teach and delight" *(dulce et utile)*.

Beyond just teaching and delighting, literature exists in the main as a corrective to human folly, as a humanizing agent, and as the uplifter of our souls through *its affective* powers. As a well-recognized discipline in the humanities, literature appeals to our sense of order, restraint, discipline, imparting in its wake a sense of decorum and proportion, and especially the virtue of humility. "I owe everything to poetry" asserts Maurice de Guerin:

> I owe to it whatever I have pure, lofty, and solid in my soul. I owe to it all my consolation in the past; I shall probably owe to it my future.[1]

We must agree then, that education in the humane letters is to be trusted to uplift our souls, to refine our behaviour, and to move us away from the path of vulgarity by smoothening all the rough edges in our behaviour. And a man uplifted by his education above the current, vulgar febrile pursuit of the false symbols of life (the present malaise of our society) is more likely to be a man of ethics, of lofty morals, and a man of God. Such a man, through the subtle refinements of his sensibilities (we do not hear of that word *refine* nowadays in Nigerian society, except with reference to petroleum products!) is to be trusted to appreciate beauty and art and to live a life of self-fulfilment. Didn't Browning tell us in "Fra Lippo Lippi":

> If you get but simple beauty and naught else
> You get about the best thing God invents

Since good literature *refines* and *uplifts* us through its affective powers, we must avoid reading bad literature because it might

---

[1] Matthew Arnold: "Essays in Criticism, First Series," in *Victorian Poetry and Poetics,* ed. W. Houghton and R. Strange (Boston, 1964), p.519.

vulgarize and *debase* us. T. S. Eliot tells us:

> The author of a work of imagination is trying to affect us wholly, as human beings, whether he knows it or not; and we are affected by it, as human beings, whether we intend to be or not.[2]

All the more reason we should avoid bad literature, especially in these troubled times when our society is in a state of anomy where individuals have lost their moral bearings and find themselves adrift in the flotsam of moral wreckage because of the mad rush for power and material wealth. The best hope for the redemption of our society from its present moral bankruptcy, I insist, lies in good, serious literature. Fortunately, our most serious writers are up to the task. A glance at the concerns of the most serious writers in our midst, reveals their deep commitment to, and concern for moral values in our society.

We must naturally begin with Achebe. In two celebrated novels, *No Longer at Ease* and *A Man of the People*, Achebe displays his concern for morality and ethics in the Nigerian society. Samuel Johnson tells us in *The Rambler*:

> Vice, for vice is necessary to be shown, should always disgust; nor should the graces of gaiety, nor the dignity of courage, be so united with it, as to reconcile it to the mind Wherever it appears, it should raise hatred by the malignity of its practices, and contempt by the meanness of its stratagems ... It is therefore to be steadily inculcated, that virtue is the highest proof of understanding, and the only solid basis of greatness; and that vice is the natural consequence of narrow thoughts; that it begins in mistake, and ends in ignominy.[3]

So, Achebe, in *No Longer at Ease* lays bare for us a society steeped in bribery and corruption, where the lone voice for moral probity in the person of Obi Okonkwo succumbs finally to the moral failure of the society. It is not enough, Achebe tells us, to begin like Obi Okonkwo by mouthing moral platitudes backed by high falutin idealism. An untested virtue is no virtue at all. No one can give what he has not got, and so, Obi Okonkwo who has neither

---

[2] T. S. Eliot, "Religion and Literature" in *Five Approaches of Literary Criticism*, ed. Wilbur Scott (New York, 1979), p.48.

[3] Samuel Johnson, *The Rambler, in 18th Century Poetry and Prose*, ed. Louis Bredevold, et al. (New York, 1956), pp•690-691.

the moral courage to withstand pressures from his parents against marrying a girl who is *osu* (even though he knows them to be wrong) nor the public responsibility to influence others to be better cannot be banked upon to change his society. The kernel of the idealism with which he returns to Nigeria is maggot-ridden at the core: Obi Okonkwo is the proverbial glass jar in which is planted a sprouting oak tree. He had seen that "there was nothing in him with which to challenge his problems". When Obi Okonkwo at last succumbs to bribery, he gives credence to Mr. Green's seemingly arrogant statement that "the African is corrupt through and through". Events prove Mr. Green right. Nigeria is a country steeped in corruption. Obi Okonkwo first encounters it at the customs and tries to fight it; he sees it at work on the highway where the policeman takes bribes to accept a "certificate of road worthiness" for an 'unworthy' vehicle and tries to fight it; girls applying for scholarship tempt him with their bodies and he tries to resist them (since he understands bribery to mean "the use of improper influence"); the civil servants who swarmed the courts on the day of his trial were there after bribing doctors who grant them "sick leave". When Obi finally succumbs and is finally jailed for his offence, Achebe brings the lesson home: evil must be punished. The fall of Obi Okonkwo is the defeat of idealism. Obi Okonkwo's conception of 'tragedy (quoting W. H. Auden); that "a real tragedy takes place in a corner, in an untidy spot...the rest of the world is unaware of it" becomes ironic and an understatement. His own tragedy as well as other real tragedies, has cosmic implications. Obi Okonkwo's tragedy is the tragedy of the Nigerian society. And as Achebe insists in the novel, we are all worse off for it.

After writing *A Man of the People* Achebe had hoped (in an interview with Semuraga):

> But I think the next generation of politicians in Nigeria, when we do have them, will have learned one or two lesions, I hope, from what happened to the First Republic. This is the only hope I have and if it turns out to be in vain, it would be terrible.

As the recently concluded elections, "Verdict '83" have shown, the moral of A *Man of the People*, has not been learnt. In the novel, Achebe identifies and indicts several ills in post-independence Nigeria, especially those ills connected with the political life of the people: (a) election malpractices (breast-feeding the ballot box, use of thugs to eliminate opponents, use or abuse of the police by those in power to influence election results, rigging, and use of violence); (b) ostentatious life style by the ministers of state who collude with foreign companies to loot the nation's treasury; (c) abuse of power and megalomania by the power brokers (d) intolerance of the opinions or even the existence of those in opposing political camps (e) politics of self-aggrandisement through blatant acts of , bribery and corruption by those entrusted to preserve the country's hard-won independence. The landslide of political abuses is endless.

The hard lessons Achebe wants Nigerians to learn from *A Man of the People* (lessons that have unfortunately fallen on the nation's politically deaf ears) are that nemesis overtakes both the populace and the rulers who abuse the political system, even though they know the rules of the game, and that as long as the intellectuals leave the government of the country to illiterates who make a mockery of democracy, there will never be salvation for Nigeria, and by extension, for Africa. As some critics have tried to point out, the two protagonists Chief Nanga (Honourable, Chief, Dr., M.A., M.P.), who is illiterate but who wields power and carries the people whom he cheats with him (although devoid of any worthwhile political ideology), and Mr. Odili (who is enlightened and has some worthwhile ideas but has no political following), are like the two proverbial knives in the house .of a widow: the one that is sharp has no handle and the one that has a handle is not sharp. Nigeria, therefore, can only attain salvation when the dirty game of politics attracts the more honest elite who have worthy political ideology. In the absence of this, only God will save us all: the suggested *deus ex machina* at the end through military intervention.

Soyinka in *The Interpreters* and *Season of Anomy* is another writer that is concerned with moral issues in the Nigerian society. These two works, set also in post-independence Nigeria expose corruption and crime in the Nigerian body politic and a kind of conspiracy of silence among the elite (who act as the "Interpreters"), who are ineffectually fiddling in bars and party halls while their country is burning. Effete intellectuals talk of "moral turpitude" while in their private lives live very immoral lives and are depicted in hilarious scenes that are not funny at all; what with their endless frivolities, cheap gossip, endless drinking orgies—all showing wasted talent adrift in the moral wreckage of the country while the corrupt chairman of the council and members of the Board of Interview are busy frustrating innovative engineers like Sekoni. In *Season of Anomy* Soyinka presses his point further. The term "anomy" was first coined by the French sociologist, Emile Durkheim, to refer to several aspects of society where the conditions necessary for man to fulfil himself and to attain happiness were not there. These conditions are that conduct should be governed by norms, that those norms should form an integrated and non-conflicting system, and that limits should be set to the pleasures attainable in life. Any state where there are unclear, conflicting or unintegrated norms, in which the individual has no morally significant relations with others or in which there were no limits set to the attainment of pleasure, is in a state of anomy.[4] Both the individual and the society in a state of anomy have lost their moral bearings, lost their moral roots, and are cast adrift in a situation where neither the society nor the individual has any standards to uphold and is thoroughly vulgarized. A state of anomy thus subsumes conflicts between value systems resulting in stress and anxieties plus the deterioration of values and standards and the disintegration of values at large.

One must, of course, observe, that Achebe first hinted at Nigeria in a state of anomy in *No Longer at Ease*. Obi Okonkwo was the first among the educated elite to suffer, having come home to find himself in an anomie society. Thus, Soyinka's famous novel becomes a mere re-statement and an expansion of a situation first glimpsed by Achebe who thus robs him of originality But Soyinka's Aiyero, exploited and brutalized by the profit-hungry cartel reflects in depth the dangerous and harassed path which the Nigerian society currently treads. The activities of the cartel and the bloodletting unleashed on fellow citizens of the Cross River led by Zaki Amuri are re-enactments of events in Nigeria before the civil war. Wanton destruction of life and property are moral issues; unfair election practices and bribery and corruption are moral issues dwelt on by our novelists. The Nigerian novelist, therefore, is not a helpless onlooker but a courageous fighter against the moral decadence in our society. Achebe and Soyinka tackle these problems by making satiric thrusts at the ills of our society.

Okara in *The Voice* tells a not-so-gory tale, but the subtlety of his artistic vision is very penetrating. The activities of Chief Izongo

---

[4] *A New Dictionary of Sociology*, ed. G. Duncan Mitchell (London: Routledge and Keegan, 1979), p. 7.

who buys people's consciences and intimidates them into compliance and acquiescence are etched in very vivid light. Then, a moral voice, quiet and insistent is introduced: that of Okolo ("the voice"). This voice makes Chief Izongo and his cabal rather uncomfortable and all of them collude to destroy Okolo. Okolo's obsessive quest: asking people if they have got it threatens the immoral and timid elements of the society, for he is asking them if they were satisfied with the way they were governed, with the quality of their lives, and whether they have allowed Chief Izongo "to buy the insides of all the people". And he goes further to ask Abadi who has got his M.A. and Ph.D. but not "it" why this is so. Okolo, that voice in the wilderness crying for the moral regeneration of his society, accuses the rulers and politicians of having accepted "the shadow-devouring trinity of gold, iron, concrete", reminding them that the worst enemies of the society are those who say like the messenger: "As for me ... if the world turns this way, I take it. Any way the world turns, I take it with my hands. I like sleep ... so I do not think"; and like the elder who thinks nothing can be done when he says: "If they do anything I agree, since they do not take yam out of my mouth". All these people Okolo condemns as "think-nothing people" who are "like logs in the river" and "float and go whither the current commands." These, of course, are the people of Sologa who bundled Okolo and Tuere and exiled them in a floating canoe, with their limbs tied up, so that they inevitably drowned in the whirlpool.

What Okara tells us in *The Voice* is that the onus of moral regeneration in our society lies with the intellectuals. Nietzsche had said that "society needs an elite that will set a pattern and curb the thoughtlessness of the masses". This Okolo tried to do and lost his life. This Odili of *A Man of the People* tried to do but had not the power base to accomplish. To this The "interpreters" of Soyinka's novel woefully failed to address themselves. All the authors discussed so far have one common premise: the burden of ridding our society of bribery and corruption and of immorality lies with the intellectuals. The Man and the Teacher in Armah's *The Beautyful Ones Are Not Yet Born* perform also the functions of the intellectuals in their society. But they are too apathetic, too detached to influence the society for the better: hence the tragedy of Ghana. For those who have never put the facts together, here it is: our most serious writers, those preoccupied with morality and immorality in our societies have always laid at the door of the intellectual, the burden of redeeming our society from moral decadence and that the duty of the elite is that of applying correctives to the ills in our society. Silence, therefore, from the intellectuals is fatal to the cause of moral regeneration in our body politic.

The famous critic, T. S. Eliot tells us that serious literature addresses itself to definite ethical and theological issues, and that "the greatness of literature cannot be determined solely by literary standards", because literature must be backed by great ethical and religious support, for great works of literature have been and "probably always will be judged by some moral standards."[5] Nigeria, at present is at the threshold of moral decadence. In setting up the National Ethical Re-orientation in 1982, President Shehu Shagari admitted that our society is in need of ethical and moral re-orientation when he charged the committee:

> To study the nature and extent of causes and the apparent breakdown in our national ethic and discipline in all its ramifications

In this "season of anomy" individuals who steal, rob, commit murder and commit suicide are reacting in extremely unpleasant ways to the stresses in our society, after realizing that none of the essential decencies with which a decent society is associated can be taken for granted any more, as most of the things held sacred are collapsing before them. Dwelling, therefore, on ethical and moral issues in our literatures is therefore imperative in these times when society has benumbed itself with the inordinate quest for materialism, when worship of ill-gotten goods has become our non-Sunday religion. We, therefore, need a moral tone in our literatures to teach the youth (are writers of the Drumbeat and Pacesetters series listening?) that evil doesn't pay, and to stress moral probity, 'honour and integrity as goods worth cultivating. Creative writers are our merchants of light and our elite are to be trusted with carrying that light to the darkest corners of our society. Let our creative writers and the intellectual elite be the bearers of light in this darksome era. As Portia, in a light hearted mood, tells Nerissa after saving Antonio's life in *The Merchant of Venice*:

> How far that little candle throws his beams
> so shines a good deed in a naughty world

---

[5] T. S. Eliot, *op. cit,* p.43

> May our writers and the intellectuals in our midst be that
> little candle that shines like a good deed in our naughty world.

Although this study has concentrated on the novel, I would like to end it with a citation from Collier's comment on the moral import of drama:

> The business of plays is to recommend virtue, and discountenance vice, to show the uncertainty of human greatness, the sudden turns of fate, and the unhappy conclusions of violence and injustice: it is to expose the singularities of pride and fancy, to make folly and falsehood contemptible, and to bring everything that is ill under infamy and neglect.[6]

---

[6] Jeremy Collier, "A Short View of the Immorality and Profaneness of the English Stage," in *English Literary Criticism: Restoration and the 18th Century*, ed. Samuel Hayes (New York: Appleton-Century Crofts, 1963), p.97.

12

The unhappy woman in Nigerian fiction: a mythic interpretation of the archetypes*

From the Edenic myth to modern times beautiful women have been depicted as angels with feet of clay, and as purveyors of unhappiness both for themselves and their men counterparts. Eve plucked the apple in the Garden of Eden, in man's first act of what Northrop Frye calls *Proairesis:* the use of freedom to lose freedom, and unfortunately she involves Adam and all mankind. By Milton's account in *Paradise Lost* Eve was a perfect beauty even if narcissistic, and Adam falls deliberately so as not to separate his life from that of his perfect beauty. Adam falls because he was uxorious. In Greek mythology Eris, in what has come down to us as Troy Tale, threw the apple of discord into the garden where the marriage of Peleus and Thetis was being celebrated and indirectly triggers off the Trojan War, for the apple on which was written "to the fairest" was awarded to Aphrodite by Paris to whom she had promised "the most beautiful woman in the world" if she (Aphrodite) won the apple as "the fairest". To make good her promise, she (Aphrodite) helped Paris elope with Helen of Troy who was then married to Menelaus, king of Sparta. And this precipitated the ten-year Trojan War.

---

* First appeared as "Mythology and the Unhappy Woman in Nigeria Fiction" in *Calabar Studies in African Literature*. Ibadan, Heinemann (1987), pp. 45-54.

Helen of Troy becomes the first anima image in classical literature, sowing sorrow, war, and confusion among her people in classical times. Her "dangerous beauty" caused her and her people a lot of woe. In the wake of Helen's example, dangerously beautiful women who act as sirens luring men to perdition and death are called the *femme fatale* or the dangerous woman, who either denies a man his man-hood or acts as a "castrating" figure who emasculates a man by making him a slave to her beauty. Circe who turns men into swine in Homer's *The Odyssey* becomes *par excellence* the archetypal woman as *femme fatale*.

Literature records many other perfectly beautiful women, temptresses who sometimes unwillingly or because of something beyond their control have a pact with the devil for the destruction of the hero. As we shall see in this study, Nigerian writers—Chinua Achebe, Wole Soyinka, J. P. Clark, Elechi Amadi, Flora Nwapa, and Onuora Nzekwu have used this idea of the *femme fatale* to depict unhappiness in the heroines of their own creation. If those women are fecund and prolific in child bearing, that blessing becomes the source of their unhappiness. If they are very beautiful and perfect models among their kind, their very perfection brings them unhappiness, for they are denied what every woman longs for—children. That these Nigerian writers lodge the source of this unhappiness in mythology is a *tour de force* on their artistic insights, for most often no earthly reason could be adduced for what causes this unhappiness for a woman who is loving, industrious, a model of good behaviour, and infinitely desirable to their men folk to whom they often bring disaster (Ihuoma in *The Concubine*) or unhappiness (Peter Obiesie in *Wand of Noble Wood*). According to Northrop Frye:

> The demonic erotic relation between man and woman becomes a fierce destructive passion that works against loyalty or frustrates the one who possesses it. It is symbolized by a...witch, siren or other tantalizing female, a physical object of desire which is sought as a possession and therefore can never be possessed.[1]

Before we, proceed further, it should be clearly stated that in Nigerian literature, especially in literature of the Igbo, ritual accounts for and communicates a myth, and divination becomes a

---

[1] Northrop Frye, *Anatomy of Criticism* (Princeton, New Jersey: Princeton University Press, 1971), p.149.

ritual method of communicating hidden myths gleaned from common knowledge in society, and the priest-diviner becomes the custodian and interpreter of these myths. In each case, divination becomes a ritual method of interpreting the myth of the sea-king (Elechi Amadi in *The Concubine*), or the myth of Uhamiri (Flora Nwapa in *Efuru*), or the incidence of *Abiku* or *ogbanje* or *Iyi-ocha* (Onuora Nzekwu in *Wand of Noble Wood*). The archetypes revealed above coalesce around those of the anima or *femme fatale*—archetypes already identified in western literature. Excessive beauty in a woman, it must be re-stated, does not come in the collective unconscious of the Igbo people, "empty-handed". It drags along with it an incubus, because of the belief that perfection cannot be found in a mortal. This is a kind of fatalism, for the Igbos believe that God gives with one hand and takes away with another. A beautiful woman who is fecund cannot be allowed to be perfectly happy since children make for a woman's fulfilment both in life and marriage—to allow her to enjoy her beauty and at the same time enjoy the joys of motherhood would be too much of a blessing for one mortal.

Such a woman is either afflicted with *abiku* children—those children who come and go and refuse to survive infancy. Or if she is beautiful and has surviving children, she cannot be allowed to have everything, so she is most often afflicted with an unhappy marriage. If, on the other hand she has surviving children, is beautiful, and is happily married, extreme poverty denies her perfect joys. But most often, beautiful women who are happily married are denied the joys of motherhood, the ultimate affliction which is infertility or barrenness. All these reflect fatalism in a people who take suffering as an inevitable concomitant of existence in a world full of inscrutable occurrences. In the mythopoesis of the Nigerian, especially the Igbo, the gods who apportion happiness and suffering in an inscrutable world ensure that no woman has all the desirable things of the world. A quick glance at the poetry of Christopher Okigbo's "Silences" reveal in the song of the "silent sisters" who vow each to die in the bloom of youth a most terrifying aspect of the *abiku* syndrome. One chooses to die the moment she goes to the stream to fetch water; the other chooses to die the day she is married; the other chooses to die at child-birth. And at the moment of death, others in their group who had taken the oath will gather around her and sing a song reminding her (in case she is reluctant) of her oath and Promise. Thus, these silent sisters who die in the bloom of their youth, spread sorrow and heart-break in their wake—to mothers, their newborn babies, their sweethearts and their newly-wed bridegrooms. What follows below is an expansion, with concrete examples from Nigerian literature, of the promise stated above.

II

Unhappiness for women in Nigerian fiction is reflected in various local myths which act as quarries for our poets and novelists. One example is the cause of unhappiness for fecund mothers—these blessed with many children. The "joys" of motherhood are celebrated by our male and female writers and found their apogee in Buchi Emecheta's title in one of her novels. In looking closely at that novel, irony skirts those "joys" as Emecheta clothes them with ambivalence. In any case the myth of *Abiku* or *ogbanje* has become an incontrovertible strain in the works of Achebe, Soyinka and J. P. Clark. Fecund mothers ("What we are all praying for are children. What else do we want if we have children" says Flora Nwapa in *Idu*) can be unhappy, and the source of that unhappiness is lodged in myth, for the concept of fate cannot escape prolific mothers. The myth of *abiku* provides the answer. Ezinma, a clear case of *Ogbanje* or *Abiku*, gives many anxious moments to her mother, Ekwefi, in *Things Fall Apart*, with her erratic behaviour and "sudden bouts of sickness", and Ekwefi was not to know peace of mind until Ezinma's *Iyi Uwa* was located and dug up by a medicine man.

In Igbo mythology, and this seems no different from the mythology of non-Igbos as recounted by J. P. Clark (Ijaw) and Wole Soyinka (Yoruba), an *abiku* or *obganje* is one who goes through a continuous cycle of birth and death as a result of some primeval oath taken in the spirit world by the *abiku* before its birth, and the oath is binding throughout the votary's short - life-span. The object of the oath is usually hidden away from ordinary human sight and usually buried underneath or nearby a huge tree or in the person's palm. Most often an *ogbanje* never knows that he or she is one (even though under the spell he or she communicates telepathically with other kindred spirits or fellow *ogbanjes* until a fortune teller or another *ogbanje* under the spell points out the fact.[2]

Unhappiness for mothers of Abiku stems from the child's constant sickness, erratic behaviour, and sudden death. Since the Abiku comes and goes, anxious and heartbroken mothers try to discourage a repeat through punitive measures like scarification, singeing a part of the dead Abiku before burial, and so on.

In *Things Fall Apart*, Onwumbiko, Ekwefi's child who died as *ogbanje* "was not given proper burial when he died."[3] The medicine man had mutilated his body and dragged it on the ground to the evil forest wilt re he was buried (p.69). Because unhappiness for mothers of *ogbanje* is stressed, Achebe tells us that "By the time Onwumbiko died, Ekwefi had become a very bitter woman" (p.69). He further tells us:

> Ekwefi had suffered a good deal in her life. She had borne ten children and nine of them had died in infancy, usually before the age of three. As she buried one child after another her sorrow gave way to despair and then to grim resignation. The birth of, her children, which should be a woman's crowning glory, became for Ekwefi mere physical agony devoid of promise. The naming ceremony after seven market weeks became an empty ritual. Her deepening despair found expression in the names she gave her children. One of them was a pathetic cry, Onwumbiko—"Death I implore you". But death took no notice; Onwumbiko died in his fifteenth month. The next child was a girl, Ozoemena— "May it not happen again." She died in her eleventh month, and two others after her. Ekwefi then became defiant and called her next child Onwuma—"Death may please himself". And he did (pp.67-68).

J. P. Clark in his celebrated poem "Abiku" stresses this unhappiness for afflicted mothers as the poor anxious mother in this poem pleads with and appeals to the child to "Step in and stay/For good" because "her body is tired/Tired, her milk going sour". She prays the child to stay even if "it leaks through the thatch/When floods brim the bank."[4]

Wole Soyinka depicts in his poem of the same title a defiant,

---

[2] Ogbolu Okonji, "Ogbanje: An African Conception of Predestination," *The African Scholar*, Vol.1, No.4 (1970), p.1.

[3] Chinua Achebe, *Things Fall Apart* (London: Heinemann, 1958), p.68. Subsequent page references will be cited in the text.

[4] See D. I. Nwoga (ed.), *West African Verse* (Longman, 1967), p.61.

stubborn Abiku who comes to torment its mother and cause her despair by boasting of its exploits, for, as it boasts: "In vain your bangles cast/Charmed circles at my feet."[5]

But if our writers attribute fecundity or fertility as the cause of unhappiness in women, they also, as can be expected, depict more unhappiness in women who don't bear children. This is first seen in Flora Nwapa's *Efuru*. Flora Nwapa digs into mythology for the cause of Efuru's infertility and hence, the source of her unhappiness. Efuru is a model of good behaviour and none is more pretty. In addition, she is industrious, considerate, and a loving wife but she is burdened with a cleft foot, a disability, the woman's feet of clay. In a society where women are child-hungry—Efuru has no children. The reason? The water-goddess, Uhamiri, has chosen her as her votary and a woman so chosen or so branded will never know "the joys of mother-hood". Her only daughter from her first marriage had died and her marriage had gone awry and subsequently collapsed because she could not bear another child. Her subsequent remarriage went the way of the first for the same reason. The choice of Efuru by the water-goddess, Uhamiri, becomes a blessing that carries in its train a mighty curse: infertility and the subsequent childlessness.

Uhamiri, the water-goddess when first seen by Efuru was "an elegant woman, very beautiful, combing her long black hair with a golden comb."[6]

When Omirima, in a conversation with Gilbert's mother heard that Efuru is now a worshipper of Uhamiri, she said in a voice full of disappointment:

> She has spoilt everything. This is bad. How many women in this town who worship Uhamiri have children?...all right let's count them: Ogini Azogu...She had a son before she became worshipper of Uhamiri, since then she has not got another child. Two, Nwanjafor Ojimba, she has no child at all. Three, Uzoechi Ngenege, no child. They are all over the place. Why do we bother ourselves counting them (p. 203).

So, Efuru is a great woman with flawed grandeur. The villagers admit to Gilbert's mother:

---

[5] Ibid., p.62.
[6] Flora Nwapa, *Efuru* (London: Heinemann, 1966), p.183. Subsequent page references will be cited in the text.

Your daughter-in-law is good, but she is childless. She is wealthy but riches cannot go on errands for us (p.205).

So, in spite of the established fact that by her choice of Efuru the water-goddess enhanced her beauty and made her wealthy, respectable, and a great woman in her society, Flora Nwapa ends her novel with an ambivalent question: since those women favoured by her "never experienced the joy of motherhood, why then did the women worship her?" (p. 281).

Next, Elechi Amadi's *The Concubine* engages our attention. The same irony, the same ambivalence shrouds Ihuoma's "good luck" in being chosen as the wife of the sea-king. The name Ihuoma according to Elechi Amadi is "beautiful face" or "good luck."[7] What good luck is it, one may ask, which ensures that Ihuoma who is fecund and has several children, would never know the joys of conjugal love? Her good luck bears in its train the curse of unhappiness, of repeated widowhood, of never knowing the joys which come from living for long with the marked men for whom she unwittingly purveys death as their concubine. Hers is the one clear case of the *femme fatale* although she never intends to be one. When her friend, Nnenda praises her beauty she protests: "I don't want to look beautiful...Beauty seems to carry sorrow with it...Ugly people do not seem to suffer as much as the beautiful" (p.35).

Indeed, Ihuoma's remarkable beauty tinged with sorrow bewitches all beholders, both men and women: "the tired look on her face gave way to a sweet youthful expression, softly alluring, deeply enchanting, which had a bewitching subtlety that only deep sorrow can give...Young men and even the old gazed at her irresistibly" (p. 36). That beauty of hers occasions unsolicited comments from friend and foe alike. The author laid it on with a trowel in scattered comments:

> Ihuoma's complexion was that of the ant-hill. Her features were smoothly rounded and looking at her no one could doubt that she was "enjoying her husband's wealth" (p.10).
> Her smiles were disarming. Perhaps the upper row of her white regular teeth did the trick. At that time a gap in the teeth was fashionable. Any girl who was not favoured with one employed the

---

[7] Elechi Amadi, *The Concubine* (London: Heinemann, 1966), p.203. Subsequent page references will be cited in the text.

services of carvers who could create them (p. 11).

But more phenomenal was her perfect behaviour, her being etched in the role of a model for all women:

> She was sympathetic, gentle, reserved. It was her husband's boast that in their six years of marriage she had never had any serious quarrel with another woman. She was not good at invectives and other women talked faster than she did ... In this way her prestige among the women-folk grew until even the most garrulous among them was reluctant to be unpleasant to her. She found herself settling quarrels and offering advice to older women (pp.11-12).

Ihuoma's good nature was so undisputed that the unheard of happened: potential rivals in love were willing to yield her pride of place if their husband decided to bring her in as a second wife. Amadi might have stretched the point quite far, but Wolu, Madume's first wife was glad to yield her place as number one wife in their household, should her husband decide to marry Ihuoma. In scattered comments she says:

> She's just a well-behaved woman who takes good care of herself...She is about the best woman in the village...I would gladly be the second wife where she is the first; not the reverse...she is...better than I (pp.54, 55).

When Ekwueme first told his mother, Adaku, that he was contemplating marrying Ihuoma, she expressed reservations because Ihuoma was too good for him:

> If you are thinking of Ihuoma, forget her.
> She is easily the best woman in the village.
> She can't do anything shameful (p.92).

With her graceful carriage, Ekwueme "came near to worshipping her," and

> The women adored her. Men were awestruck before her. She was becoming something of a phenomenon (p.153).

But Ihuoma was not happy. Elechi Amadi took recourse to the myth of the sea-king as the cause of unhappiness for this perfect model with a curse on her head. When Ekwueme told her to her face that she was beautiful, she protested:

> I am not responsible for my beauty...Besides, beauty does not always mean happiness. I have not been a very happy woman (p.214)

Events prove her right. Her first husband, Emenike had suddenly died of lock-chest. Big-eyed Madume who had manhandled her and later contemplated marrying her had committed suicide when a spitting cobra blinded him. And when Ekwueme became her second husband and she had looked forward to being happy again, her son's arrow kills Ekwueme. Why all this concatenation of unhappy occurrences? Amadi has recourse to mythology to prove that these occurrences are not just happenstance. As Anyika divined later:

> Ihuoma belongs to the sea. When she was in the spirit world she was a wife of the Sea-King, the ruling spirit of the sea. Against the advice of her husband she sought the company of human beings and was incarnated. The Sea-King was very angry but because he loved her best of all his wives he did not destroy her immediately she was born. He decided to humour her and let her live out her normal earthly span and come back to him. However, because of his great love for her he is terribly jealous and tries to destroy any man who makes love to her (p.195).

The diviner also confirms that "as soon as Emenike married Ihuoma his life was forfeit and nothing would have saved him"; and that "Madume's real trouble began after he assaulted Ihuoma while she was harvesting plantains. Added to this was the fact that he had a secret desire to make Ihuoma his lover or maybe marry her. All this was too much for the Sea-King and he himself assumed the form of a serpent and dealt with his rival" (p.195).

In Nigerian fiction, Ihuoma is the best realized example of the *femme fatale* which enunciates the myth of the "castrating female" or the dangerous woman who is a siren luring men to their death with her bewitching beauty and song. Ihuoma's beauty prompts

Ekwueme to a death wish: "If" he says, "marrying a woman like her is a fatal mistake I am prepared to make it. If I am her husband for a day before my death my soul will go singing happily to the spirit world" (p.197). And so it came to pass! In Ihuoma's role as a *femme fatale* we have subsumed in one, the role of Eve, of Helen of Troy, of Clytemnestra, of the wicked sirens of mythology, of Circe.

Of these anima images in literature as they relate to the wishes of Ekwueme just quoted, Carl Jung makes a significant statement. He asserts that man

> imagines his worst enemy in front of him, yet he carries the enemy within himself—a deadly longing for the abyss, a longing to drown in his own source, to be sucked down to the realm of the mothers...This death is no external enemy, it is his own inner longing for the stillness and profound peace of all-knowing non-existence, for all-seeing sleep in the ocean of coming-to-be and passing away.[8]

Ekwueme's death-wish has been fulfilled. He has answered the call of the siren.

Onuora Nzekwe's *Wand of Noble Wood* completes the circle. The heroine of *Wand of Noble Wood*, Nneka, has all the makings of the tragic heroine whose very beauty and perfection are the source of sorrow, for nature gives with one hand and takes away with another. She is both beautiful and a great dancer:

> She is tall, about five-feet six. She has a nice shape and a good gait and she is slim. Men turn to admire her when goes along the street. Women she envy her. She is not proud. She comes from a good family. She is a good girl and I am sure she'll make a good wife.

But she adds polish to these natural attributes. In addition to being "the best dancer of the lot" (p.101), she is also educated, an accomplishment that *Efuru* and *Ihuoma* lack.

But Nneka has the same disability of the cleft foot. She is an object of beauty with a curse on her head. Like the Abiku, while she was still in her mother's womb, she became the subject of a curse

---

[8] Carl Jung, *Symbols of Transformation* (New York: Harper Torch Books, 1952), p.356.

which must be exorcised before she could marry happily. Her mother had bought cloth from a cloth-seller and had thought she paid the seller which the seller denied. It was later discovered that the money was left in the house. In anger, the cloth-seller cursed Nneka's pregnant mother and the child in her womb was Nneka. As she narrates it to Peter Obiesie to whom she has just been engaged:

> "the cloth-seller cursed the pregnant woman and the child in her womb. She called on a deity, an *alusi* called *iyi ocha*, to take revenge on them for cheating her...Daddy says the curse is upon me too. He does not want it to be visited upon you, as it certainly will be, if you marry me" (pp.129-130)

In spite of expensive ritual sacrifices undertaken to exorcise the curse, a wicked agent, Ikem Ono, a rejected suitor of Nneka, had removed a vital ingredient necessary for the exorcism and Nneka took her life on the night preceding her wedding to protect her intended husband from inheriting the curse. Her mother told her of this in a vision:

> "Nneka, the white stone, the most important item in the *iyi ocha*, was missing from the bundle on which the curse on you was said to have been lifted. Without it no *iyi ocha* curse can be revoked; so you see the curse has not left you. If you marry Peter Obiesie, he will die at the hands of *iyi ocha* on the night your marriage will be consummated. Take the advice of your mother; do not bring misfortune on yourself and on others" (pp.206-207).

So, Nneka, a potential carrier as *femme-fatale* takes her life to avert dragging others along with her to their ruin. Her suicide becomes a tragically noble gesture undertaken to save others from the fate of the cursed, of which she is a victim

We are done. It remains for me to extend kudos to the writers examined in this study for delving into other myths to explain away the cause of unhappiness in women who are their tragic heroines. Why women are looked upon in Christian and other mythologies as creatures of misfortune, why Freud says they suffer from a "castration complex" from the point of view of psychoanalysis, and why the English call them "woe-man" (woman) has not been adequately explained from the rational logical point of view.

Feminists might rebel and blame the church and men generally, for this "debasement" of the female image in our literatures, but the myth persists in all societies and all mythologies, and Flora Nwapa, a feminist in her own right, has not helped matters for feminists by creating Efuru. What one can say finally is that explaining the origins of myths is beyond us, be women ever so unhappy in the way myth affects them negatively. But the use of what Soyinka terms "the African self-apprehended world in myth and literature' by our writers is encouraging, and only in their continued use will African literature be finally decolonized. According to Soyinka, African literature should continue to be "engaged in what should be the simultaneous act of eliciting from history, mythology and literature, for the benefit of both genuine aliens and alienated Africans, a continuing process of self-apprehension whose temporary dislocation appears to have persuaded many of its non-existence or its relevance."

13

The "Sons of Achebe": example of John Munonye*

There is no organized academy of writers known as "the sons of Achebe", although the term has been used quite often by literary critics. But for the purposes of this chapter, I identify as "sons of Achebe" all those first generation of African men and women who took to their literary calling in the footsteps of *Things Fall Apart*.

The sons of Achebe are those early post-Achebe writers who were so fascinated with the subject matter and technique which Achebe so admirably perfected that they set out consciously or unconsciously to imitate him. Outside Nigeria, Ngugi wa Thiong'o and Ayi Kwei Armah are Achebe's disciples by writing in that tradition of Achebe's novels identified as "archetypal" and which describes the impact of the coming of Europeans on African societies and the conflict and attendant disintegration of such societies as a result. And they are not absolved from writing another brand of novels inaugurated by Achebe and identified by Larson as "the situational novel" which exists to present a group-felt experience so that whatever happens to the protagonist is felt by all the people involved in the story because the individual identifies

---

* First published in *Kriteria*, vol.1, No.1 (February, 1988), 1-13. In an interview with Munonye, Nnolim had asked him whether he was "one of what they call 'the sons of Achebe'", as if he had "consciously set out to imitate him". Munonye's reply: "No, no, no... I don't think my style in any way resembles his." For the interview: See *Okike* 24 (June, 1983): 77-90.

with his society and acts as that society's consciousness. Armah and wa Thiong'o also follow in Achebe's tradition by their treatment of post-independence African societies displaying a 'colonial' mentality, and full of 'imperialist' stooges who collaborate with the imperialist to milk their countries dry for the benefit of post-colonial masters. Armah's *The Beautyful Ones Are Not Yet Born* and *Fragments* and Ngugi wa Thiong'o's *Weep Not Child*, *The River Between*, and *A Grain of Wheat* are in the Achebe tradition.

Within Nigeria, John Munonye *(The Only Son, Obi, A Wreath for the Maidens, Bridge to a Wedding);* Elechi Amadi *(The Concubine, The Slave, The Great Ponds);* Onuora Nzekwu *(Wand of Noble Wood, Blade Among the Boys);* T. M. Aluko *(One Man, One Wife, One Man, One Matchet, Chief the Honourable Minister);* Flora Nwapa *(Efuru, Idu),* are writers that must be identified as the "sons" of Achebe in more ways than one.

Beyond trying to copy Achebe in subject-matter as mentioned above, the "sons of Achebe" try, like Achebe, to weave the local proverb into their narrative, to use our native myths, rituals, ceremonies, and legends unashamedly in their stories, and to promote awareness of what is really great and dignified in our culture. On a more subtle level, the "sons" of Achebe revel like him in ancestor worship and follow his tradition of cultural nationalism by trying, like him, to rehabilitate the dignity of the black man bruised and denigrated by the colonial master. This study intends to demonstrate that in writing *The Only Son* and *A Wreath for the Maidens,* Munonye could not have ignored Achebe's *Things Fall Apart* and *A Man of the People,* and did not ignore him in the least; in fact he did set out, perhaps unconsciously, to imitate Achebe, if not in those quirks and mannerisms called style, at least, in setting, subject matter, and narra-tive point of view. Let us then begin with *Things Fall Apart* and *The Only Son.*

To begin with, Achebe set his *Things Fall Apart* in Umuofia (children of the forest) and set out to record the rise of Okonkwo who, through a mischance ran to Mbanta (his mother's place) for protection. In his absence, the white man came to Umuofia with his destabilizing religion and civilization. Munonye set *The Only Son* in Umudiobia (children of strangers) and set out to record the precarious life of an only son, Nnanna, who (after a fight) escaped to Nade (his mother's place) where he met the coming of the white man with its destabilizing religion and civilization. But while

Okonkwo returns to die in resisting the white man, Nnanna stays on to embrace and prosper from the allure of the white man's religion and civilization. The ending of each of these first novels at once reveals the philosophic outlook of each writer: while Achebe's story wears the face of tragedy in its record of a collective loss, Munonye's story wears the face of comedy in its record of progressive gain for the protagonist, in spite of the disappointment expressed by Nnanna's mother, Chiaku. Characteristically, Achebe's *Things Fall Apart* is a closed novel ending with the death of Okonkwo, while Munonye's is an open novel, ending in pregnancy for Chiaku (with the hope of a new life) and further adventures for Nnanna who joins Father Smith at Ossa, to chart a new course for himself. We must immediately observe that while Achebe sketches the cosmic implications of the colonial intrusion in Umuofia which ends in the death of a way of life for the Igbos, Munonye paints the picture of a seemingly minor impact of the same colonial intrusion on the household of a widow who, instead of succumbing to her own discomfiture and committing suicide, chooses a better alternative that leads to a new life and happiness through remarriage. Although there is no room to discuss it in detail here, we must bear in mind that Achebe, is essentially a writer of the tragic vision while Munonye's vision is, for the most part, comic.

In writing *The Only Son*, Munonye used Achebe's *Things Fall Apart* as his obvious quarry. In the latter, we remember that missionary activities provided the ammunition for many a do-or-die confrontation between the natives and the zealous converts. In *Things Fall Apart*, the natives looked at the misguided missionaries with benign amusement and allowed them to establish their church in the evil forest if that was where their demented sensibilities wanted to domicile their headquarters. This was the point of the greatest interest for Munonye and the main area of artistic indebtedness to Achebe. As in Umuofia, Nade was equally accommodating. Following Achebe, Munonye says that "when baldheaded Francis Osita, *alias* Ositason, arrived in Nade to start the church, hardly anybody took him seriously. The rulers merely left him at the mercy of the most prominent witch doctors of the land" (72). But soon the point at issue in both works centred around Christian defiance of the sacred sanction and the breaking of the taboo and the consequences of such brazen behaviour. In *Things Fall Apart*, it was Okoli who killed the sacred python out of zeal, and the consequence

> He had fallen ill on the previous night. Before the day was over he was dead. His death showed that the gods were still able to fight their own battles (145)

Compare the above with Munonye. In *The Only Son*, it was the same category of people we have *in Things Fall Apart* who first embraced the Christian religion — the *efulefus;* outcasts, and cult slaves – and they were the most zealous, and the same fate awaited those breakers of the sacred sanction. Munonye says:

> Take the two friends, David and Dominic. Throughout Nade, these two men were better known as ex-slaves than as anything else. Slavery had been abolished; but that did not mean that a freed slave, was equal to a free-born... Over the years, David and Dominic had fretted under jibes of this nature. Then the church arrived and preached, among other things, equality of all human beings, great or small, man or woman, slave or free, before the Maker. Taking advantage of the teaching, they rebelled against their status. They were the very first converts George made in the town... Unknown to him, they proceeded to Igwe's shrine which was about three hundred yards away. About twenty minutes later, a mournful cry arose from there. "Igwe has been assaulted!" the voice said.
>
> Nade seldom acted in a hurry, and they did not in this case. Full twenty-eight days passed. On the morning of the twenty-ninth, David and Dominic were both reported dead. The story went that each of them had died quietly, and in his own house. It was Igwe that did it (74-75).

Several facts from Achebe come together in the above passage; the status of the converts, their overzealous impudence, their iconoclastic tendencies, and the residual powers of the traditional gods which still mustered enough powers to demonstrate their continued potency against breakers of the taboo. Achebe had said in *Things Fall Apart* that none of the converts

> was a man whose word was heeded in the assembly. None of them was a man of title. They were mostly the kind of people that were called efulfu, worthless, empty men...Chielo, the priestess of Agbala, called the converts the excrement of the clan and the new faith was a mad dog that had come to eat it up (128).

Now, Munonye's David and Dominic also share the same social status with Achebe's Enoch. While the former were freed slaves, the latter was an *Osu*, a cult-slave, since "his father was the priest of the snake cult" (159). Any wonder that Enoch's zeal knew no bounds. The zealous Enoch that unmasked the *egwugwu* (an act that caused the destruction of the church by enraged masked spirits and precipitated the imprisonment of important men in Umuofia, including Okonkwo) was the same zealot that "had killed and eaten the sacred python" (159). And the fate of Okoli in *Things Fall Apart* which resembles the fate of David and Dominic in *The Only Son* is extended in a watered-down fashion in the latter novel to show the continued power of the old over the fledging adherents of the new. When bald headed Francis Osita, *alias* Ositason, in *The Only Son*, defied the masked spirits, "then, before him, the masquerade waved the small, black idol in its hand, after which, it ran away, the attendant following closely behind. A few days later, Francis discovered big leprous patches all over his body. He left Nade before the story spread" (73).

The above recreates the activities of zealous converts in the first novels of the two authors under study. Munonye published his novel eight full years after Achebe, and it would be instructive to see how both novelists represented the missionaries themselves, their characters, and their proselytizing techniques. What Munonye did was a simple inversion of Achebe's mode of presentation. In Achebe, Mr. Brown, the first missionary in Umuofia, was a tactful, cautious man who was on the side of com-promise and accommodation, in order to give his church a firm footing in a hostile environment. Mr. Brown was replaced by the no-nonsense hard-liner, Mr. Smith, under whose tough stand the neophyte church came to grief in Umuofia. According to Achebe, "there was a saying in Umuofia that as a man danced so the drums were beaten for him. Mr. Smith danced a furious step and so the drums went mad" (165). Naturally, under Mr. Smith's lead, characters like Okoli and Enoch emerged. And Enoch's devotion to the new faith "seemed so much greater than Smith's that the villagers called him the outsider who wept louder than the bereaved" (165).

Munonye in *The Only Son* inverted the order of the appearance of the missionaries—all protestants in the two novels. While in Achebe, the tactful Mr. Brown is followed by the heedless zealot, Mr. Smith, whose fanaticism fuelled the events that brought grief to the church, in Munonye, the first to arrive were that fanatics bringing along their sound and their fury before a wiser, more tactful missionary came to Nade to give the church a firm footing. Mr. Ositason had foolishly confronted a masked man who afflicted him with leprosy. On his leaving Nade, Mr. George, more fanatical and ear-clouting, next arrived:

> Some of the audience...called him a lunatic orator; some just snapped their fingers in their horror at the things that were coming out of the lunatic's mouth (73).

When George left Nade, blinded in one eye by his jealous wife for ogling the girls in his church, he was succeeded by Joseph who was

> quite cool-headed and calculating in his ways. Francis had offended the masquerade world and that had ruined him, he told himself. George had been too aggressive in his approach. He was going to move cautiously...he would start a school...Joseph's success was phenomenal (75-76)

Achebe's *Things Fall Apart* draws attention to Okonkwo's reaction when his son joined that miscreant crowd, the Christians. Munonye's *The Only Son* equally re-creates Chiaku's reaction when Nnanna joined the church. To each parent, each son's conversion signals that part of the break-up of the cohesiveness of the old order which the coming of the white man was a harbinger. But while in Achebe, the cosmic implications of the break-up of the older order lends sublimity to *Things Fall Apart,* in Munonye, the ripples of that break-up seem to be confined to the discomfiture of a widow who in a swift reaction, charts for herself a new, more comforting course through remarriage. This underlines the basic philosophic outlook of each writer. For Achebe, his tragic vision shows itself through loss; for Munonye, his comic vision is seen through regain. But in both Achebe and Munonye, no matter the opposition from the natives, the new order prevailed and gained a firm foothold in the societies mirrored.

In *Things Fall Apart,* Nwoye's callow soul drinks in the poetry of the new religion, as he abandons the harshness of his father's aggressive ways for the pacific ethos of the new religion. With his eyes on Achebe, Munonye creates the as the tempter, who dazzles Nnanna with the magic of the new alphabet and the new literacy which the church and the school had brought in their train We recall that when Okonkwo's brother, Amikwu, told Okonkwo that Nwoye had joined the new religion, Okonkwo awaited Nwoye's return, and then "sprang to his feet and gripped him by the neck... He seized a heavy stick that lay on the dwarf wall and hit him two or three savage blows" (136), as Nwoye tried to free himself from the choking grip. Compare this to Munonye. When Chiaku learnt from her brother, Oji, that Nnanna had joined the new religion, she "leapt up and pounced upon Nnanna. A second later, she had wound her hands round his neck, crushing it and choking him with her masculine strength" (112).

Munonye continues to be faithful to Achebe's method. After the savage blows from his father, Nwoye "walked away and never returned... He went back to the church and told Mr. Kiaga that he had decided to go to Umuofia, where the white missionary had set up a school to teach young Christians to read and write" (136-137). After Chiaku, following what she considered Nnanna's treachery, announced she was going to marry Okere, Nnanna goes to his teacher, announcing: "Master I want to leave our house...You told us something last week about the Reverend Father who will visit here soon... Master, I would like to follow him" (175-176).

Now, the pathos surrounding the aftermath of the confrontations between father and son (in *Things Fall Apart*) and mother and son (in *The Only Son*) bears close resemblance, showing Munonye's fidelity to his source. After Nwoye's departure following the savage blows from his father, Okonkwo brooded:

> Why, he cried in his heart, should he, Okonkwo, of all people, be cursed with such a son... Now that he had time to think of it, his son's crime stood out in its stark enormity. To abandon the gods of one's father and go about with a lot of effeminate men clucking like old hens was the very depth of abomination. Suppose when he died all his male children decided to follow Nwoye's steps and abandon their ancestors?
>
> Okonkwo felt a cold shudder run through him at the terrible prospect, like the prospect of annihilation. He saw himself and his fathers crowding round their ancestral shrine waiting in vain for worship and sacrifice and finding nothing but ashes of bygone days,

and his children the while praying to the white man's god (137).

The same touch of pathos surrounds Chiaku's knowledge of Nnanna's conversion. What one may call "the lament of Okonkwo" becomes "the lament of Chiaku", though Chiaku's is more attenuated and restricted in its cosmic implications:

> Chiaku broke into tears, sobbing spasmodically. But the load in her heart could not be washed out by tears alone. She opened her mouth..."Why should I continue to weep in this life where every broad road seems to end in bush... I've laboured and laboured to obtain our living. What did I not suffer from Amanze and his wives! That was at Umudiobia from where we fled. And yet, I had to bear everything because of my child. That's the child that has gone mad now
>
> I fled to Nade, to my father's land. Here to start life afresh and live in peace. Suitors have come and I have turned them out. I tell them I have a son who is my husband. Just because I don't want to live away from him. That's the child that has gone mad now" (115).

To sum up, then, one must assert that John Munonye found Achebe's *Things Fall Apart* an irresistible quarry. As he was trying to find his feet as a fledgling novelist he could not resist looking closely and hard at Achebe's subject matter and technique in pulling off so resoundingly his first famous novel. He found the pre-colonial setting of *Things Fall Apart* irresistibly fascinating. But Munonye moved beyond merely finding Achebe's work fascinating. The impact of Christianity and colonialism for both authors, however, provided the ammunition for different visions of life. For Achebe, it was tragic, as he created Okonkwo who perished while he blindly opposed the new order, and his death signalled the collective collapse of a way of life. For Munonye, it was not so tragic for while a few souls like Chiaku suffered the pangs of this new order, the ultimate outcome provided fresh challenges for self-improvement. Hence, at the end of the trilogy in *Bridge to a Wedding*, Nnanna (now Mr. Kafo) has profited from his encounter with the white man; has offered education to all his children; has his daughter, Rose, married off to a graduate; and returns to Umudiobia (now Mudi) with its own modern network of roads, pipe-borne water, and electricity.

A few more examples and we round off Munonye's indebtedness to Achebe in *The Only Son*. Okonkwo's power-name is "the roaring flame", while Nnanna's (after many coaxing names called him by his adoring mother) is "the lion"—given to him by the teacher, after he scaled the wall to catch a truant classmate. Furthermore, in *Things Fall Apart*, Achebe waxes lyrical on the magic and power attendant on a dreaded masked spirit:

> A sickly odour hung in the air wherever he went, and flies went with him ... Many years ago another egwugwu had dared to stand his ground before him and had been transfixed to the spot for two days. This one had only one hand and with it carried a basket full of water (108-109)

Again, compare this to a similar passage from Munonye on the powers of Ezedibia's fetish as narrated to Chiaku during her efforts to stop Nnanna from following the ways of the white man. Ezedibia, in the manner of Achebe's masked spirit, had transfixed thieves to the spot so that they were easily caught the next day, and at one time or the other, he had also carried a basket full of palm wine:

> While they (the thieves) were gathering the yams in the dark night, something which Ezedibia planted there in the barn commanded them to stand still, The next morning they were all apprehended...He had done some incredible things. I remember the day he filled a small basket with palm-wine and carried it about, from one end of the market to another, without a single drop escaping (135-136)

It is significant that the two incredible doings of Achebe's masked spirit narrated in one passage, metamorphose into two similar doings in Munonye, accomplished by one medicine man, and equally in one passage.

In moving beyond the two works just discussed, one notes that Achebe, the writer of the tragic vision, pursues Nwoye's grandson, Obi Okonkwo, to an ignoble and disgraceful fall from grace, to a prison term in *No Longer At Ease*, while the optimistic Munonye, by the end of his trilogy in *Bridge to a Wedding*, paints the picture of a glorious return by Nnanna (now, Mr. Joseph Kafo) to Umudiobia from Sankia where he has prospered. We must, of necessity, skip *No Longer At Ease* and Obi for a larger fish in *A Man* of the People and A Wreath for the Maidens. Munonye might continue to deny that he set out to imitate Achebe,' but cleavages both in style and subject matter of the two novels are self-evident. Achebe published *A Man of the People* in 1966, while Munonye's *A Wreath for the Maidens* appeared in 1973, after the Nigeria-Biafra war. Both novels are topical in the sense that each chose a political historical epoch in Nigeria and made scathing and scurrilous remarks about the operators of the system through the agency of imaginative literature. The lament of misrule is Achebe's major theme in *A Man of the People,* while the same lament is a major part of Munonye's theme in *A Wreath for the Maidens.*

Both *A Man of the People* and *A Wreath for the Maidens* read like *a roman a' clef* in which actual historical events are documented in a vaguely fictionalized form, but while Achebe chronicles the failings of Nigeria's first Republic and prophesies its demise through a coup d'état which actually takes place, Munonye recreates events leading to the Nigerian civil war and the mismanagement of the war by corrupt officials who turned a war of self-defence into a war of mutual self-destruction through greed, corruption, and selfishness.

We remember that Achebe, the intellectual, uses Odili as his mask, and the narrative point of view is "I" as witness or "I" as minor character; Munonye, following this narrative vein, uses another intellectual, Roland Medo, whose narrative point of view is also "I" as witness. Three parties vied for election in *A Man of the People:* The POP (People's Organisation Party, led by Teacher Nanga in Anata); the PAP (Progressive Alliance Party; and the CPC: (Common People's Convention—a party of intellectuals led by Odili in Urua but which carried the fight right to Chief Nanga's doorstep). Compare these to the four major parties in Munonye's *A Wreath for the Maidens:* the PIP (People's Independence Party - led by Eduado Boga in Oban Constituency and to which Chief Lobe also belongs); PNDL (People's National Democratic League, led by Sunday Umelo); NIP (National Independence Party-led by Michael Ebo); and the RDP (The Real Democratic Party-led by Ubakile and which Mr. Roland has joined to oppose Chief Lobe who has just snatched his girl-friend, Ruth Aniedo).

Odili, the intellectual, moves from observer of the political scene to an active involvement in party politics in order to fight Chief Nanga of POP who had just snatched his girl, Elsie; Roland Medo, the intellectual, also goes from the position of observer of the political scene to active involvement in party politics in order to oppose Chief Lobe of PIP who has snatched his girl-friend, Ruth Aniedo. But while Odili could not defeat Chief Nanga although he won the latter's intended second wife, Edna, Roland Medo has the satisfaction of his party defeating Chief Lobe although he did not win back Ruth who already had five children for Chief Lobe.

A Man of the People dwells on the state of anomy in politics caused by a vacuum created by the fact that knowledgeable intellectuals who should be involved in piloting the affairs of state have culpably left the stage for illiterates and uncouth practitioners like Chief Nanga who tells Odili: "Leave the dirty game of politics to us who know how to play it" (113). Achebe tells us: "But what else can you expect when intelligent people leave politics to illiterates like Chief Nanga" (73). Likewise, in *A Wreath for the Maidens*, reasons are advanced why the uncouth and the illiterate have a field day in the political arena while the soft; educated intellectual is relegated to the background. Now, in *A Man of the People*, Chief Nanga was appointed the Minister of Culture in spite of his near illiteracy, and his sordid display of ignorance provided the reader with many a condescending chuckle as Chief Nanga "announced in public that he had never heard of his country's most famous novel and received applause" (62). He went on to cap this embarrassing announcement with a greater *faux pas* when, lifting his eyes off a prepared speech on great literary figures of the world, he added extemporaneously "Michael West and Dudley Stamp" (62). Munonye equally found this episode irresistible. He creates Chief Eduado Boga, the "uncultured Minister of Culture" (31) who is among those "not quite in a position to discuss affairs of state with good understanding" (17-18), and who is also made to read from a prepared speech he did not understand, and from which he received "frequent applause", until he also came to the last paragraph over which he stumbled until he abandoned the speech altogether in midstream complaining that the speech-writer, the Permanent Secretary, "had composed the heavy speech purposely to embarrass him before the public, and before the constituency"(32).

It is also interesting to note that in *A Man of the People,* Chief Nanga came to bribe Odili to step down for him by offering him a scholarship to study overseas, garnished with a personal cash gift of two hundred and fifty pounds sterling. This Odili turned down (112). In *A Wreath for the Maidens,* Chief Lobe had come to offer a similar bribe to Roland Medo through Biere Ekonte. Roland Medo equally turned this offer down and his party went on to defeat Lobe.

It is also instructive to note that in *A Man of the People*, Chief Nanga and his ilk collude with foreign companies to rape the nation. We are informed that the British Amalgamated made a free gift of ten luxurious buses to Chief Nanga, each costing six thousand pounds sterling, while "the European building firm of Antonio and Sons whom Nanga had recently given the half-million-pound contract to build the National Academy of Arts and Science" (92) had given him a modern four-storey structure as "dash". In the same vein, we learn in *A Wreath the Maidens* that the Honourable Minister of Local Government and Chieftaincy Affairs had directed that for the construction of a new market "only well-established contractors should be considered; and that expatriate firms must be given a chance" (35). The reason for this directive soon becomes clear "there had been some firm understanding already between the Honourable Minister and the monopolistic firm of Shaws and Sharp Limited, Civil Engineers" (35), whom we soon learn "are going to finance the elections for the PIP" (37).

One easily notes, too, that while Odili resigns his teaching job and was assigned a Volkswagen car as a candidate for the CPC (Common People's Convention), Medo also resigns his teaching job and was assigned a Volkswagen car as the Publicity Secretary of the Real Democrats. And while in *A Man of the People*, Max compromises the moral stance of the CPC by accepting one thousand pounds sterling from Chief Koko (intended to bribe Max to step down for him) and bought a minibus for running their campaign, the chairman of the Real Democrats, Mr. Ubakile, compromises the moral stance of their party by accepting a red Volkswagen car from Mr. Lukter of the Premier Oil Company, also for running their election campaign, in spite of Medo's demurral that it was a "dangerous gift" (44).

There is a point where both Odili and Medo display their youthful idealism. Odili, the idealist thinks elections can be won without dirtying one's hands (hence, his rebuke to Max for accepting Chief Koko's money and using it to fight him), plus his expecting a man like Chief Nanga or a junior Minister to resign "on a matter of principle" (79). Medo, on the other hand thinks elections could be won simply by sticking to the rules and principles and by not spending money on the electorate, because "the party has enough spontaneous goodwill to carry it through" (49).

Finally, we should note the pervasive corrupt political practices in the two works under study. In both novels, massive election rigging (Achebe) and census fraud (Munonye) and the confusion attendant on the violence let loose in the body politic ended with a coup d'etat by the army. Achebe ends his novel on this note, while hinting that "a coup might be followed by a counter coup and then where would we be?" (139), while Munonye goes further to enact the counter-coup, the massacres and the civil war which inevitably followed. But the same irony that informs *A Man of the People* reveals itself in *A Wreath for the Maidens*. Independence which promised freedom and political utopia to the societies examined in both works, actually brought ethnic rivalry, exploitation of the masses, election rigging, census fraud, and fratricidal bloodletting.

Munonye admits that he admires Achebe and that he "was very much encouraged" by Achebe's success. The extent of his admiration and how far Munonye went in following in the footsteps of Achebe I have tried to sketch in this study although, I admit, all this may have been unconscious on Munonye's part. The rest is for scholars and critics to judge.

Works cited

Achebe, Chinua. *Things Fall Apart.* London: Heinemann, 1959.
... *A Man of the People:* New York: Anchor Books, 1967.
Munonye, John. *The Only Son.* London: Heinemann, 1966.
... *A Wreath for the Maidens.* London: Heinemann, 1973.

14

African feminism: the scandalous path*

The trajectory of the more recent movements of African feminism draws an arc that is most disquieting in its implications. Polygamy under Islamic religion seems to be the foul dust that floats in the wake of most African radical feminist writers. The Nigerian Flora Nwapa, the Senegalese Mariama Ba and the Egyptian Nawal el Saadawi—all are in league to push the tenets of feminism to scandalous, even criminal and murderous levels.

We may begin by drawing attention to the plethora of feminist theories that are making the rounds in current headlines in the landscape of feminist ideas. The contours of that landscape are uneven and zigzag in a seesaw of confusions. As Achebe tells us in *Things Fall Apart:* as a man dances, so are the drums beaten for him. To paraphrase him further, some African feminists are dancing a furious step, and the feminist drums have gone mad. Gynandrism has sucked African male writers into the cesspool of their confusing theories; gynandrists being men with female empathy. Femalism, a mish-mash, a conflation of undigested ideas about feminism and the female point of view, urges on us and fellow feminists

---

* First published in Beyond the Marginal Land: Gender Perspective in African Writing. Port Harcourt, Belpot 1999. pp. 46-56. I am indebted to Margaret Nutsukpo for most of thew categorizations in her unpublished Ph.D. Dissertation: "Feminist Consciousness in the Novels of Nawal el Saadawi and Ifeoma Okoye: A comparative Study", University of Port Harcourt, 1998.

consciousness-raising without much opposition to the enemy man, who is benignly tolerated as partner-in-progress, as long as man allows woman opportunities for self-actualization and self-reclamation. This is not to be confused with womanism whose ideals according to Ogunyemi, are for black unity:

> Womanism is black-centred. It is accommodationist...It wants meaningful union between black women and black men and black children, and will see to it that men will change from their sexist stand. This ideological position explains why women writers do not end their plots with feminist victories. (5)

Men and women could have lived comfortably with this ideology if restless feminists did not invent more ideologies. Catherine Acholonu dreams up a new term, *Motherism*:

> A multi-dimensional theory which involves the dynamics of ordering, re-ordering, creating structures, building and rebuilding in cooperation with mother nature at all levels of human endeavour. (110-111)

Motherism further advocates "love, tolerance, service mutual cooperation for the sexes, not antagonism, aggression, militancy or violent confrontation" plus "protection and defence of family values" (111-112). Now, how this is different from womanism, one is hard put to it separating both concepts. But there it is to add to our feminist vocabulary.

Opposed to accommodation femalism and motherism is radical feminism (the focus of this study) which arrogantly claims that feminine values of nurturance, intuition and affectionate relationships are superior to the masculine values of objectivity, rationality and quest for power while advocating the overthrow of patriarchy and the men behind it through a revolution energized by female bonding, sisterhood practices, and consciousness-raising. These are the dangerous ideas and tenets of Bell Hooks, Shulamith Firestone, and Leslie Steeves - European feminists who have dangerously infected the writings of our African feminist sisters.

Arrayed to do battle with men are all feminist shades or groups originally based in Europe and America, under all categories and nomenclatures:

Suffragettes: Lucretia Mott, Elizabeth Stanton, Mary Wollstonecraft Godwin, Harriet Mills, Abigail Duniway. These successfully fought for the right of women to vote resulting in women suffrage in Britain

Women Liberationists: Alice Paul, Elizabeth Boyer, Judith Hole. These feminists, realizing that voting rights for women did not go far enough to obtain total equality for women, fought for total emancipation for all women including sexual freedom with a warning to all women that romantic love is a trap to subdue women's identity. They further pushed the idea that total equality with men in jobs must be realized based on individual capacity, training, expertise, and skill.

Socialist Feminists: Kate O'Hare, Emma Goldman and Christine Obbo. These were trade union oriented, while urging fellow women to emancipate themselves from the shackles of motherhood through birth control. Sexual emancipation was the watchword.

Liberalist Feminists: Mary Ritter Beard, Julia Lathrop, Shana Alexander. These are traditional in outlook and they assume that women's rights, in a world dominated by men can only be obtained through legal efforts and all sorts of litigation to enforce those rights.

Marxist Feminists: Simone de Beauvoir, Kate Millett, Michelle Barrett - These held capitalism responsible for the inferior status of women, because capitalism allots inferior occupational jobs and lower pay for women.

They condemn in strong terms the use of women as cheap labour and limiting employment of women to nursing, teaching and secretarial occupations.'

European theorists on feminism have depended on the merit of logic and legal means to persuade men to see reason. If Mary Wollstonecraft Godwin *(Vindication of the Rights of Women);* Simone de Beauvoir *(The Second Sex);* Germaine Greer *(The Female Eunuch);* Betty Friedan *(The Feminine Mystique);* and Kate Millett *(Sexual Politics),* have written and theorized so persuasively for the total emancipation of women, none ever advocated the murdering of men or criminality to theorists urged their case further through organizations and group pressure that at worst included heckling and some shouting. We have in mind the National Organisation of Women and The National American Woman's Association both in the United States of America whose aim, among others, according to Betty Friedan is "to bring women full participation in the mainstream of American society ... in truly equal partnership with men." The Beijing Conference in China also happened because, through superior organization by women throughout the world, such and similar conferences were organized to push to the front burner, burning issues of women's rights and their emancipation to a world that was ready to listen.

In Africa, a Decade of Women's Conference in Nairobi was fully backed by the United Nations in 1985. We also have is Africa, The Movement for Muslim Women, Association of University Women, Women in Nigeria, and the National Council for Women's Societies. Their combined and collective pressure through conferences, demonstrations, seminars, workshops and in extreme cases litigation can positively and without bloodshed, change the future of women and create an atmosphere of self-definition for all women. My assessment is that through these organisations and conferences, women have built a formidable case for feminism and the world is much better for it. Through logic and group pressure, organized resistance to the abuse of women's rights has and will surely guarantee a better future for both men and women for no one should remain passive in the face of oppression. So far for theorizing feminism.

II

As we now turn to African feminist writers, one is gravely worried by the excesses of their radical practitioners. We have in mind the heretical and dangerous ideas propagated by many of them through their literary and creative works. We have in mind Flora Nwapa *(One Is Enough* and *Women Are Different);* Mariama Ba *(Scarlet Song);* and Nawal el Saadawi *(God Dies by the Nile* and *Woman at Point Zero).*

First to Flora Nwapa. For her, radical feminism meant breaking all known society's mores and elegant decorum. It started innocuously with Efuru's dignified self assertion when, in breach of age-old traditions she moved in to live as a wife with Adizua who was so poor he could not afford the bride price. Efuru's self assertion by defying the traditional marriage customs was hailed as one of the ways in which a woman could break out of the shackles of patriarchy and tradition because the end result was marriage, a sacred institution. She may have suffered for her decision to marry a will o' the wisp, but that was her decision. The problem with Nwapa's feministic preachments in the creation of her strong-willed females was the condoning of immortal behaviour in her independent women. Economic independence should not be advocated for, or achieved through destruction or flouting of society's most cherished values. There must be another method of achieving self-actualisation in a dignified manner.

So when we come to Amaka in *One is Enough,* her manner of becoming independent through questionable behaviour debases rather than enhances the image of women. Why, one wonders, does she not create a feminist self-assertive woman who is a role-model for younger women. Why must Amaka sleep her way through an Alhaji and a supposedly celibate priest to achieve selfhood? Why are Nwapa's women so irreligious? Why must money and wealth be their non-Sunday religion? Why are they almost anti-society and anti-God? The men in Nwapa's canon may not be saints—Adizua, Gilbert, Obiora, Izu Mclaid—but must the women in their lives be demonised, must they corrupt the system and abuse their own persons to declare their emancipation.

Yes, indeed, Nwapa's women are different in *Women are Different* where women's peculiar demonism knows no God, no religion, and is no respecter of society's moral tenets. Yes, women have a right to abandon an irresponsible and uncaring husband for their own psychological health. Yes, women have a right to flout custom to marry any man they fancy. Yes, a woman has a right to pursue and achieve economic independence. But why must a mother advise her daughter to be unfaithful as Amaka's mother in *One is Enough* encourages Amaka to be. She tells Amaka:

> But you refused to take my advice. You were being a good wife: chastity, faithfulness my foot. You can go ahead and eat virtue. (35)

Why must Zizi, the daughter of Agnes in *Women are Different* be made to go into full prostitution at fifteen by living in a brothel, snatch other women's husbands at eighteen, begin trafficking in dangerous drugs (121, 123) and just two weeks after her fabulous wedding to Theo, take a lover? But most disconcerting and scandalous is the authorial support for these aberrant behaviours. When Chinwe in the same novel went ahead and "married a married man" whom she dumped as soon as his fortunes waned, the authorial voice announced to all and sundry its heretical preachments:

> Chinwe had done the right thing. Her generation was doing better than her mother's own. Her generation was telling the men that, there are different ways of living one's life fully and fruitfully. They are saying that women have options. (119)

Must a dubious and loose life-style (Amaka) and drug trafficking plus home-breaking doctrines be the only avenues for self-actualization? When no holds are barred, when women who are custodians of morality are in the vanguard of scandal ridden behaviours, society must then be on its way to self-destruction. There is little in Nwapa's women that is uplifting. It is always scandal and debauchery.

We next turn to Mariama BA whose first novel *So Long a Letter* started on a sober note with the character of Ramatoulaye and gave signs of positive feminism in the character of Aissatou who broke from Mawdo Ba in a most dignified manner. But Ramatoulaye's cigarette-smoking daughters that ended in Aissatou's unwanted pregnancy began to give cause for worry, for society's mores began to be infringed. And the liberal feminist in Mariama Ba began to give way to radicalism. In *Scarlet Song*, Mariama Ba betrayed an extremist stance that stunned even her most ardent admirers. When Mireille decided to kill her own son, Gorgui, and attempted to murder her husband, Ousmane Gueye, because he married Ouleymatou according to Islam, Mireille became the sow that eats her own farrow.

Any woman converted or nurtured in Islamic religion who murders or goes insane because of love or a sense of betrayal is thoroughly self-deceived. True, an educated woman who is "in love" may feel betrayed when her husband, exercising his full rights as a Muslim, takes on a second wife. But she should have known that his act of betrayal is not due to callousness or lust but a right conferred by both religion and tradition. When a mother or wife goes beyond a dignified outrage under Islam because her husband is a polygamist, neither society nor custom nor religion will come to her sympathy. Modou Fall, Ramatoulaye's husband in *So Long a Letter* may be sneaky in the manner he married Binetou; and Ousmane may be devious in the manner be married Ouleymatou, but no one would consider these men as callous, overtly wicked or breakers of any known laws. Society would not change or even take notice when a Muslim wife goes berserk over her own sense of betrayal. Any violence resorted to by such a woman is merely scorching the snake without killing it, for polygamy either under traditional or the Muslim religion is a native to Africa as *foofoo* and couscous.

Murdering a husband who under Islam takes a second wife in fulfilment of his religious obligations is wasting one's energy; attacking the symptoms rather than the disease. Besides, it is an exercise in futility, for as long as Islam sanctions polygamy, neither the tantrums of starry-eyed women like Aissatou Ba, Ramatoulaye Fall, Jacqueline Diack or even the *taubab*, Mireille Gueye, will bring an end to the practice. As we say in Africa, the offspring of a snake has no choice but to be long. And Mireille herself admits that "when all's said and done, black men are not the only ones who are unfaithful to their wives" (162).

Aminata Sow Fall in *The Beggar's Strike* may make a martyr out of Lai Badiane who is unhappy when her nouveau-riche husband, Mour Ndiaye, abandons her for a younger wife. Adja Awa in Ousmane Sembene's *Xala* may feel frustrated when. El Hadji Abdou Beye also behaves true to type, but the society that breeds these men takes no notice beyond each woman's support by her young but outraged and educated daughter. The point being urged here is that murder is not the solution in these feminist novels until tradition, patriarchy and society, change the religion of Islam that gives rise to these events. Unless these starry-eyed wives do something about the tenets of Islam, my suggestion is that these writers might do well to find alternatives to the expression of their outrage.

Nawal el Saadawi paints a more disturbing picture of women who suffer under the triple oppression of religion, patriarchy, and class. According to her, marriage and the family are mechanisms through which women are subjugated and oppressed, for marriage breeds a master-slave relationship where a woman is defined in terms of her husband. To eliminate men as agents of oppression, el Saadawi creates women as avengers, as killers of the wicked men in their lives. In *Woman at Point Zero*. Firdaus, that woman driven to prostitution by the wicked and oppressive environment in Egypt that destroys her life, exclaims her hatred of all men, one of whom she eventually murders:

> All the men I did get to know, every single man of them, has filled me with but one desire: to lift up my hand and bring it smashing down on his face. (6)

Feminism should never translate into criminality and murder. Firdaus knows quite well the enormity of her crime for she tells the reader early in the novel that her father told her that under the religion of Islam,

> Stealing was a sin, and killing was a sin, and defaming the honour of a woman was a sin, and injustice was a sin, and beating another human being was a sin (7)

Yes, when she kills the pimp Marzouk, her declared sense of freedom and liberation is frightening:

> I walked down the street, my head held high to the heavens, with the pride of having destroyed all masks to reveal what is hidden behind My footsteps broke the silence with their steady rhythmic beat on the pavement. They were the foot steps of a woman who believed her herself, knew where shewas going and could see her goal. (78)

In *God Dies by the Nile*, Zakeya's murder of the mayor, Sheikh Zehran, the "god" of her oppression to avenge the wrongs done her by the Mayor who caused the jailing of her son Gala and the imprisonment of her brother Kafrawi to enable the Mayor defile her nieces Nefissa and Zeinab, is touted by radical feminists as a symbol of the destruction of the class and power structure that oppress women because it is only through such destruction that true emancipation of women will emerge (Nutsukpo, 67). But we must assert that murder is murder, and murder is a criminal act under the laws of all human societies. What is a woman, symbol of nurturance doing with murder? Even a noted feminist. criti Akachi Ezeigbo admits that el Saadawi's works leave her readers "shocked and outraged" (119).

To sum up then, a few points need be stressed. It must be emphasized that the manner and method by which both Mariama Ba and Nawal el Saadawi have engaged their protagonists on a destructive and murderous course is a syndrome of misplaced aggression that must be condemned by all feminists, for the real oppressors of women in a Muslim society are the religion of Islam, plus patriarchy and class. In *So Long a letter, Scarlet Song, God Dies by the Nile* and *Woman at Point Zero* as long as the likes of Modou Fall and Mawdo Ba *(So Long a Letter)*, Ousmane Gueye *(Scarlet Song)*, Sheikh Zehran *(God Dies by the Nile)* and Marzouk Mahmoud and Bayoumi *(Woman at Point Zero)* exist, so long will they use the religion of Islam to wreak havoc on the womenfolk.

Feminism, in all its phases on the African literary scene, it must be admitted, has enriched African literature and given that literature a sense of balance. That balance can only be promoted and enhanced when, and only when feminist writers create a positive atmosphere of collective self-definition and self-actualization for fellow women. For mankind and all societies stand to gain only when it enjoys that complementarity between man and woman that will ensure a better future for all. For extremist radical feminism that ends in murder and crime may be counter-productive, creating bloodshed and wastage of human potentials. How many men can disgruntled feminists actually kill to gain complete emancipation, especially under Islam?

Finally, all fair minded readers believe that feminism has done mankind a lot of good. We say yes to the right of women to fight for equality and parity with men in all fields of endeavour. We all believe in all efforts of all women for collective self-definition and self-actualization. We all encourage bridging the gender gap between men and women. And we should all encourage all efforts of all women towards positive female-bonding and sisterhood practices as long as these lead to full liberation and emancipation from the unwholesome shackles of tradition, class, patriarchy, religion and custom. We encourage personal upliftment through education and economic independence for women. But we all should equally condemn all feminist efforts at shoving before our noses all unwholesome freedoms that lead to immorality, murder and crime.

On a final note, we urge the use of woman's power to influence society for good, through all legal means. Why, for example, are very educated and influential women both in the North and South of

Nigeria so ominously silent while Sharia dehumanizes their sisters in Zamfara State? Why are our educated and influential women standing by while their sisters in the North are inferiorized, marginalized, under-educated, while they could engage the powers that be in the North in all manners of litigation through their various organizations? After all, the man (or woman) dies in him who is silent in the face of oppression. Have our feminists not understood that the oppression, suppression and subjugation of one woman in the Muslim North is equivalent to the subjugation of all women in Nigeria? Why this silence in a country where a system like Islam oppresses half of their members in the North? True feminism in Africa in general and Nigeria in particular should go beyond promoting effete ideas to positive action through mass demonstrations, legal action and effective lobbying to ensure that all women in Nigeria are truly free and fully emancipated.

Works cited

Acholonu, Catherine. *Motherism: The Afro-Centric Alternative to Feminism*. Let's Help Humanitarian Project, Women in Environmental Development Series, Vol. 3, Owerri, 1995.

Ezeigbo, T. A. "Technique and Language in Ba's *So Long A Letter*, el Saadawi's *Woman at Point Zero* and Warner Vieyra's Juletane," *Currents in African Literature and the English Language*, Vol. 1, No.1 (March, 1997); 113-123.

Nwapa, Flora. *Women Are Different*. Enugu, Tana Press, 1986.

Ogunyemi, Chikwenye. "Woman and Nigerian Literature", *Perspectives on Nigerian Literature*, Vol.1 (Lagos: Guardian Books, Nigeria Ltd., 1988), pp. 60-67:

Saadawi, Nawal *Woman At Point Zero*. Trans. Sherif Hetata. London: Zed Books, 1983.

15

Contemporary Nigerian fiction

I take contemporary Nigerian fiction to be fiction (the novel) written between the year 2000 and the present. We shall state from the outset that most of the fiction we shall discuss are blemished in numerous ways, succinctly put by Osofisan in a recent the in *African Literature Today* captioned: "Eagles in the Age of Unacknowledged Muse: Two major Writers in contemporary Nigerian Literature, Akachi Ezeigbo and Promise Okekwe" I need to quote him in full:

> Naturally, in these strenuous circumstances, the results are not always successful. They cannot be, given the enormous costs of publishing, the near absence of editing services, and also, sometimes, the low level of education of the people involved. Such is the impatience and eagerness of the young authors to get into print and establish their names, that they are quite often unwilling to go through the necessary apprenticeship and training required to (hone) their skills. Thus many books come out with several avoidable errors, mostly relating to the feeble control of language and a murderous assault on grammatical laws. Especially for those who publish themselves, the lack of intermediary editorial processes is too obviously needed. This is why the quality of the output is frequently uneven, and sometimes even embarrassing (22).

With the above in mind, any wonder why the first edition of the Nigeria Liquefied Natural Gas prize for Literature found no contemporary Nigerian novel worthy of its prize.

Contemporary Nigerian fiction writers belong to the third generation of African writers. Where the first generation of African writers (Achebe, Soyinka, Oyono, wa Thiongo, Peter Abrahams,

Denis Brutus and Alex La Guma) had a general thematic focus, Africa's cultural encounter with Euope and the fight against apartheid and colonialism; the second generation (Osofisan, Sowande, Iyayi, Omotosho, El Saadawi, Buchi Ernecheta, Ama Ata, Aidoo, Sembene Ousmane); fought ideological battles for social equality, for feminism contemporary African writers (identified in this study as mainly Nigerians who always act as the weather-vane for trends in African literature), lack a clearly defined thematic focus. If anything, they have depicted a people adrift, hedonistic, cowed finally by the long incursion of the military in the body politic. It is this lack of thematic focus that Shuaibu Abdul Raheem describes thus:

> Perhaps it would be more appropriate to say that we are confronted with a literary jungle-rich with varieties of life and growth, awe-inspiring and full of breath-taking surprises, where it is no longer possible to tell the trees from the shrubs, the climbers from the creepers or the thorns from the bushes. It is the spectre of unregulated growth which has not only induced perfunctory nods from but also constituted the challenge to a bemused critical establishment over the closing years of the twentieth century (12).

We are now going to wade into this jungle of creepers and thorns. Ben Okri is the harbinger of the contemporary Nigerian novel, the link between the old and the new. In *The Landscapes Within*, Omovo the protagonist makes a statement that will haunt the reader of Nigeria's contemporary fiction: "I think ours is another damned generation of loss." Earlier Nigerian literature had talked of a "wasted generation". Furthermore, Okri as a harbinger had set his two novels Flowers and Shadows and The Landscapes Within in Lagos. Lagos as setting, has come to assume a special place in contemporary Nigerian fiction enough to assume a character all. its: .own, enough to become a symbol in its own right, symbol of the corruption, hedonism, debauchery and shenanigans, in contemporary Nigerian fiction. Moreover, it was Okri who defines the main thematic insights that will preoccupy this study, the depiction of Lagos as the *locus classicus* harbouring a society and people adrift. This is captured in "scumscape", a painting by Omovo seized by the authorities, where Keme desclibes the painting as "disturbing, a commentary on our society showing people on a drift, a scummy drift" (48).

It is, therefore, the position of this study that contemporary Nigerian fiction depicts a society adrift and a people lost in the imbecilities of futile optimism, hoping that materialism and the pursuit of dirty lucre will compensate for the loss of the nation's soul; for the Nigeria we encounter in its contemporary fiction is a nation without a soul, without direction, without a national ethos it is a rudderless ship a-sail amidst the jetsam and flotsam of a directionless voyage to nowhere.

II

Maik Nwtasu's Alpha Song is the engine-room of Nigeria adrift. Since in reality Nigeria is operated on the principle of base indices rather than merit-catchment, geographical spread, federal character, educationally disadvantaged states; in its fiction, the individual's response is each one for himself and God for us all, So, in Maik Nwosu's *Alpha Song*, the protagonist, Tanba (later Beneta), recognizing that "life is a terminal disease" (p,2), hopes to "depart this world at night" (p.3) thus making his night his day. And at night, he is most active, most alive. The novel is a collection of people really lost who come to Lagos from uprooted backgrounds. Tamuno who boasts: "I manage the night...Anything at all that goes on in the night, brother, I've got a little finger in it. Anything you want done in the night or anything you want the night to do for you, just whisper to me" (12) runs the night club "The Owi".

Tamuno "had been abandoned at birth, dumped outside an orphanage (117). Then we have Yellow, the albino, who lives in the streets and never sleeps. Once Taneba confronts him:

"In the night you are here. In the day too. When do you sleep?"
"I no dey fit sleep. Na the problem wey I get be that" (p.43)

Yellow, we are told "had been rejected at birth because his father could not believe it was he who had fathered an albino" (131). So Yellow spent a great part of his life, "tossing about in search of stability" (p.131). Colonel Briggs, so rich, so powerful is also addicted to night life:

"When we get to power" he would say, "the first thing we will do is to set up a ministry of Night. Yes, a ministry for night affairs ... You see, the problem is that those in power do not realize there is a powerful army of the night constantly being enlarged by the policies of the day ... I can tell you now that all the changes of government that have taken place in this country were initiated and perfected at night" (180).

Maik Nwosu's *Alpha Song* is a dissertation on night life which has attraction for drifters who are debauched, 'irreligious, men and women thinking with their crotch. The night clubs in Nwosu's Lagos are numerous and celebrate with gusto, the abode of those trying like Taneba to run away from their roots. The clubs are: The Owi, the Sundown, Seventh Heaven, Tamuno Heaven, Kabila, The Red Hat, Nightingale, and in far away Australia, The Tamarinde. Night clubs would be nothing without the ladies of the night. And Taneba indulged himself: Lovelyn, Mairo, Aisha (her majesty, the only one who resisted him), Toshiba, Jacqueline, Angel (Who drifted to Spain for more opportunities for whoring), Eve whom he "married", made pregnant and abandoned.

Maik Nwosu's *Alpha Song* sets the tone for contemporary Nigerian fiction in which characters engage themselves in "seeking for a great indefinable essence but finding only small definable pleasure" (12), where daylight time is of no productive consequence while the night sits as the queen of drunkenness and whoredom. Maik Nwosu has thus established what may be termed the fleshly school of writers in contemporary Nigerian fiction. To that school belong Toni Kan Onwordi (*Ballad of Rage*), Jonah Ageda (*God's Own Country*), Wale Okediran (Dreams *Die at Twilight*), Omo Uwaifo (*Fattening House*), Chim Newton (*Under the Cherry Tree*), and Fola Arthur-Worrey (*The Diaries of Mr. Michael*).

The fleshly school of writers are those authors whose main characters are in dire pursuit of the flesh, writers for whom the excitements and satisfactions of the body are far more important than the sanctity of the soul; for whom the pleasure of the flesh are of more moment than the essence of the spirit. In *Alpha Song* Maik Nwosu has said through his protagonist Taneba:

> My race with the night has been that of the flesh and I had been rewarded accordingly with the paradigms of flesh, all amounting to nothing more than sheer waste of the possibilities of my Spirit (p.215).

We may have to explain that debauchery alone is not the only defining principle for the fleshly writer. The main characters of Wale Okediran's *Dreams Die at Twilight* pursue more than prurient interests. In fact, Leemy the protagonist is a pervert who is not satisfied with consorting with prostitutes, accessory to drug trafficking and a murderer, but indulges in necrophilia-raping dead bodies of women in the morgue. His friend, Jimi Gomez is no more than a procurer, fetching one woman after another for his psychopath friend Leemy (Lamid Bello) whose sordid performance with women leads him to ridicule and opprobrium. But that Leemy, a lame, misshapen pervert who wreaks havoc in his environment, a murderer and accessory to trans-national drug trafficking, a necrophile who indulges in raping female cadavers gets rewarded in the end with appointment as vice-chancellor of Lagos State Southern University, offends the reader's sensibilities, and the readers belief that crime should not pay. But this is Nigeria where, according to the blurb, "anything is possible. Anything".

The fleshly writer delights also in depicting characters who, in addition to debauchery indulge in bribery and corruption with gusto, characters who suffer no sanction or disability through their inordinate quest for power and whose corrupt practices catapult them into higher and higher positions of power and authority. Such is Omo Uwaifo's *Fattening House*. Ejike, the protagonist, after a career marked by, brazen self enrichment plus other scandals with the support of the nation's president is appointed ambassador to the U.S. where he indulged in further peccadilloes before his recall. When this inveterate womanizer and graft kingpin was appointed ambassador, the press squirmed:

> Meanwhile the country's press looked, at gjthe's past and cried out. They said that it was only in a country such as it is that anyone could have worked for so long, with a record as unclean as a sewage dump. The Statesman asked if it was state policy to export the worst to the rest of the world. "what sense is there to make a man-a loud symbol of moral decline-an ambassador?" asked the paper (224)

Mr. Ejike who ended up as the leader of his country's ruling national party has a wife, Morin, with her own sordid and despicable past. Morin, shameless whore, had displaced her elder sister, Doyin, and taken over her husband. She equally broke the wedding plans of Ayi Johnson '(Sophie)' to Nath Ndem by seducing Nath Ndem on his bachelor's eve: Of her the author comments:

She looked at her self and her mind told her that se was a' bitch. She touched her pearl necklace and she felt a mane. Her dress was a coat of hair. Her eyes heard Ayi call her a whore (186).

Yet, she and her husband emerged as fit for ambassadorial appointment and as a couple at the helm of the ,country's national party.

Toni Kan Onwordi's *Ballad of Rage* captured Nigeria, as a country adrift and debauched. He tells a depressing story of a nation populated by characters with no worthwhile pursuits. It is a well-woven narrative of a staid old doctor, a nymphomaniac and egregiously promiscuous wife, and a marijuana-smoking Rimless lover boy. It is a story of mass rape, abortion, infidelity, prison riots and killings, sodomy, and murder. The futility and purposelessness of life are etched in this work.

Movement is a defining aspect of the new Nigerian novel. It defines a group of people on the move, flitting as it were from one Nigerian city to another, while also restless within the city (mainly Lagos), in which night clubs, bars, hotels and choice restaurants engage their waking hours. Contemporary Nigerian fiction is, therefore, more spatial than temporal. The characters, epicureans all, engage in an orgy of sensuality signifying the disintegration of social values in time of moral anarchy. Emphasis is on the lusty, the physical aspects of living-food, wine, women, and indulgence in armchair discussions on what is wrong with Nigeria without suggesting or doing anything positive to reclaim her.

We have arrived at a roaring age where the automobile has become a symbol reminding us of one America's roaring twenties during which Scott Fitzgerald wrote The Great Gatsby depicting similar careless and immoral people on the move. The automobile, the aeroplane, the motorcycle ensure that characters do not stay for long in one environment, but must move from one city to another, even from one continent to another. There is a restlessness, a search for new experiences, an excitement about a brave new world of the internet, and the computer, hence the drift, the general unsettledness that sends characters on a quest which no one village or city can satisfy.

The third generation of Nigerian writers under study pitch their tent with Fola Arthur-Worrey (The Diaries of Mr. Michael), and Chim Newton (Under the Cherry Tree). The works of these writers are about a restless group of characters on the move.

Characters in Fola Arthur-Worrey's The Diaries of Mr. Michael are restlessly on the move. It is a disquisitory novel where characters are mouth pieces for opinions they espouse; where discussions on every thing wrong with Nigeria takes centre stage, analysed, and condemned, as Mr. Michael Barnes a foreign journalist joins Nengi, Dede, Ude, Collins and Chuks to traverse every nook and cranny of Lagos. The subjects they discuss-the lack of maintenance culture,- the chaotic transport system, the garbage heaps that assault the doorway of the eyes-all make for depressing reading unrelieved by humour. There is no hope for the future it seems. Thee is no character development, no climax, and a doubtful denouement as Michael Barnes, the journalist never sits down to write his diaries and never returns to England. In the true tradition of the fleshly school, this journalistic documentary provides vignettes of enjoyment when the group routinely stops to unwind in a restaurant, a night club, or in one of he drinking bars that Lagos is rich with.

The central theme of *The Diaries of Mr. Michael* is disorder in a wasteland full of God's bounty, with the unanswered question:

> Can any person out there propound some basic, rational, explicable, logical, sociological, anthropological, spiritual or even metaphysical explanation for our endemic and recurring decimal disregard, shamelessness, dishonesty, violence, incivility, disorderliness, credulity, and laggardliness can anyone out there encapsulate , the reason why we import what we already have and export what we need; why no humanly designed system solely and exclusively manned by Nigerians, be it administrative, managerial or technological has ever worked in Nigeria in spite of massive capital investment and a huge skilled work force complemented by professionals in every field; why no town or city in ... Nigeria is free of filth, bad road, poor I" motorcycle riders, open gutters, disorganized and dirty motor parks and markets, area boys or street urchins ... Why we are incapable of enthroning a culture of maintenance, attention to detail, and observance of deadlines and schedules? (7)

Fola Arthur-Worrey's novel is a depressing novel pictured from the eyes of a visitor from abroad who tours our cities while thoroughly enjoying our food, our beer, our women.

Perhaps, because of the catalogue of woes just quoted from Fola Arthur-Worrey's *The Diaries of Mr. Michael*, young Nigerians are depicted as a people "on the move", underlining further the spatial nature of contemporary Nigerian fiction. Jonah Ageda's *God's Own Country* highlights Nigerian youths who drift abroad to America, *God's Own Country*, to seek their own fortunes, hoping, Horatio-Alger fashion, to make it from grass to grace. But the youth carry along with them the Nigerian factor: they won't have the grace or the patience to make it through the American work ethic. They would rather join the mafia, engage in drug trafficking, and corrupt the system. *God's Own Country* is written in the thriller tradition but with an unhappy ending for the protagonist Tobi Agboola, a handsome, recklessly ambitious whiz-kid whose incautious sense of adventure propels him into immorality, homosexuality gangsterism, drug addiction and drug trafficking, that eventually led him to his grave. Ageda's thriller encompasses the normal rhetorical topoi of that sub-genre-adventure, man-hunt, suspense, the cop-and-robber chase, plus sensational snippets of romance. For balance, of course, Joseph Tile, Tobi Agboola's fellow adventurer in Uncle Sam's land by maintaining the puritan ethic of honesty and hard work, achieved the coveted green card. But he didn't drift back to Nigeria. Jonah Ageda belongs to the fleshly writers for it was mainly the temptations and indulgence in fleshly excitements that proved Tobi Agboola's undoing.

A final glance at reasons adduced by the characters in Jonah Ageda's novel, would reinforce the notion that Nigeria is the proverbial sow that eats its own farrow. Tobi Agboola wants to drift to America to escape the deprivations which Nigeria epitomizes to join the "haves". Those

> for whom life is one lifelong party ... they lent their time and energies to more agreeable causes such as flying in private jets and helicopters and cruising in yachts. They drove in chauffeured limousines, changing them like handkerchiefs. They lived in mansions with gardens and swimming pools and had the mansions dotted in all around the world. They globe trotted ... Owned business empires and had eight, nine or ten bank accounts. They ate banquets, drank choicest wines, had the best women and wished the binge would go on for ever (8-9)

Chim Newton's *Under the Cherry Tree* continues unabated the fleshly tradition and motion without movement or rather the restlessness and debauchery which have preoccupied the characters in works so far discussed in this study. K. C. Chuba's weakness for women is the major scandal of this depressing book. And there is no virtuous man or woman in the novel. All the girls are scandalously promiscuous because the head of the family cannot control them, himself too debauched to assert his moral authority. Nne already has two love children from two different men, Sam and Enudi. Sally carries a pregnancy plus a love child for Dibe. Ogonne, daughter of the hunter Panam is carrying a pregnancy for Zino. The family of Chuba who keeps bringing to his household loose women ("wives") who arrive with bastard children of their own-all make Chuba's household a school for scandal. The poverty, the witchcraft, the venereal disease reveal a group of people 'pursuing no worthwhile ends in life—a people adrift: It is ironic though, that from Chuba's household emerges one of their children, Dibe who becomes a prize-winning writer, a light leaping out of darkness.

IV

Contemporary fiction in Nigeria is not without its women: Chimamanda Adichie (*Purple Hibiscus*), Theodora Akachi Adimora Ezeigbo (*House of Symbols*), Promise Okekwe (*Groaning Passage*), and Bina Nengi-Ilagha (*Condolences*). One surprising aspect about contemporary female writers in Nigeria is the total absence of the ideology of feminism which preoccupied, even energized their predecessors. Flora Nwapa, Buchi Emecheta, Zaynab Alkali, Ifeoma Okoye—all were consumed with the theme of the empowerment of women whom they saw as disparaged, sidelined, and even brutalized by male writers like Ekwensi, Achebe, and Soyinka. They therefore went on a demolition campaign of the male image in our literatures and a reassertion of the importance of women. Nwapa's Adizua, Gilbert, Amarajeme and Obiora were as good as useless as husbands and Emecheta's Nnaife was repulsive.

But contemporary female writers have transcended all that. They seem not to have been affected by the traumatic experience of military rule that set adrift the characters depicted in contemporary male fiction. The women have reverted to the hearth, to the home, to family life. In Chimamanda's heralded *Purple Hibiscus*, the home with a domineering father is the centre of the of Papa Eugene, a pious monster, an ogre who indulges in wife-bashing and child abuse. How Papa, a canting Christian, a heathen-hater, was finally done in through his self-effacing, unassertive wife to create space for herself and find her children to grow is the thematic point of *Purple*

Hibiscus. Kambili, naïve narrator, maladroit and seemingly uncoordinated daughter of Eugene can now flower and her find her feet and outgrow the physical and psychic wounds inflicted on them by Papa. Those wounds inflicted on wife and children, symbolized by the purple hibiscus will surely efface as Jaja returns from prison, and mama lives a normal life without a tyrannical spouse; and the children will come into unfettered adult estate.

The hearth is what extremely matters in Akachi Ezeigbo's House of Symbols. An illusion is created that the gender war has been fought and won and men and women are now co-equals in family matters; in fact, that when it comes to running a home, the man is merely like a freak in a side show. How did we arrive at this position; Akachi Ezeigbo had, in The Last of the Strong Ones written a counter history: that the war against colonial intrusion was not fought, as Achebe tried to present it, by the men alone (by the likes of Okonkwo and Ezeulu) but by the collective efforts of men and women (the Oluada). By the time Ezeigbo wrote, the men had been crippled enough, as Alkali in The Stillborn depicted a sobered, crippled Habu Adams walking side by side with crutches handed to him by his wife Li. With Alkali, the gender war had been won by the women, and Ezeigbo has assumed this womanist stance as a given in House of Symbols.

So, in *House of Symbols*, Ezeigbo, a new star in the firmament of African female writers, mounts the podium with loudspeakers, urging fellow women to relax, for the gender war has been won no victor no vanquished. So, Ezeigbo establishes a matriarchy (where Achebe had established a patriarchy) and seems to ask: why the fuss, why the agitation since women have quietly but confidently ruled the world on equal basis with the men, whether it is Ejimnaka in *The Last of the Strong Ones* or Eaglewomen in *House of Symbols*. In *House of Symbols*, women have no more need to sing "We shall Overcome", for the complementarity between men and women long sought after by women has long been on ground. Ezeigbo, should be congratulated for the superiority of her vision, having restored women to a primordial status where she presumes there never existed any gender conflict between men and women, where the issue of superiority or inferiority between men and women never arose. House of Symbols is therefore, a notch beyond feminism.

Therefore, in *House of Symbols*, the sharing of resources between Eaglewomen and her amiable and supportive husband,

Osai, was never discussed. There is a common pool in this perfect relationship between man and women. There is no provider in the conventional way in which Igbos address a wife as the consumer of the husband's wealth. House of Symbols is utopia of marital relationship, in a gender-issues free zone. Men and women in reality have achieved complementarity, have indeed become partners in progress; in a brave new world of gender harmony. Women in Ezeigbo's *House of Symbols* are role models in which the Eaglewomen is exemplar. Even the ward maid in Atagu Maternity Home wipes "her pretty face with a blue handkerchief" (12). With her achievement in House of Symbols, the gender-issues vehemently reopened by Eaglewomen's highly educated daughters in *Children of the Eagle* are, without Ezeigbo knowing it, a retrogression, a step back into ideological axis.

The hearth is the nerve-centre, the engine-room around which Bina Nengi-Ilagha's *Condolences* and Promise Okekwe's *Groaning Passage* gravitate, albeit, sadly. As I hinted earlier, while the men were eviscerated by the power-play in the unending years of military rule as evinced in the characters they create in contemporary fiction, the female writers, tired of the sound and fury of the many faces of feminism in the twentieth century, made a volta-face in the twenty-first, and faced the hearth. Bina Nengi-Ilagha's brilliant *Condolences* imbues the hearth with a deep sense of loss. The innovative subject (the signing of the condolence register at the death of the head of the family), the suspenseful narrative which etches vignettes of various aspects of the deceased's character corrals in the process ugly glimpses into every aspect of Pere Alazibo's character - his womanizing, his philanthropy, his business acumen, his irreligion. The sense of loss surrounding death is painfully renewed with the arrival of each new mourner.

One of the achievements of Bina's narrative skills is how she achieves characterization of each mourner through satire, through sly digs at their insincerities, their bare-faced lies, their subtle mockery of the dead. Bina's ingenuity in maintaining a protracted atmosphere of mourning till the actual burial and aftermath. is amazing. We encounter people relieved by Pere's death (Senator Ogbeiyefa who owes Pere millions of naira); people hurt by Pere's death (Daisy); people shamefully exposed (Trisha); and people genuinely touched by his death (the L.G.A. chairman). In a well-controlled narrative structure, and in the midst of the obsequies,

Bina found space to smuggle in her other thematic concerns: ugly wife disinheritance practices, levirate marriage, and environmental degradation of the Niger-Delta by multi-national oil companies.

As Bina Nengi-Ilagha mourns the death of Pere Alazibo, promise Okekwe mourns the osu caste system practices by Igbos in *Groaning Passage*. How the hearth wounds the heart of people in love is what preoccupies Okekwe in this novel. Nadi Igu genuinely loves and puts Saruwe in the family way, but he is prevented by his family from marrying her because, as she protested to him.

> You believed too, that I am evil because my ancestor chose to take refuge at the shrine of a merciful god rather than be sold into slavery to bestial white folks by his bestial blood brothers. His blood brothers, your people decided he would no longer be part of them (18).

When Nadi Igu confronts his own father insisting he must many Saruwe, his father tells him

> "I am afraid you can't marry her. She is from a tribe where nobody goes?"
> "What do you mean? She is from Iseke village"
> "Precisely, Iseke village is an osu village. It is a whole tribe of osu. They are outcasts, my son, and the free born will have nothing to do with an osu" (46-47).

After the above confrontation, Nadi Igu goes berserk, and later mad, walking about naked and feeding from compost heaps. In recent Nigerian fiction, there is no love so deep and no commitment to marry a woman one loves so tenacious that Okekwe devotes the rest of the novel to the reunion and rehabilitation of Saruwe and Nadi Igu by Saruwe' daughter, Ona, and her wonderful husband Otmar. In the process is a hint that the freeborn and the outcast have started a sort of association. It is a an engaging and passionate novel where character of Saruwe's mother, Souzu-Bella assumes mythical and epic proportions

V

We have ranged far enough in this tentative study of contemporary Nigerian fiction. We hay.: established that there is a definite break in contemporary Nigerian fiction from its antecedents in the twentieth century. There are no heroes in our recent fiction, there is no national cause to fight for, no charismatic or ascetic character willing to make sacrifices for the common good. There is to populist leader likely to, cry like Horace: *dulce et decorum est, pro patria mod* (it is sweet and fitting to die for one's country). And where there is no 'vision, the scriptures tell us, the people perish (Proverbs 29: 18).

African literature in the twentieth century had its high, even sublime moments. There was colonialism to confront. There was independence to aspire to. There was racism to declaim against and counter through Negritude. There were heroes and martyrs in our literatures- heroes willing to die for the national cause: Ikem in *Anthills of the Savannah*, Dedan Kimathi in *Dedan Kimathi* (drama), Bakayoko in *God's Bits of Wood*, Karega in *Petals of Blood*. There were visionaries who wrote *Facing Mount Kenya* (Kenyatta) and *Zambia Shall Be Free* (Kaunda).

But in recent Nigerian fiction, with the exceptions we noted among female writers, there is a corruption of the Nigerian dream, there is absence of a national ethos, there is a sense of estrangement, of cultural disinheritance and we have alienated people who have abandoned "home" and converged in Lagos (a no man's land), searching for quintessential pleasures through the sluice-gates of debauchery, drinking, motoring, as doubtful palliatives and suspect compensations in bars and brothels.

In spite of the proliferation of churches, God is dead in recent Nigerian fiction, completely edged out by materialism and epicurean tendencies. Hedonism is the new non- Sunday religion. No major character in new Nigerian fiction goes to a religious service on Sunday and none kneels down to pray for God's intervention in moments of crisis. In Maik Nwosu's *Alpha Song*, is it the night club addict and womanizer, Taneba, that we expect to pray, or the nymphomaniac wife of the doctor in *Ballad of Rage*, or even the graft king cum male prostitute, Ejike, in *Fattening House*? Or even the pervert necrophiliac, Leemy, in *Dreams Die at Twilight*?

I had said in elsewhere that twentieth century African fiction with its sense of loss, its fight against slavery and colonialism, was not a happy one. From our observations here, recent Nigerian writing is not more cheering, for the Nigerian dream destroyed by prolonged military rule, leaves Nigerian is a nation without a soul. The image of Nigerian in contemporary Nigerian fiction is a depressing one. To paraphrases Matthew Arnold, it is only in criticism that the thought of an era becomes articulate and crystallized.

Works cited

Abdul Raheem Shuaibu "Reconstructing the Road Map of Nigerian Literature: Reflections on Recent Fiction Writing". Annual Lecture of the Nigerian Academy of Letters, Kano, March 18, 2005.
Adichie, Chimamanda. *Purple Hibiscus*. Lagos: Parafina Books, 2004
Ageda, Jonah. *God's Own Country*. Makurdi: Cornerstone Enterprises, 2004.
Arthur-Worrey, Fola. *The Diaries of Mr. Michael*. Lagos: Griffith Audio-Visual Company, 2003.
Dorsch, T. S. (ed). *On the Art of Poetry*. London: Penguin, 1965.
Ezeigbo, Akachi-Adimora. House of Symbols. Lagos: Oracle Books, 2001.
Nengi-Ilagha, Bina. *Condolences*. Yenagoa: Treasure Books, 2002.
Newton, Chim. *Under the Cherry Tree*. Lagos, 2003.
Nwosu, Maik. *Alpha Song*. Lagos: House of Malaika and Beacon Books, 2001.
Okediran, Wale. *Dreams Die at Twilight*. Lagos: Malthouse Press, 2001.
Okekwe, Promise. *Groaning passage*. Lagos: Oracle Books Ltd, 2003.
Onwordi, Toni Kan. *Ballad of Rage*. Lagos: Hybun publications, 2004.
Osofisan, Femi. "Eagles in the Age of Unacknowledged Muse: Two Major New Writers in Contemporary Nigerian Literature, Akachi Ezeigbo and Promise Okekwe." *African Literature Today*, No. 24 (2004), 21-42.
Uwaifo, Omo. *Fatterning House*. Lagos, Hanon Publishers, 2001.
Wotton, Henry. Quoted in Henry Reeves, *The Critical Sense*. London: Heinemann Educational Books, 1955.
Others cited in this work are S. T. Coleridge and John Dryden.

16

The writer as patriot

> Force and right are the governors of this world; force, till right is ready. (Jourbert in *Pensees*)

In this chapter, I have chosen to focus on the writer in national development and on writing as a patriotic act and the writer as a patriot. George Orwell tells us in "Why I write" that people write for "egoism, aesthetic enthusiasm, historical impulse, and political purpose."[1] Before we ask the Nigerian or African writer why he writes, let us first take care of a few nagging issues about the purposes of art and that ultimate hiatus between art, the artist and his audience.

All art is propaganda even if it is propaganda in its most subtle form. But what matters to the writer who is an artist is not whether art is propaganda but whether the propaganda in his art impedes aesthetic considerations;[2] whether he has forgotten that the final difference between propaganda and art is that all art is an aesthetic endeavour that must end in an aesthetic experience. The writer must never forget that "all art" according to Schiller, "is dedicated to joy, and there is no higher and no more serious problem than how to make men happy. The right art is that alone which creates the highest enjoyment."[3]

If, like many writers past and present throughout the world,

---

[1] George Orwell, quoted by Adrian Roscoe in *Uhuru's Fire: African Literature East to South*. Cambridge University Press, 1977, p.174.
[2] Theodora Ezeigbo, "Functionality in Literature, Art and Propaganda", *Savannah*, Vol.10, No.1, June, 1989, p.79.
[3] In *Oxford Anthology of English Literature*, Vol.2, ed. by Frank Kermode. Oxford University Press, 1973, p.992.

writing for you is, in Orwell's suggestion, a political act, then you are a patriot, not, we are definitely certain, in the sense in which Dr. Samuel Johnson describes patriotism as "the last refuge of a scoundrel" but in the sense that you are genuine lovers of your country willing to die for her in the pursuit of truth; ready to risk even life and liberty because, according to Senator Fulbright, "to criticize one's country, to tell her that it could do much better, is to pay it the highest compliments" for this, in itself, constitutes the highest patriotism; provided that your loyalty or patriotism is not to one regime or junta, but to an indivisible country and to all her peoples.

If, then, for you writing is a political and patriotic act, you are warned of the risks which you run, of the dangers along your path. Torture, detention, exile, death by letter bombs—these are the occupational hazards of a majority of those who tread this path and they should imagine in front of them a placard in bold letters with the inscription:

Writing May Be Hazardous To Your Health

One might recall the fate of artists and writers over the centuries. In mythology, King Minos of Crete imprisoned Daedalus and his son Icarus in the labyrinthine mazes the king had ordered the artificer Daedalus to construct for the, Minotaur. The myth of the escape of Daedalus by fashioning wings for himself and his son (who flew too high and plummeted to earth for disobeying his father's instruction) has become the myth of the artist fashioning the mode of his own salvation. But note that the harassment of Daedalus and his son is the harassment which all artists face.

But that is myth. In history, the story of Socrates, that questing gadfly who made uncomfortable even a democracy as established as the Greeks must arrest our attention. Did they not arrest him, detain him, condemn him to death and give him hemlock to drink, on these charges:

> that Socrates is a criminal and a busybody, prying into things, under the earth and up in the heavens, and making the weaker argument the stronger, and teaching these things to others; that Socrates is a criminal who corrupts the young and does not believe in the gods whom the state believes in, but other new spiritual things instead.[4]

---

[4] *The Great Dialogues of Plato*. ed. Eric H. Warminton and Philip G. Rouse. New York:

You will remember how Socrates, the one man the Delphic oracle pronounced "the master of them that know" quipped: "what a blessing it would be for young people if the whole nation of the Athenians makes them (the youth) fine gentlemen and I alone corrupt them," and then refused to escape from prison in a boat smuggled in by his friends for that purpose, because it would confirm his accusers in their false belief that he is a criminal who now has made himself a fugitive from justice. Such an escape, he argued, would destroy the laws of Athens and render them nugatory. He, therefore, decided to stick by the truth, for truth, as he ingeniously argued, is a cleansing from vices, and wisdom commands him to obey the laws of the state and accept the punishment.

In our own days, we all remember how Aleksandr Solzhenitsyn, the 1970 Nobel Laureate, defied the KGB and published *The Gulag Archipelago* (1973), a documentary expose of the Soviet secret police, its prison camps, and its methods of terror and torture. The stir caused by this publication both in Russia and the West led to a dramatic development. After refusing to answer the summons to appear before government investigators ("before asking that citizens obey the law, learn to obey the law your-selves" he told the government), Solzhenitsyn, who had spent eleven years in Russia's prison camps, was accused of high treason, stripped of his Soviet citizenship, had a decree read to him ordering his deportation without his family, and was hustled aboard an airliner and flown to West Germany. That was on February 12, 1974. *Writing may be hazardous to your well-being.*

In apartheid South Africa, the scattering of her black writers abroad through banning orders is fresh in our memories. Dennis Brutus tells us how in 1965, he was imprisoned and tortured in Robben Island and "banned from publishing anything." In Kenya writing has proved also to be a risky enterprise. On December 31, 1977, Ngugi wa Thiong'o, the maverick Kenyan writer, was arrested and detained in Kamiti Maximum Security Prison in Kiambu, Kenya where he said: "I was kept behind stone walls and iron bars for a whole year." He had protested that "detention without trial is really a denial of the democratic rights of a Kenya national...I have

---

Mentor Book, 1956, pp.425, 430.

never, even now, been told any specific reasons for my detention."[5] And in Nigeria, Wole Soyinka was detained from August 1967 to October 1969. He had declared in an entry in World Authors: "I have one abiding religion—human liberty" and he avowedly uses art to challenge unacceptable situations in society, having allegedly held up a radio station to forestall Chief Akintola's victory address in a rigged election, and having declared elsewhere:

> I believe implicitly that any work of art which opens out the horizons of the human mind, and intellect, is by its very nature, a force for change, a medium for change.[6]

Soyinka did not close the door to the harassment of the artist in Nigeria. Achebe was reportedly questioned about the coincidence between Nzeogwu's coup d'état and the publication of A *Man of the People*, 1966, and Festus Iyayi lost his job at the University of Benin.

Now, having highlighted the plight of those whom writing has put in trouble, having put you on the "red alert", I must ask you to examine your conscience and find out why you write. Is yours an exercise in the famous art for art's sake; in the pursuit of "the poem *per se*"; in the service of a meretricious, abstract beauty for your own privatist, ego-inflating purposes: *Quo Vadis?;* in what direction? Are you with or against your society; are you an activist in the service of man and the betterment of your society or are you a safe writer, suffering from that ashen paralysis of will which numbs action? Are the polite chronicler of events merely, or even an accessory in the face of crimes against society by the mighty and powerful, through silence, knowing that evil persist because good men say or do nothing? Are you an Abadi (in Okara's *The Voice*) who has got his M.A. and Ph.D. but not "it"? Are you the old messenger in the same novel who says: "As for me...if the world turns this way, I take it. Anyway the world turns I take it with my hands. I like sleep...so I do not think," Or have you allied yourself with the elder in the same novel who thinks nothing could be done: "if they do anything, I agree, since they do not take yam out of my mouth." Are you one of Okara's "think-nothing people" who are like logs in the river that float and go whither the current

---

[5] *The Weekly Review.* Nairobi: January 5, 1979, p.30.
[6] *In Person: Achebe, Awoonor and Soyinka.* Seattle: Washington Institute of Comparative and Foreign Area Studies, University of Washington, 1975, p.135.

commands"?⁷

As I just mentioned above, evil persists, moral theologians tell us, because good men do nothing The African writer must ask himself: Am I a writer for whom? Are you writing to make vague noises in the press or, worse still, are you taking up writing as an extended letter to your countrymen in defence of an obnoxious status quo or regime, hoping to find your name in the list of the next ministerial appointments. Or are you, as you should be, a questing gadfly asking, for instance, Nigerians like Okara's Okolo if they allowed the powers –that-be "to buy the insides of all the people?" Are you, as you should be, an Osime Iyere (in Iyayi's *Heroes)* urging the promotion of a third army to oppose and change the status quo? One should use this occasion to re-examine the purposes of one's profession.

The Nigerian writer, for instance, as Emmanuel Obiechina argues should have a special allegiance to the down trodden in the Nigerian society, to the socially handicapped, to the women, the children, the unemployed, the sick; all those who are not able to fight their own battles. The writer should put on his armour and charge into battle in defence of the defenceless. It is my view that the writer in Nigeria of today has to take his position against the oppression of the people, all forms of brutalities, and of unwarranted violence against the masses.⁸

This should be applied to any other country. In the light of the above, it is clear that the reader demands of our writers some measure of commitment, some degree of courage to challenge the status quo, to change our society long in anomie. The writer must definitely tell us where he stands. He must, in his works, confront the problem of good and evil in his society, differentiate them and take sides; and in taking sides, he must tell us where he stands. If he is not writing on the side of society; if he is not for the masses of his country; if he is not for us—the masses of his country—then, he can-not but be against us. He cannot, therefore, be a hypocrite—chasing with the hounds and at the same time running with the deer.

A majority of our writers, if not all, started on a patriotic

---

[7] Gabriel Okara. *The Voice.* London: Heinemann, 1964.
[8] Emmanuel Obiechina, "The Writer and his Commitment in Contemporary Nigerian Society," *Okike*, Nos. 27/28, March 1988, p.4.

note—each was a writer with political radar. Each saw his job as that of reconstruction, of rehabilitation, of defence against the psychological wounds and denigration inflicted upon the people by the colonial invaders. Read Nnamdi Azikiwe and see his defence of Africa's dignity, of our place in world history denied us by European writers. Azikiwe tells us in *Renascent Africa* (Accra, 1937): Educate the renascent African to be a man. Tell him that he has made definite contribution to history. Educate him to appreciate the fact that iron was discovered by Africans, that the conception of God was initiated by Africans, that Africa ruled the world from 765 to 713 B.C., that while Europe slumbered during the "dark ages" a great civilization flourished on the banks of the Niger, extending from the salt mines of Therghazza in Morocco to lake Tchad. Narrate to him the lore of Ethiopia, of Ghana or Songhay. Let him relish with the world that, while Oxford and Cambridge were in their inchoate stages, the University of Sankore, in Timbuctoo, welcomed scholars and learned men from all over the Moslem world, as Sir Percy put it. (P.9)

Mbonu Ojike, the boycott king of Nigeria, had also patriotically reacted against the false social theories propounded by Leo Africanus, Gobineau and Levy-Bruhl. *My Africa* (New York: 1964), by Ojike was a defence of Africa's dignity, a rehabilitation of the African personality. The European, he asserts, assumes that the African has neither laws nor political organizations; that the society is therefore chaotic, living in a miasma of tribal disorder...I wonder how much longer these fictions can blind the West (p.192).

With the above in mind, Achebe's dictum below has an accredited and noble ancestry:

> Here then is an adequate revolution for me to espouse—to help my society regain belief in itself and put away the complexes of the years of denigration and self-abasement.[9]

Africa's earlier writers, it will now be seen—these writers critics refer to as Negritudinists including Achebe, were concerned with reconstructing Africa's image distorted and bruised by colonial intrusion, especially by white writers who saw in Africa a savage people without humanity, saw in its climate an impenetrable and uninhabitable jungle teeming with wild animals, dispensing only

---

[9] Chinua Achebe, "The Novelist as Teacher", in *Morning Yet on Creation Day*, London: Heinemann, 1975, p.44.

illness and death to the white man; and saw in Africa's culture and traditions a senselessness that made an entire continent irrelevant in world history. These early pioneer writers have risen to the challenge of giving valency to our traditions and cultures by demonstrating through their works the logic in our traditional legal systems, the soundness in our healing ways, the meaning in our rituals, and the beauty in our art. This is what Obiechina calls "cultural nationalism" among African writers which aims at "rehabilitating the autochthonous culture;" For the Nigerian writer, like his other African and black counterparts, must possess at all times the highest measure of social consciousness. And, as Chinweizu and his group cogently put it:

> The function of the artist in Africa, in keeping with our traditions and needs, demands that the writer, as a public voice, assume a responsibility to reflect public concerns in his writing ... because in Africa we recognize commitment is mandatory of the artist.[10]

This social commitment wears many faces. Having chased away the colonial fox from without, the Nigerian writer, for instance, came home to admonish the barn-yard hen within. This he did by writing pungent satirical works that focus on what Nigerians have made of themselves since independence, attacking especially the corruption, the bribery, the failure of leadership, the kleptomania by people in positions of power, and the usurpation and abuse of power by the military elite.

While Achebe (in *A Man of the People*) and Aluko (in *One Man One Matchet*) merely held their protagonists up for ridicule, Soyinka of this older vanguard was not as patient or as subtle. He is for revolution, as he argues in *A Shuttle in the Crypt*

> Take justice
> In your hands who can
> Or dare, insensate sword
> Of power
> Outherods Herod and the law's outlawed
> ...Orphans of the world
> Ignite! Draw

---

[10] "Towards the Decolonization of African Literature", *Okike*, Vol. VII, June 1975, pp.78-79.

your fuel of pain from earth's sated core

'In *Season of Anomy,* Soyinka unabashedly insists on a bloody revolution to remove an oppressive regime. Demakin the Dentist urges his men:

> Extract that carious tooth quickly before it infects others...But we must also set up a pattern of killing the more difficult ones. Select the real kingpins and eliminate them. It is simple, you have to hit the snake on the it harmless... The harmattan... is the insurrections. Fires burn faster, the winds fly drier, people's anger spirals swifter in the dust of devil-winds building up into the cyclone that in their oppressors.[11]

The younger ideologues...those hankering after- socialist utopia of a class-less society—ally with the masses and, like Soyinka, urge a revolution that would cleanse society of its present ills and usher all into nirvana. These ideologues see literature as an instrument of liberation from the oppressors who invariably belong to the ruling class, urging the masses to rise up and overthrow the oppressive system. In Iyayi's *Heroes*, the protagonist urges a third army to rise up and liberate the cheated and betrayed masses, while Osofisan in *Once Upon Four Robbers* creates hoodlums who are bent, Robin Hood style, on forcible redistribution of the nation's wealth, by robbing the rich and sharing the loot among themselves who represent the masses.

But with the antennae of current works by Iyayi, Odia Ofeimun, Sowande, Osofisan, and Omotoso pointing toward revolutionary trends, Achebe's mature vision in *The Anthills of the Savannah* urges reform rather than revolution, the consequences of which might be cataclysmic. We might need to heed this voice of the elder:

> Experience and intelligence warn us that man's progress in freedom will be piecemeal, slow and undramatic. Revolution may be necessary for taking a society out of an intractable stretch of quagmire, but it does not confer freedom, and may indeed hinder it ... Reform may be a dirty word then but it begins to look more and

---

[11] Chinua Achebe, *Anthills of the Savannah.* Ibadan: Heinemann, 1988 p.99.

more like the most promising route to success in the world.[12]

The more practical minded among us may begin to wonder where all these are leading us. He may ask when Matthew Arnold says that poetry would save us, whether literature has saved any nation or any people. Suppose his skepticism about it all, leads him to discover anew Don Lee's poem:

> I ain't seen no poems stop a .38
> I ain't seen no stanzas break
> a honkie's head
> I ain't seen no metaphors stop a tank

Is he to despair; or do we urge him to replace pessimism with optimism in Amiri Baraka's counter stance in his call for

> Assassin poems, poems that shoot guns
> Poems that wrestle cops into alleys
> And take their weapons, leaving them dead

The level-headed thing to do is to steer the middle course. No, we cannot point to a society "saved" by literature. And yes, literature has been influential in changing societies and individuals. In fact, literature has once helped save a soul. Emile Zola's *J'Accuse* (1898) inspired by the Dreyfus Affair led to the release of Captain Dreyfus; and Andre Gide's work *Voyage au Congo* led in modern history to the termination of King Leopold's hold on that nation, by exposing the atrocities perpetrated by Belgians against the Congolese people.

So, as we turn our attention briefly from the writers to their products, we may ask: what has literature done for Nigeria, for instance? Why does it deserve a place in the scheme of things, in our educational system? Well, we may ask: has it ever occurred to any one of us that while technology could be "transferred" literature and the arts belong uniquely to a people. Literature like tradition and culture, is autochthonous; and if we allow literature and the arts to die through neglect, our very humanity, our identity as a people will

---

[12] Chikwenye Ogunyemi, "Women and Nigerian Literature," in *Perspectives on Nigerian Literature, Vol.1*, Lagos: Guardian Books (Nigeria) Ltd., 1988, p.66.

not only be under threat but it will disappear and our very identity in world culture will face complete effacement. Nigeria, of course, need no longer entertain any such fears. We are not only the pathfinders in African literature; we are the undisputed leaders in that field. Our literatures have indeed fostered patriotism and nationalism. Every Nigerian anywhere in the world because Achebe, Rotimi, Niyi Osundare, Festus Iyayi, Ben Okri are indigenes of this great country of literary giants. Nigeria's most valued export commodity is not petroleum products but her literatures which have won international prize including the Nobel Prize. Achebe's works alone, by the latest count, have been translated into fifty different languages outside Africa. Through her literatures mentioned above, Nigeria exports her culture to other parts of the world and, through these literary works, exposes to the world the very foundations of her national consciousness.

At the level of society, the aesthetic experience fosters mutual sympathy and understanding which will normally help on a larger scale to draw men together, to draw our country together, since all shared experience helps to bring people together in friendship and mutual respect, for any group of people who share the same aesthetic experience have a bond between them and feel united under a common identity. So, Nigerian literatures unite Nigerians more than politics or science or religion. It is true of any nation. Nigeria today stands tall before the international community because of the collective endeavours of her writers. While our politics and the shenanigans of our business deals most often sell Nigeria's private shames in the international scandal market, it is through the collective endeavours of Nigerian writers (and sportsmen) that Nigeria stands redeemed and enhanced in the eyes of the world, since the onus of moral regeneration in our society has always lain with our writers, as if in response to Nietzsche's call that "society needs an elite that will set a pattern and curb the thoughtlessness of the masses."

Nigerian writers have accomplished this by establishing what I refer to as the Nigerian tradition in literature—a tradition that has set a pattern for the entire continent. It is that tradition which makes use of and expresses allegiance to our folk culture *et cetera,* in giving expression to our national culture by stridently stressing what is indigenous to Nigeria. Tutuola, Achebe, Soyinka, Elechi Amadi, Okigbo, Ola Rotimi, and many others were all concerned with cultural assertion and were pioneers in what we have come to regard as cultural nationalism in Nigerian literature: in their stressing the innate dignity of the Nigerian, in their concern with the rehabilitation of the image of the black man in general, and the Nigerian man and woman in particular—that image damaged and distorted by white writers. They have all established this tradition mainly through myth-making, through the mythopoeia of group identity and group experience, thereby transmitting culture, pursuing an ideology of cultural renaissance, emphasizing our communal and collective philosophy, stressing the success stories or failures of communities rather than the fortunes or misfortunes of the individual, calling attention to a rural rather than an industrial or technological way of life that has led to a fulfilled way of existence. They have done this by bending, twisting and proverbializing the English language or revealing, the innate wealth of our vernacular languages.

And one should not leave the Nigerian female writer out of this discourse. Again it is the Nigerian female writer, Flora Nwapa, who set the pace both for Nigeria and the entire continent as the trail blazer in modern African female fiction writing, and is therefore historically important. She saw it as her duty to redeem and correct the disparaged and debased image of the Nigerian woman as the women saw it depicted by male writers like Achebe and Cyprian Ekwensi - women created helpless, dependent brutalized, disparaged, living either as prostitutes, concubines or "kept women", destined in the words of Chikwenye Ogunyemi "to carry *foofoo* and soup to men discussing 'important matters'."' Nwapa set the pace for the feminist trend in Nigerian literature, quickly joined by Buchi Emecheta, Zulu Sofola, Zaynab Alkali, Ifeoma Okoye, and a host of others by preaching the dignity and economic independence of the Nigerian woman in captivating titles like *Women Are Different* (Nwapa) and *Double Yoke* (Emecheta). Far from being parasites, far from being dependent on their men, the feminist Nigerian woman is highlighted as dignified in comportment, economically independent, highly industrious and possessing superior and higher moral values than their male counterparts. Through their writings, the image of the Nigerian woman as equal in all respects with her male counterpart is now firmly established.

In sum, the writer is a patriot who, for love of his country has taken great risks to ensure that we live in a free and democratic society where no one is oppressed. The ultimate end toward which the writer tends is utopia for whether the writer is revolutionary or reformist in orientation, every writer is essentially a dreamer envisaging a heaven on earth, freedom from racial, colonial and neo-colonial abuse, in short, a golden era of opportunities. Writers are finally the interpreters of our culture, the enemy of sinister forces in society, the conserver of our values, the terror of bad governments. "Force and right are the governors of this world; force, till right is ready," says Jourbert. And force is the terror of all writers. That is why writing may be a hazardous profession and one could die in the cause of that calling. The only consolation is that one, in the world beyond, will be dining with a noble and select group of humans: Homer, Sophocles, Euripides, Virgil, Shakespeare, Flaubert, Hemingway, Dostoyevsky, Tolstoy, Nwapa, Richard Wright, and Du Bois. Where else would there be more distinguished company?

Epilogue

In search of new challenges: African literature and criticism in the twenty-first century

From its beginnings written African literature in the nineteenth and twentieth centuries from Phyllis Wheatley and Gustav Vassa, down to Achebe and Ngugi wa Thiong'o, was an unhappy one. It was lachrymal. It was a weeping literature, a literature of lamentation, following Africa's unhappy experience with slavery and colonialism. It was Hippolyte Taine who suggested in *History of English Literature* (1864) that we could recover from the monuments of literature a knowledge of the manner in which men thought and felt at a particular epoch in their history. The sociologist, Taine, had remarked that the distinguishing mark between the early literatures of Great Britain and those of France was that the former was the literature of a defeated people while the latter was the literature of a conquering people.

Having lost her pride through slavery and colonialism, modern African literature arose from the ashes of her past experiences. It became a literature with a strong sense of loss; loss of our dignity; loss of our culture and tradition; loss of our religion, loss of our land; loss of our very humanity. Any wonder that the titles of our most celebrated literary works highlighted these losses. Have we forgotten Achebe's *Things Fall Apart; Ngugi* wa Thiongo's *Weep Not, Child;* Alan Paton's *Cry the Beloved Country?* And protest literature over Apartheid further irrigated Africa's tears because of man's inhumanity to man, to a people dubbed "the wretched of the earth".

This study will, therefore, be Janus-faced. It will cast a backward glance at African literature and criticism in the twentieth century and, in the process, look forward to the challenges of the twenty-first century. While conceding that modem African literature (its written version) arose weepingly in, reaction to, slavery and the colonial experience, one must, of necessity, draw attention to Africa's pre-history, to a time its oral literature stood toe-to-toe with the best celebrated epics of Europe. *The Ozidi Saga*, the *Mwindo Epic*, the *Sundiata epic* and so on, stood toe-to-toe with the epics of Greece and Rome, and with other European epics which all started also from their oral tradition: the Sanskrit (Indian) epic, *Mahabharata*, the Spanish *El Cid*, the German *Niebelungenlied*, the Greek *Iliad* and *Odyssey*, the Roman *Aeneid*, the French *Chanson de Roland*, and the English *Beowulf*. Each of the above epics both African and European, sang of a noble people in noble pursuits.

Once the above is established, it would be easy to understand that modern African literature (its written version) arose after the psychic trauma of slavery and colonialism which made her literature in the twentieth century one with a running sore, a stigmata that forced her literature to dissipate its energies in a dogged fight to re-establish the African personality. African literature in the twentieth century thus operated on a narrow canvas, a point that will be pursued later in this study.

The lachrymal nature of modern African literature made it inevitable for that literature to start by blaming the white man for everything wrong with us, castigating him for exploiting our resources and debasing our humanity. We also blamed the white man for not granting us, at least, flag independence to allow us develop our-selves. And when the white man threw in the towel, our eyes were opened to the rapacity, greed; myopia, and the corrupt tendencies of our indigenous politicians.

Before the white man left, and to pay him in his own coins for the haemorrhage he inflicted on our collective psyche, the literature of Negritude was born. The philosophy of Negritude became finally enthroned in the motto of the University of Nigeria: "to restore the dignity of man". There may be no space here to recount the obvious, or to repeat all the platitudes surrounding the Negritude movement whose trajectory became over-arching from the Harlem Renaissance through the Rastafarian movement in Jamaica to indigenism in

Haiti. But after regaining our equilibrium through the Negritude movement, and after unsurefooted attempts by Ayi Kwei Armah at psychic reconstruction in *The Healers* and *Two Thousand Seasons,* African literature in the twentieth century seemed to have reached a point of mild exhaustion.

As we know, literature is judged always in relation to its social function; the better the function is fulfilled, the better the literature. A spiritual vacuum seems to have crept in toward the end of the twentieth century, among African writers; an ashen paralysis that has not spared our most celebrated writers of that epoch. "Art", Camus tells us, "is of small importance in the face of suffering." It seems that the devastations of the economic order, the instabilities of governments in most African countries south of the Sahara, the frequent disruptions of thee democratic order through military rule, and the ravages of disease, especially, the HIV/AIDS pandemic, have taken their toll in the area of literary production.

First, the publishing houses suffered a demise. Time was when publishing houses like Heinemann, Evans, Brothers, Oxford University Press, Longman, African Universities Press, Malthouse, Spectrum Books, offered advance royalties to budding writers to complete their work. Toward the dying hours of the twentieth century, the publishing houses turned around to demand large sums of money from budding writers in order to have their works published. Soon, they were joined by new "publishing" establishments in Nigeria: Kraft Books, ABIC, which insisted on publishing a writer's work on a cash-and-carry arrangement: and before a new writer could catch his breath, countless but nondescript desktop computer "publishers", or rather, printers who had cornered ISBN numbers joined the field with no facilities for marketing or distribution of their product. These newcomers to the printing business saw no need to evaluate a manuscript or even offer advice before proceeding to print what the author told them was a novel, a play or a book of poems. With countless self-published books in the field, it became almost impossible to separate the chaff from the grain with the exception of the incomparable Niyi Osundare.

In Nigeria the only hope for discrimination among new books and new authors may lie in the efforts of the poorly funded Association of Nigerian Authors (ANA) through its yearly awards. But the major problem with ANA is its award of prizes for unpublished manuscripts and its lack of promotion of books it considers worthy of attention. ANA, therefore, needs to source for funds to establish a publishing house in order to publish, promote, and market its award-winning authors. *Things Fall Apart,* for example, may have remained an obscure but excellent novel, had Heinemann not undertaken to publish and promote it worldwide.

Since Achebe, Wa Thiong'o, Denis Brutus, Ayi Kwei Armah, Soyinka, La Guma, Peter Abrahams, Buchi Emecheta, Meja Mwangi and Cyprian Ekwensi have definitely passed their prime, carrying with them the youthful vibrancy of the 1960s and 1970s, African literature at the turn of the century has experienced a disquieting lull except for the residual voices of Ben Okri, Nuruddin Farah and Niyi Osundare.

At the onset of the twenty-first century, something has definitely happened in the lives of old and new writers that has deprived us of the ebullience and revolutionary spirit of the 1960s and 1970s. As Malraux declared at the Congress of Soviet Writers in 1931:

> Art is not an act of submission; it is a victory. The victory of what? Of emotions and the spirit of expressing them.

If, as Malraux asserts in the above declaration, the work of art is seen as a "conquest, a struggle between the artist and his world, an accusation against forces that hold humanity in servitude" in order to make men "conscious of the hidden greatness and dignity in themselves", a new image of the African personality needs to be fashioned, to reposition Africa for the take-off of the twenty-first century. We need a new world order. Our writers, in this new epoch of globalization dominated by a technologically oriented new world order must create a new Africa, a new spirit of optimism, an Africa full of promises, able to feed its teeming populations, with a healthy and vibrant people not dependent on Europe and America for sustenance.

I hinted earlier at the smallness of canvas of the African writer in the last century. The reason for that smallness of artistic canvass was, as discussed earlier, the defensive nature of our literatures and our preoccupation with re-establishing the African personality, glancing backwards to a glorious past, in the process of which looking forward imaginatively eluded us.

Our writers should now look forward to the twenty-first century as one with positive challenges. The white man has been described as belonging to a minority race with a majority complex, while the African portrays himself as belonging to a majority race with an inferiority or minority complex. The twenty-first century offers the African writer opportunities to position himself as one at par, at least imaginatively, with the white race. This century offers the African writer opportunities to carve out a new humanism devoid of the complexes of the twentieth century that made him so defensive as a second-class citizen of the world.

The African writer in the twenty-first century should forget the complexes of the past and be more imaginatively aggressive and expansive, invading other continents and even the sides is new setting, striving to have a global outlook in his creative output, mounting a new international phase and not limiting his canvas to the African soil. He should break away from *the retour aux sources* fixation that informed the Negritude aesthetic of the last century.

Let me explain. The European writer of the nineteenth and twentieth centuries set his sights beyond Europe. Rider Haggard's *King Solomon's Mines,* Orwell's *Burmese Days,* E. M. Forster's *A Passage to India,* Conrad's *Heart of Darkness,* Edgar Wallace's *Sanders of the River—these* displayed the wide canvas of the European writer. Henry James, the American novelist, developed what critics called his "international theme" in *Daisy Miller, The Ambassadors, The Portrait of a Lady,* depicting the gaucheries of naive Americans, among sophisticated Europeans. The European writer widened his literary canvas in writing science fiction. Jules Verne, the French fiction writer invaded the skies in the 1960s with *Froth the Earth to the Moon* predicting a journey to the moon from a rocket launched from Cape Canaveral. One hundred years later, man landed on the moon in a rocket launched from the same Cape Canaveral in the U.S. He further invaded the sea under the earth with *Twenty Thousand Leagues under the sea.* The American science fiction writer Alvin Toffler wrote *Future Shock* with his futuristic insistence that we should be "educating for change", that we should be "preparing people for the future" while warning that "unless man quickly learns to ,control the rate of change in his personal affairs, we are doomed to a massive adaptational breakdown."

It becomes clear when one draws attention to the narrow canvas of the African writer in the twentieth century, busy as he was weeping over the losses inflicted on him by past colonial wasters, preoccupied with blaming the African politician or military leaders for leading us into political and economic quagmire, that the time has come for a more forward looking vision.

The twenty-first century beckons Africans to embrace new challenges in this epoch of globalization. If African literature in the twentieth century had suffered from imaginative timidity, it has no reason to be so confined in the twenty-first century. Our literature should no longer be contented to be fixated on our cultural moorings Europe invaded Africa and the world with their civilization, religion, and technology and all of us have since then been transfixed. What prevents the African writer in the twenty-first century from re-inventing Europe and from there develop an international theme in our literatures. The Europeans wrote about Africa after a mere trip (Conrad), or domiciling there for a few years (Elspeth Huxley), why can't Africans write about Europe of America? We have travelled to Europe and America, worked there, studied there, married their women, and lived there. Are we so unperceptive not to observe, so blind not to see, so analphabetic not to write about them or about us in their midst?

The idea of science fiction even at its most elementary levels has eluded African writers. African writers must face the future by developing an international theme, by engaging in futuristic literature, by looking forward to the fulfilment of "the African dream". The African dream was partially achieved in the twentieth century...the rehabilitation of our humanity through the negritude aesthetic. We should look forward and project a forward looking utopia for Africa, not the backward looking utopia of the twentieth century that merely healed our psychic wounds. A forward-looking utopia for African writers should project a truly independent Africa politically stable, able to feed her starving peoples, standing toe-to-toe with Europe and the West, possessing enough coercive force that will earn her respect in the international arena, and become the last refuge for the oppressed all over the world. This is the challenge twenty-first century for African writers.

II

The wind follows the sun, we read in geography books, just as critical trends follow trends in creative writing. Criticism of African literature in the last century rose in vigorous, to spirited and passionate creative output by most celebrated writers...Achebe, Soyinka, Ngugi wa Thiong'o, Kwei Armah, Okigbo, Denis Brutus, Flora Nwapai Emecheta, Mariama Ba, Cyprian Ekwensi, Peter Abrahams, Alex La Guma. Their central theme which began with of culture-contact with Europe captured in its sweep arising from post-independence, moving on to feminism, socialist concerns and then the various wars in Africa. Expectedly our most respected critics rose to the challenges arising from the concerns of the writers. Emenyonu engaged Bernth Lindfors on who is most qualified to be the critic of African literature. Nnolim aroused Achebe's ire on the source of one of his novels. Soyinka and the troika (Chinweizu *et al.*) locked horns over what the former called "Neo-Tarzanism" in African Literature.

Toward the *Decolonization of African literature* made waves in the critical annals of African Literature. Debate over the proper language of expression still lingers among our critics, and establishment of what constitutes the accepted aesthetic of African literature is unresolved. Women soon joined the fray. Chikwenye Ogunyemi, vigorously aided by Omolara Ogundipe-Leslie and Helen Chukwuma in promotion of the feminist cause, attacked male critics tagging them with the indelicate sobriquet "phallic critics". From here oppositional criticism by radical voices engaged in discursive relations between classes in their theoretical constructs, politicized the cultural basis, on which our autochthony was anchored. Although they enjoyed the appellation "radical", their Marxist socialist fulminations hardly led to new rationalities in the African literary domain. The failure of the Marxist/Socialist ideologues to move African literature forward was resounding. After all, the ultimate aim of the Marxist/Socialist school was utopian: to re-order society so that the dictatorship of the proletariat would take root on the African soil. This informs the fact that they started criticism as class warfare, highlighting the skirmishes of the downtrodden against the powers-that-be.

Now, the twenty-first century seems to have taken the African writer and critic by surprise. Pioneer writers like Achebe and his contemporaries have fallen silent or are now playing into what soccer enthusiasts refer to as "injury time". Ben Okri, Nuruddin Farah, Niyi Osundare and a few others are holding the field, but the enthusiasm, the vibrancy of the 1960s and 1970s are definitely lacking. That leaves the critic with little to do. Who is the new writer on the literary scene today whose message is large enough to elicit spontaneous response from the critics because the critic feels challenged by the depth of the writer's insights?

This is not to forget that critics whom I refer to as "children of de Saussure" are alive and active. They are keen students of structuralism, post-structuralism, modernism, deconstruction and post-colonialism. With the exception of post-colonialism, the regular diet of critical discourse of these children of de Saussure has always in its menu high falutin terms like *ecriture, archiecriture, aporia, semiology, semiotics*. For these scholars, writing should be seen as *ecriture* and the literary text as one species of social institution where, in the process of *lecture* (reading) which must be "creative", at which point, according to post-structuralists, the reader has reached the state of *recuperation*. A text must be *lisible* (readable) and if it is not (according to Roland Barthes in *S/Z*) it becomes *illisible* (unreadable) denying the reader the *plaisir* or *jouissance* (orgasmic ecstasy) that Roland Barthes harps upon in *The Pleasure of the Text*.

To be able to follow and popularize the terms mentioned above, the student must have read vital works in the area: Derrida's *Of Grammatology*, and *Writing and Difference* (on deconstruction); Jean Piaget; *structuralism,* Jonathan Culler-*structuralist Poetics,* Roland Barthes: *Elements of Semiology* Claude Levi-Strauss: *Structural Anthropology* (all of structuralism). Some more adventurous among these critics may complete their readings with Jacques Lacan: *The Language of the self;* Michel Foucault: *The Archaeology of the self;* Gerrard Genette: *Narrative Discourse.* And to belong, one has to be familiar with Julia Kristeva's theory of *intertextuality*.[1]

The point at issue is that since the critic is a mediator between art and its audience and is there to arouse enthusiasm for the work while pointing out the worth, of the work, is he still at one with his

---

[1] See entries on "Deconstruction" and "Structuralist Criticism" in M.H. Abrams A Glossary of Literary Terms, 4th ed. (New York: Holt, Rinehart and Winston, 1981).

audience when in these life-denying exercises? Isn't the primary social of the critic to make a text easier to understand for find it hard; to be a midwife between hard text and a non-understanding reader?

With all humility one might ask how these dry exercises in structuralist discourses conduce to solving problems (at least imaginatively) besetting Africans at the turn of the century? How does deconstruction as a critical engagement address life-denying issues confronting Africans at the beginning of this century ... poverty, unstable governments, the 'HIV/AIDS pandemic? How does deconstruction create, in Matthew Arnold's dictum, "a current of true and fresh ideas" and propagate "the best that is known and thought in the world"?

The preoccupation of critics I refer to as "children of Saussure" is critically life denying and leads to a critical cul-de-sac because one sees them as gradually moving away from the primary questions posed by criticism; what is art? What is its use? Why is it studied? Is it good or bad art?' Of what value/worth is art to man? Deconstruction or dismantling of structures may be where Europeans have arrived after four thousand years of their art history. But African written literature and its arrival on the world scene are barely sixty years old. Don't we need to walk before we run, to build before we dismantle? Moreover, deconstruction, and its allied studies seem to deflect and distract the critic from his primary; even elemental functions: to be of some use to the reader by helping him understand the work; to propagate, according to Matthew Arnold, the best that is known and thought in existing works of art; to legislate taste and insist on decorum; to act as a guide to writers through suggestion, advice, demonstration; to explicate, work by showing that it has or lays definite claims to ultimate values ...the good, the true, the beautiful? Finally, it is the function of the critic to discriminate among competing works of art and to defend the work of art against those who doubt its validity.

A new trend in the criticism of African literature which is not likely to lead to a critical cul-de-sac is post-colonialism with its tripartite implications of "New English Literatures", "third world literature", and "commonwealth literature". Post-colonialism further encompasses within its circuitry of discourse the following:
a. Works by and about the post-colonial adventure, the white man who finds himself in an alien environment and writes about it

in his own language as we find in Australia, New Zealand, Canada. He is also found in other settler colonies in India, and Africa (Zimbabwe, Kenya, South Africa).

b. Work about the Caribbean experience where the post-colonial has experienced dislocations through slavery or indentured labour, finding himself in an alien environment where he struggles with. a new language and a totally new experience.

c. Works by and about the colonial as we see in Africa and India where the colonial subject is forced by the intrepid imperialist adventurer, to remain in his own environment with no loss of his inheritance but is forced to express his experience in the colonial master's tongue. The tensions between the colonized and the colonizer involved in literature of post-colonialism provide a mine-field of unexplored discourse.[2]

In sum, it is the position of this study that African literature and its criticism have suffered a decline at the turn of the century. The causes of this decline are manifold. The downturn in our economic order, the demise of the publishing houses that made availability, distribution, and marketing of new literary texts impossible; the fact that our best writers reached their peak in the late 1980s so that their most productive years have suffered exhaustion...these plus the fact that what kicked the African writer in the 1960s and 1970s are no longer current. All contributed to the lull in literary creativity and its attendant criticism at present.

It is imperative, therefore, that a change of vision and a new attitude of the mind should govern and efforts in this century. As Ebong asserts, Africa

> is ripe for a revolution. It is not the promiscuous, violent, bloody revolution of permissive wantonness to life and property, nor is it the cultural revolution of black humanity asserting itself in protest against the indifference of the west. The revolution for contemporary Africa presuppose the reorganization and the restructuring of the African mind and psyche (71).[3]

---

[2] A good work on post-colonial literatures is the *Empire Writes Back: Theory and Practice of Post-Colonial Literatures* by Bill Ashcroft, Helen Tiffin and Gareth Griffith. (London, Routledge, 1989).

[3] Inih Akpan Ebong, "Towards the Revolutionary Consciousness: The Writer in Contemporary Africa", in *Literature and Society: Selected Essays on African Literature*,

If great writers do not emerge in the twenty-first century shall we ever again have great critics with the kind of insight that produced *The Writings of Wole Soyinka* (Eldred Jones); *Christopher Okigbo: Creative Rhetoric* (Sunday Anozie); *The Novels of Ayi Kwei: Armah* (Fraser); *Cyprian Ekwensi (Emenyonu); The Poetry of Okot p'Bitek* (Heron); *Peter Abrahams* (Wade); and *The Novels* and *Plays of Ngugi wa Thiong'o* (Killam). And were great writers to emerge by miracle in the early days of this century, where would one find the supporting encouragement from publishing houses like Evans Brothers and Heinemann that promoted both the creative output and its attendant criticism of the last century? With self-published works suffering the disability of non-distribution and non-availability, would one be tagged a doomsayer if one predicted that the immediate future of African literature and its attendant criticism are bleak?

Finally, if as we have tried to establish, the creative sun is followed inevitably by the critical wind, what new writers on the African creative horizon are there to excite the critical responses of a new Izevbaye, a new Irele, a new Lindfors, a new Emenyonu. So, *quo vadimus?* Where is African creative writing headed in the twenty-first century? What is the dream of African writers in this century? If the dream of the African writer in the last century was to recapture our lost humanity and project the African personality, the African writer in this century is challenged to envision a new Africa, which has achieved parity (politically, technologically, economically, and militarily) with Europe and America. And he has to widen his canvas as Nuruddin Farah is trying to do and as Ali Mazrui definitely did in *The Trial of Christopher Okigbo*.

---

ed. Ernest Emenyonu, (Oguta: Zim Pan-African Publishers, 1986, 71-83).

Index

1984 -46, 50, 81
A Dance of the Forest -102
A Grain of Wheat -95, 97,182
A Hen Too Soon -121
A Man of the People -46, 95, 109, 135, 161, 162, 165, 182, 190, 191, 192, 193, 222, 225, 235
A Portrait of the Artist as a Young Man -93
A Question of Power -42
A Shuffle in the Crypt -225
A Traveller from Altruria -51
A Wreath for the Maidens 1973 -64, 67, 78, 182, 190, 191, 192, 193
A.D 2050 -51
ABIC -233
Abiku 171, 172, 173
Abiku -173
Abriba -6
Accommodationist -117, 122
Achebe's
  -ancestor worship 137, 138
  -fictional world -130
  -masked spirits 137, 138,145, 147
  -novels -1
  -philosophic pessimism -130
  -sons of -74, 181, 182
  -sources -26
  -tragic heroes -127, 128,129
Africa -86
African -58, 59
  -traditional religions -45
  -writers 51
African aesthetic -86
  -in literature -86, 87, 101, 103, 108, 109
African
  -art & folk & oral tradition -87
  -art -89
  -artist -109
  -artists -89
  -creative writing -241
  -fiction -217-20th century -217
  -folkway & oral tradition -90
  -literacy artistes -88
  -literacy critic -31
    --mission of -32
  -literacy scene -110
  -movement -52
  -orature -35
  -tradition 90
  -writers & critics -37, 38
African English Literature 1965 -32
African literature -1, 31, 35, 38, 85, 98, 107, 108, 111 131, 156, 157, 217, 227, 234, 236

-aesthetic of -151
-and criticism in 20th century -232
-and it's criticism -239, 240
-challenge of 157, 158
-challenges of 21st century -232
-contemporary -149, 158
-critic of -31
-criticism -23, 35
-criticism of -151, 237
-critics -42, 128, 149
-cultural nationalism in -91
-evaluations of -32
-expatriate criticism -37
-female writers -123
-feminism in -113
-feminist house in -115
-feminist trend in criticism of -41
-in 19th century -231
-language use -42, 107
-modern -231
-modern -232
-neo tarzanism in -237
-pioneer in -130
-problem of language -106
-progress of modern 110
-scientific criticism of -153
-state of -31
-trends in criticism of -149
African Literature Today -37, 151, 205
   -no. 15, 1987 -42
   -no. 3, -42
   -no. 11 1980- 41
   -no. 5, 1971 -35
   -no. 7, 1975 -36
African Literature: What Does it Take to be it's Critic? -35
African Universities Press -233
African Writers Series -151
Africart -89
Afro Cubanism 52, 53
Ainsi Parla L' Oncle -54, 100
Alpha Song -206, 207, 208, 217
America -50, 51
American constitution -113
American Was Promises -50

An Introduction to African Novel 1972 -150
Anatomy of Criticism -34
Ancestor worship -91, 93
Anthills of the Savannah -67, 217, 226
Arcadia -51
Aristotle's observation about tragedy -135
Arochukwu -5
Arrow of God -1, 2, 3, 4, 9, 11, 12, 15, 16, 18, 22, 23 24, 25, 26, 27, 29, 41, 63, 74, 94, 98, 102, 128, 129, 133, 137, 138, 144, 146, 147,
   -myth & ritual in -41
Art -40, 233, 234, 239
   -for arts sake -89
   -pragmatic theory of -61
   -what is -239
As Grasshoppers and Wanton Boys: The Role of the Gods -41
Association of Nigerian Authors (ANA) -233
Association of University Women - 197
Axiology -32
   -African -35
   -expatriate -35, 36
   -western -35
Azania 59
   -people of -59
Ballad of Rage -210, 217
Batouala 1921- 97
Been to English -106
Behind the Cloud -122, 123
Beijing Conference -198
Biafran war -66, 67
Black Orpheus -37
Blade Among the Boys -74, 182
Blanchitude -100
Brave New World -46, 50
Bridge to a Wedding -77, 182, 188, 189
Brothers Karamazou -33
Burmese Days -235
Cabalistic Societies -89

Cahier d' un Retour au Pays Natal - 53, 100
Calabar Studies in African Literature -37
Canon -72
Chaka -106, 107
Chanson de Roland -232
Chief Igwe Gbe Odum: the Omenuko Of history -28
Children of de Saussure -238, 239
Children of the Eagle -215
Christopher Okigbo: Creative Rhetoric -151, 241
Climbie -65
Colonialism -55
Come Thunder 1984 -67
Condolence -213, 215
Congo question -64
Congress of Soviet Writers 1937 - 234
Course in General Linguistics 1916 - 34
Critic -32
  -best -33
  -formalistic -33
  -of African literature -33, 43
    --challenges of -43
  -stylistic -43
Critical Perspectives on Chinua Achebe -127
Criticism -32
  -European -34
  -feminist -42
  -Marxist approach to -157
  -mission of 32
  -myth -158
  -of African art -37
  -of European literature -33
  -of literature of European & west -33
  -psycho analytic -33
  -structuralist -37
Critics -137, 150, 151
  -bourgeois -40
  -colonialist -36
  -expatriate -32, 149
  -female 123

Cry the Beloved Country -98, 231
Cubism -34
Cultural nationalism -63, 99
Cultural relevance -137
Cyprian Ekwensi -151, 241
Dark Child -92
De Vulgari Eloquentia -103
Decade of Woman Conference -198
Decameron -103
Deconstruction -43
Dedan Kimathi -217
Defense Illustration de Lang Francaise 1549 -103
Destination Biafra -42
Devil On the Cross -41
Divided We Stand 1980 -67
Dolls and Statutes -19
Double Yoke -229
Dreams Die at Twilight -208, 209, 217
Drefus Affair/Episode -64, 227
Duke Theodore of Gothland -109
Education -160
Efuru -42, 65, 75, 118, 171, 174, 182
El Cid -232
Elements of Semiology -238
Equal Rights Amendments -113
Erewhon -46
Eurafrica -100
European aesthetics -109, 110
European colonialism -99
Evans Brothers Limited -150, 241
Evbu My Love -122
Eve -123
Existentialism -34
Fables -91
Facing Mount Kenya -217
Fattening House -208, 209, 217
Feast of the new yam -20, 21
Femalism -195, 196
Feminine in African Literature 1994 -42
Feminism -114, 124, 197, 198, 202, 203
  -African -125, 195
  -European theorists -197
  -in African literacy scene -115

-radical -196
-true -204
Feminist(s) -115, 116, 123, 180, 197
  -critics & writers -116
  -dilemma of -114
  -house in African literature -115
  -types -115, 197
Femme fatale 170, 171, 175, 177, 178
Festival of pumpkin leaves -11, 12
Fiction
  -contemporary Nigerian -207
  -Nigerian -172, 177
First African Literature Association Conference -3
Flowers and Shadows -206
Folktales -91
Forty-eight Guns for the General 1976 -67, 78
Fragments -182
From the Earth to the Moon -49, 235
Future Shock -49, 50, 235
Gender Issues in Nigeria: A Feminine Perspective 1996 -42
God Dies by the Nile -198, 202, 203
God's Own Country -208, 212
Gods Bit of Wood -41, 65, 157, 217
Goethe and His Age 1947 -33
Golden age -45, 50, 51
Great German influenza -28
Greek
  -aesthetic -87
  -art 86, 87
  -artist -86, 87
  -mythology -169
  -tragedy -77
Groaning Passage -213, 215, 216
Gynandrist -118, 195
Hamlet -33
Harlem Renaissance -52, 53, 232
Healthy Nationalism -104
Heart of Darkness -234
Heinemann educational books -151, 233, 234, 241
Helen of Troy -123, 169
Heneid -231
Heroes -223, 226

History of English Literature 1864 - 95, 231
Home Coming -54
House of Symbols -213, 215
Ichu -6
Idu 65, 75, 76, 118, 172, 182
Igbo
  -culture -1
  -mythology -172
  -society -26, 138
Ijele mask -13
Ikenga -24, 23
Ikolo -12, 13
Iliad -232
In the Ditch 1972 -120, 125
Indigenism -52, 53, 232
  -in Haiti -53
Indirect rule -24
Interpreters -94, 107
Israelites -47
J' Accuse -64, 227
Jagua Nana -82
Jewish state -48
Judaic legacy -48
Julius Caesar -3, 45
King Solomom's Mine -235
Kingdom of God -48
Kolera Kolej -41, 65
Komfess artistes -40
Kraft Books -233
Kunapipi -37
L'Etranger -34
Lagos -206
Law and Authority in a Nigerian Tribe -23
Le Docker Noir -65
Legacy of Europe -49
Legend of Umunama -7
Legends and epics -91
Liberalist feminist -197
Literacy critic -1, 2
  -activities -64
  -godfathers -63
  -periods -61
  -voice -159
  -work -95
Literary criticism -32, 40

-approaches -40
-in Europe and west -34
-job of -32
Literature -170, 226, 227, 239
  -African -180, 240
  -African aesthetic in -95
  -African oral -159
  -aim of - 45
  -and politics -64
  -committed -111
  -cultural traditionalism in
  -difference between France and Britain's -95
  -fighting -62
  -function of -160
  -good 160 -bad -160, 161
  -great Britain -231
  -greatness of -166
  -national -62
  -Nigerian -170, 206
    --cultural nationalism in -74
    --earlier -206
  -Nigerian tradition in -64
  -of France -231
  -of Igbo -170
  -protest -231
  -serious -166
  -traditional African -91
  -use of language & the African aesthetic in -103 106
  -utopian -45, 47
  -written -239
Lives of the noble Grecians and the Romans -3
Local amalgamations -5
Long Drums and Cannons 1986 -32, 70
Looking Backward -46, 51, 81
Mahabharata -232
Malthouse Press-233
Marxism -42
Marxist 40
  -dictum -40
  -feminist -197
  -trend -33
Marxist/Socialist school -237
Masked Spirits -25, 137, 138, 145

-function -143, 144
Masquerades -143, 144
  -cult -140, 141, 143, 145
Matatu -37
Method of recording months -20
Modernism -34
More Than Once -142, 143
Morphology of the Folklore -35
Mother is Gold -154
Motherism -196
Mott/Stanton Submission -113
Movement for Muslim Women -198
Mwindo Epic -232
My Africa -224
My Life in the Bush of Ghost -70
Myth and ritual in African literature and art -4
Myth in Africa 1982 -41
Myth, Literature and the African World -153
Mythology -220
Myths -90, 91
Napoleon -49
Narrative Discourse -238
National Council for Women Societies -198
National Ethical Reorientation 1982 -166
National Organisation for Women (NOW) -113, 197
Nationalism -93
  -and the literature of colonial experience -93
  -and the negritude aesthetic in African Literature -99
Negrism -53
Negritude -100, 102
  -2nd important phase of -101
  -aesthetic -39, 99, 100
    --in African literature -39
    --importance -100
    -- as revolt -100
  -as celebration -101
  -cultural significance of -99
  -extremes of -102
  -ideology -100, 102

-movement -51, 52, 57, 58, 63, 109, 232, 233, 235
--poets -52
-of past -54
-of reconciliation & understanding -100
-of rejection of anti-assimilation -100
-Senghor's brand of -100
-sources -54
Negritudinists -102, 224
-archetypal novel -95
-art -219
-right -219
Negro primitivism -52, 53
Neuf Poets Camerounais -96
Never Again 1975 -67
New yam festival -3
News from Nowhere -46
Niebelungenlied -232
Nigerian broadcasting service -3
Nigerian Female Writers 1989 -42
Nigerian Fiction 216, 217
-contemporary -208, 212, 213
Nigerian Liquefied Natural Gas Prize for Literature -205
Nigerian literature
-cultural nationalism in -228
Nigerian Magazine -28
Night masks -4
Nnamdi Azikiwe -223
No Longer at Ease -94, 135, 161, 164, 189
No Second Chance -65
Novel -61, 71, 137
-archetypal African -74
-concerns of the -70- Nigerian -70, 71, 72
-genres of -81
-in west Africa -65
-new Nigerian -210
-Nigerian -159
--moral values in -159
-Nigerian -82
-Nigerian first real -72
-Nigerian tradition in the -69
-Nigerian war -67

-pioneers in development of English -73
-political -61, 62, 64, 65, 66
-situational -181
-situational -74
-tradition of -70
-war -78
-west African -62, 68
-west African protest -64
Novelist -1, 70
-first Nigerian -73
-Nigerian -81, 82, 83, 164
Novella 72
Novels by West Africans in English and French 1965 -32
O Pays, Mon Beau Peuple -64
Obi -76, 144
Odyssey -232
Oedipus complex phenomenon -33
Of Grammatology -238
Ogbanje -171, 172, 173
Ogene -13
Oil man of Obange -77
Okike -37
Okike No 6 & 7 1974, 1975 -154
Omenuko -29, 107
One is Enough -42, 65, 119, 198, 199
One Man One Machete -64, 182, 225
One Man One Wife -74, 102, 182
One Upon Four Robbers -226
Onitsha market pamplet literature -71, 72
Our Man The President -41, 65
Ozidi Saga -232
Pan Africanism -55
Paradise Lost -169
People of the City 1954 -72, 82
Petals of Blood -41, 157, 217
Petty antiquarians -31, 32
Phallic critics -116
Pidgin English -106
Pigments -100
Poetics -116, 135
Political events -61
Political novel in West Africa -63
Political novelist in West African- 63
Politics -62

-in west African novel -61
Polygamy -66
Position Review -40
Post Face to Ethiopiques -100
Prolegomenia -85
Prophecy -48
Prose fiction -97
Prospero and Caliban: the Psychology of Colonization -57
Proverbs -90
Publishing Houses -233
Purple Hibiscus -213, 214
Rastafarian Movement -52, 232
Reactionaries & Middle-of-the-Roaders -117
Reactionaries and Fence-sitters -123
Renascent Africa -224
Research in African Literatures -37, 151
Rethinking Myth -41
Revolution -226
Riddles -90
Robinson Crusoe -95
Roots -52
Rosencrantz and Guildenstern are Dead -34
Russian formalists -35
Sacrifice -65
Sanders of the River -235
Scarlet Song -198, 200, 203
Scholar -2
Scholars -1
Science fiction -50, 81
Season of Anomy -81, 163, 164, 225
Second Class Citizen 1974 -42, 65, 120
Seed yam festival -3
Seven African Writers 1962 -32, 150
Sexual politics -42, 197
Short Story -157, 158
Silences -171
So Long a Letter -42, 66, 200, 203
Song of a Goat -100
Songs of Steel 1979 -67
Sophocle's Oedipus -134
Soufflàs -91
Source study art -1

-aim -1
-genuine -2
-problems of -1
-scholar -2
Spectrum Books -233
Speech Act Theory -43
Standard English -106
Structural Anthropology -238
Structural Poetics -238
Structuralism -238
Stylistic Criticism and the African Novel 1982 -43
Suffragates -196
Sundiata Epic -232
Surrealism -34
Survive the Peace 1976 -67
Tel Quel Group -35
The African Child -63
The African woman 1993 -42
The Ambassadors -235
The Ambiguous Adventure -63
The Anatomy of "African" Criticism -155
The Anonymity of Sacrifice 1974 - 67, 78
The Archeology of the Self -238
The Archetypes and the Collective Unconscious -33
The Beautyful Ones Are Not Yet Born -64, 95, 109, 165, 182
The Beggars Strike -201
The Bible -48, 49
The black arcadia -52
The Blind Men and the Elephant -36
The Blithedale Romance -51
The Bride Price 1976 -42, 120
The Broken Calabash -121
The City of the Sun -46
The Coming Race -46
The Common Wealth Journal of Literature -151
The Concubine -74, 77, 170, 171, 175, 182
The Contract Heroes -41
The Destroyer of Guns -11
The Diaries of Mr. Michael -208, 211, 212

The Divine Comedy -103
The Double Yoke 1981 -120
The Edifice -41
The Emergence of African fiction - 74, 91, 152
The emergency -97, 94
The Epic in African 1979 -41
The Female Eunuch -42
The Feminine Mystique -42, 197
The Function of Criticism at the Present Time -32
The Great Ponds -74, 77
The Growth of the African Novel 1979 -150
The Gulag Archipelago -221
The Healers -63, 232
The Historical Novel 1955 -33
The History of Obosi -3
The History of Umuchu - 2, 3, 4, 5, 11, 18, 23, 28, 29
The Interpreter -78, 80, 81, 82, 163
The Jew -49
The Journal of Commonwealth Literature -37
The Joys of Motherhood 1979 -120
The Landscapes Within -206
The Language of the Self -238
The Last Duty 1976 -67, 78
The Last of the Strong Ones -214
The Late Bourgeois World -98
The Liberal Imagination -138
The Masks of God: Primitive Mythology -33
The Merchant of Venice -166
The Myth of Sisyphus -34
The National American Women Association -197
The Nature of "African" Literature - 155
The New Atlantis -49
The Nigerian Magazine 1964 -139
The Nigerian Society for Preservation of African Culture -142
The Nigerian tradition in the novel - 69
The Novels and Plays of Ngugi -151, 241

The Novels of Ayi Kwei Armah -151, 241
The Novels of Chinua Achebe 1969 - 150
The Odyssey -170
The Only Son -74, 76, 139, 142, 144, 182, 183, 184, 185, 186, 187 189
The Pacification of the Primitive Tribes of the Lower Niger -1
The Palmwine Drinkard -70, 90, 92
The People Wept -98
The Pleasure of the Text -238
The Poetry of Okot P' Bitek -151, 241
The Portrait of a Lady -235
The Price Between -74
The Principle of "African" Criticism -155
The Problem of Language in African Creative Writing -42
The Rambler -161
The Republic -45, 46
The Rise of the Igbo Novel 1978 - 153
The River Between -95, 182
The Road to Udima 1969 -67
The sacrifice of coverture -15
The Second Sex -42 197
The Sirens in the Night 1982 -67
The Slave Girl 1977 -120, 182
The Stillborn -122, 123, 214
The Tempest -95
The Theory of African Literature 1989 -39, 40, 41
The Time of Martyrdom -96
The Trial and Metamorphosis -34
The Trial of Christopher Okigbo -55
The vernacular style -107
The Virtuous Woman -122
The Voice 1964 -78, 79, 164, 165, 222
The Wasteland -34
The White Man's Burden -95
The Wound and the Bow -33
The Writings of Wole Soyinka -151, 214
The yams -20

Index

Theory of 'African" Literature -155
Theory of Intertextuality -238
Things Fall Apart -1, 4, 11, 24, 25, 54, 63, 74, 76, 82, 102, 92, 95, 97, 98, 128, 129, 130, 131, 132, 137, 138, 139, 140, 141, 143, 145, 147, 173, 181, 182, 183, 184, 185, 186, 187, 188, 189, 195, 231, 234
Toads of War 1979 -67
Toward a Sociology of African Literature -40, 41
Toward Defining the African Aesthetics 1982 -38
Toward the Decolonization of African Literature 1980 -36, 37, 38, 63, 152, 154, 155 157, 237
Toxophilos 1545 -103
Tradition – 69, 70
Traditional European art -88
Tragedy -127, 162
 -African 128
 -classical 128
 -European -128
 -in classical term -127
 -real -162
Tragic events -127
Tragic hero -129, 132, 133
Trail of Christopher Okigbo -82
Transition -37
Transition No. 4 1975 -154
Trends in criticism of African literature -31
Trends in criticism of Europe literature -43
Troika -88, 89
Twelve African Writers -150
Twenty Thousand Leagues Under Sea -235
Two Thousand Seasons -63, 233
Ulu -21
Umuchi -2, 3, 9, 11, 15, 20, 21, 28, 29
Un Chant Escalate -121
Un Piege Sans Fin -64
Under the Cherry Tree -208, 211, 212
Une S 'Longue Lettre -114, 121

Une Vie de Boy -64, 95, 98, 108
Utopia -46, 55, 62
 -and romantic movement -51
 -bearers of -47, 52
 -characteristics -47
 -concepts of -48
 -fruitfulness of -47
 -literature -48, 50, 51, 55, 58, 59
 --genre of -51
 -literature and the African worldview -45
 -of a golden age -51
 -of future 48
 -of past 48
 -origin of -47
 -power of -47
 -romance -51
 -writers of literature -50
Utopia -46, 81
Vernacular language -107
Ville Crueelle and The Poor Christ of Bomba -64
Vindication of the Right of Women 1792 -113, 197
Violence -41, 65
Voyage au Congo -64, 227
Voyage to Karia -46
Waiting for Godot -34
Wand of Noble Wood -74, 170, 171, 178
Warrant chiefs -24
Weep not Child -74, 94, 182, 231
West African novel -61
 -protest novel -64, 67
West
 - mind of the -50
Western writers -47
Winterbottom -24
Woman at Point Zero -198, 201, 203
Womanism -116, 196
Womanist/Accommodationist -116
Women are Different -119, 198, 199, 229
Women in Nigeria (WIN) -113, 198
Women liberations -197
Women's Right Convention -113
World Authors -222

Writer(s) -1, 33, 61, 62, 63, 131, 223
- African -36
--literature of -37
- Nigerian 219, 223, 225
-African -42, 63, 86, 94, 103, 104, 105, 106,108, 109, 110, 131, 205, 206, 219, 222, 233, 234, 235, 236, 237, 240, 241
-African earlier -224
-African female -125
-African feminist -198
-as patriot - 219
-contemporary female -213
-contemporary Nigerian fiction - 205
-creative 166
-culture -99
-English -103, 107
-Europe -235
-European -109,110
-female -42, 67, 123, 215, 217, 229
-feminist -203
-French -103, 107
-Igbo -141
-in Nigeria -223
-male -124
-marxist -65
-Nigerian -82, 123, 170, 228
-socialist -65
-west African female -65
-white 224, 228
Writing -220
Writing Difference -238
Xala -201
Zambia Shall be Free -217

Index - Authors

Abioseh Nicole -54
Abrahams Peter -42, 131, 151, 206, 234, 237
Achebe Chinua-1, 2, 3, 4, 6, 7, 8, 11, 12, 13, 15, 20, 21, 22, 24, 25, 26, 36, 42, 52, 54, 57, 63, 64, 67, 73, 74, 75, 92, 94, 95, 102, 105, 107, 108, 109, 118, 124, 129, 131, 133, 139, 142, 143, 144, 145, 147, 161, 162, 164, 170, 172, 181, 182, 183, 184, 185, 186, 187, 188, 189, 191, 193, 195, 206, 222, 224, 225, 226, 227, 228, 229, 231, 234, 237, 238
Acholonu Rose -116, 123, 124
Afigbo A. E. -28, 29
Aldous Huxley -46, 50
Aleksandr Solzhenitsyn -221
Alexander Shana -197
Alice Paul -197
Alkali, Zaynab- -116, 117, 122, 123, 124, 214, 229
Aluko T. M. -64, 74, 102, 182
Ama Ata Aido -42, 116, 123, 124
Amadi Elechi -41, 74, 77, 80, 118, 128, 170, 171, 175, 176, 177, 182, 228
Anekwe Ossie -67
Aniebo I.N.C. -67, 78
Anstophanes -88
Aqostinho Neto -96
Archribald Macleish -50
Aristotle -49, 61
Armattoe R.E.G. -96
Arnold -35
Ascham Roger -103
Auden W. H. -162
Austin J. -43
Ayi kwei Armah -42, 63, 64, 95, 165, 109, 165, 181, 182, 233, 234, 237
Bachelder -50
Barthes Roland -43, 238
Beckett -34
Bell Hooks -196
Bellamy -46, 81
Bessie Head -42, 123, 124
Betty Friedan -42, 115, 198
Bina Nengi-Ikigha 213, 215
Birago Diop -91
Boccaccio Decameron -72, 103
Bode Sowade -41, 65
Browning -160

Index

Brutus Dennis -206, 221, 234, 237
Buliver Lytton 46
Bunyan John -36, 73
Byron -88
Cabet -46
Camara Laye -42, 52, 55, 63, 92, 93, 109
Campanella Tomasso -46
Camus Albert -34, 233
Carey Joyce -72, 93
Carl Jung -33, 178
Cartey Wilfred -52
Catherine Acholonu -118, 123, 196
Cesaire Aime -53, 57, 100, 101
Chekh Hamidou Kane -131
Chidi Amuta -31, 40, 41
Chim Newton -208, 211, 212
Chimamanda Adichie 213
Chinweizu -36, 37, 88, 89, 154, 225
Chinweizu et al -237
Christine Obbo -197
Chuba K.C -213
Chukwukere B I. -42
Circe -123
Clark J. P. -36, 102, 170, 172, 173
Claude Levi-Strauss -34, 43, 238
Clement Agunwa -142, 143, 144
Collier -167
Conrad Joseph -1, 36, 73, 140, 235, 236
Dadie -65
Damsa -104
Daniel Defoe- 72, 95
Dante -36, 103
Darah G.G -40
David Diop -96
Derida Jacques -35, 238
Don Lee -226
Dostoyevsky -33, 230
Douglas Bush -2
Du Bois -230
Du Bellay -103
Duniway Abigail -196
Dylan Thomas -36
Ebong -239
Eddie Iroh -67, 78
Eddie Madunagu - 40

Edgar Allan Poe -71
Edgar Wallace -73, 235
Edmund Wilson -33
Ekwensi Cyprian-36, 63, 67, 71, 73, 75, 78, 82, 94, 118, 229, 234, 237
Ekwuru Andrew -67
El Saadawi -206
Elaine Showater -115
Eldred Jones -241
Eliot T. S. -34, 36, 160, 166
Elizabeth Boyer -197
Elizabeth Stanton -113, 196
Emecheta Buchi -42, 65, 206, 213, 229, 234, 115,116, 119, 120, 122, 125, 172, 237
Emenyonu Ernest -35, 36, 37, 39, 63, 118, 151, 152, 153, 154, 241, 237
Emile Durkhein -164
Emile Zola -64, 227
Emma Goldman -197
Emmanuel Ngara -42, 43
Euripides -88, 230
Eustace Palmer -71, 150
Ezeigbo Akachi Theodora -42, 202, 205, 213, 214, 215,
Femi Ojo Ade -118
Ferdinand de Saussures -34
Flaubert -230
Fola Arthur-Worrey -208, 211, 212
Forster E. M. -235
Foucault Micheal -43, 238
Francis Bacon -103
Frank Kafka -34
Frantz Fanon -61
Fraser Robert -151, 241
Freud Sigmund -33, 114, 179
Fulbright (Senator) -220
George Lamming -104
George Lukac -33
George Orwell -46, 50, 219
Gerald Genette -35
Gerald Jones -151, 152
German Greer -42, 197
Gide Andre -64, 227
Gobineau -224
Grabble -109

Gustaus Vassa -96, 231
Haggard Rider -235
Haley Alex -52
Hamidou Kane -63
Harriet Beecher Stowe -65
Harriet Mills -196
Hawthorne -51
Helen Chukwuma -42, 116, 123, 237
Helen Obiagele -116, 117, 122
Hemingway -230
Henry James -137, 235
Heron G. A -151, 241
Hippolyte Taine -231
Homer -170, 230
Hopkins -36
Horace -88, 160
Howell William Dean -50
Huxsley Elspheth -236
Ihechukwu Madubuike -154
Inns and Lindfors -127
Irele -241
Iyasere -152, 154
Iyayi Festus -65, 206, 222, 226, 227
Izevbaye -152, 154, 241
Jacobson Roman -34
Jacopo Sannazaro -51
Jacques Lacan -238
Jacques Roumain -54
James Joyce -34
James Frazer -33
Janheinz Jahn -101
Jean Price Mars -54, 100
Jemie -36
Jeyifo Biodun -40, 41, 157
John R. Searle -42
Jonah Ageda -208, 212
Jonathan Culler -238
Jonathan Swift -73
Jones William Ernest -33
Joseph Okpake -37
Josphe Campbell -33
Jourbert Joseph -62, 229
Judith Gleason -32 35, 150
Judith Hole -197
Jules Verne -49, 235
Julia Kriseva -35, 238
Julia Lathrop -197

Juliet Okonkwo -116, 123, 124
Jung -114
Juvenal -88
Karl Marx -65
Kate Millet -42, 197
Kate O' Hare -197
Kiekegaard -34
Killam G.D. -2, 27, 150, 151, 241
Kipling -95
Kole Omotoso -40, 41
Kwasi Wiredu -38
Laguma Alex -131, 206, 234, 237
Larson Charles -36, 74, 90, 95, 128,
    152, 154, 181
Lawton J. G -28
Leavis F. R. -33
Lenrie Peters -54
Leo Africanus -224
Leon Damas -100, 101
Leslie Steeves -196
Levy-Bruhl -224
Lewis Nkosi -92
Lincoln (President) -65
Lindfors -36, 39, 63, 151, 237, 241
Lionel Trilling -138
Lloyd W.H. -28
Longinos -105
Lotain J. G. -3, 10, 20
Lucretia Mott -133, 196
Mabel Segun -117, -123
Madubuike -36, 88
Malraux -234
Mamon -57
Maran Rene -97
Marcus Garvey -52
Margaret Laurence -32, 35, 70, 150
Mariama Ba -42, 66, 115, 116, 117,
    121, 122, 125, 195, 198, 200, 203,
    237
Marie Umeh -117
Mark Twain -50
Mary Ritter Beard -197
Mary Wollstonecraft Godwin -113,
    196
Mathew Arnold -32, 156, 218, 226,
    239
Maurice de Guerin -160

Index

Mazrui Ali -55, 56, 82, 241
Mbonu Ojike -224
Meek C.K. -23, 24, 25, 26
Meja Mwangi -234
Michelle Barrett -197
Milton -169
Mofolo Thomas -106, 107
Mongo Beti -64, 131
Moore Gerald -32, 36, 46, 81, 150, 150, 151
Morrise William -46
Mulcaster -103
Munonye John -42, 64, 67, 74, 76, 77, 78, 130, 142, 144, 182, 183, 184, 185, 186, 187, 188, 189, 190, 191, 193
Nadine Gordimer -98
Nathaniel Hawthorne -71
Nawal el Saadawi -195, 198, 201, 202 203
Ngugi wa Thiong'o -41, 74, 94, 95, 97, 109, 118, 157, 158, 181, 182, 221, 231, 234, 237
Nietzsche -228
Niven Alastair -151
Nkrumah -64
Nnolim Simon -2, 3, 4, 7, 8, 10, 11, 14, 15, 18, 20, 21, 22, 23, 27, 28, 152, 154, 237
Northrop Frye -34, 155, 169, 170
Nuruddin Farah -234, 238, 241
Nwana Peter -29, 107
Nwankwo Victor Uzona -67
Nwapa Flora -42, 65, 67, 75, 76, 115, 116, 118, 119, 120, 122, 123, 124, 170, 171, 172, 174, 175, 180, 182, 195, 198, 199, 200, 229, 230, 237
Nwodo O. -42
Nwoga -152
Nwosu Maik 207, 208, 217
Obi Wali -42
Obiechina Emmanuel -71, 99, 100, 102, 152, 223, 225
Ofeimun Odia - 226
Ogunba -151
Ogunbiyi Yemi -40

Ogundipe Omalara -115, 116, 123, 124, 157, 237
Ogunyemi Chikwenye -115, 116, 118, 121, 123, 229, 237
Okara Gabriel -36, 78, 79, 80, 164, 222
Okediran Wale -208, 209
Okekwe Promise -205, 213, 215, 216
Okigbo -1, 153, 171, 228, 237
Okot P' Bitek -42, 124
Okoye Ifeoma -116, 117, 122, 123, 124, 229
Okpewho Isidore -41, 67, 78, 89, 118, 241
Okri Ben -206, 227, 234, 238
Ola Virginia -123, 124
Olympe Bhely-Quenum -64
Omo Uwaifo -208, 209
Omotosho -206
Omovo -206
Onuora Nzekwo -74, 80, 170, 182
Onwordi Toni Kan -208, 210
Onwuchekwa Jamie -88
Onwueme Tess -116, 121, 122
Oriaku Nwosu -42
Orwell -81, 235
Osimi Ilyere -223
Osofisan Femi -40, 41, 65, 157, 205, 206, 226
Osundare Niyi -41, 227, 233, 234, 238
Otokunefor H -42
Oyono Ferdinand -64, 95, 98, 108, 131, 206
Paton Alan -98, 231
Peray -224
Petrarch -103
Philip Sydney -51
Philombe -96
Piaget Jean -238
Plato -45, 49
Plekhanou -33
Plutarch -3
Pollack T.C -155
Rabelais -88
Rebecca Njau -118, 123, 125
Regina Pedroso -53

Richards I. A. -155
Roscoe Adrian -39, 154
Rotimi Ola -227, 228
Samuel Butler -46
Samuel Johnson -161, 219
Schiller -219
Scott Fitzgerald -210
Sembene Ousmane -41, 64, 65, 118, 131, 157, 206
Senghor Leopold -54, 57, 100, 104, 109
Shakespeare, W. -3, 33, 95, 230
Shelly -88
Shuaibu Abdul Raheem -206
Shulamith Firestone -196
Simon de Beauvoir -42, 114, 115, 197
Socrates -49, 220, 221
Sophocles -230
Sowande, B. -206, 226
Soyinka, W.- 36, 42, 57, 78, 79, 80, 81, 94, 102, 107, 124, 151, 153, 154, 163, 164, 170, 172, 173, 180, 206, 222, 225, 226, 228, 234, 237
St. John -48
Stoppard Tom -34
Sunday Anoze -43, 151, 152, 241

Tchicaya U' Tamsi -96
Theocritus -51
Tibble Anne -32, 150
Tillich Paul -47, 58
Todofou Tzuetan -35
Toffler Alvin -49, 235
Tolstoy, L. -230
Toune -95
Tutuola Amos -36, 70, 71, 75, 90, 92, 228
Ulasi Adaora -117, 123
Valdimir Propp -35
Virgil -51, 88, 230
Voltaire -88
Wade Michael -151, 241
Wake Finnegan -34
Wellek and Warren -155
Wellek Rene -31
Wheatley Phyllis -95, 231
William Blake -36
Wright Richard 230
Yeats -35
Sartre, Jean Paul -34, 101, 114
Sofola, Zulu -118, 123, 229

www.ingramcontent.com/pod-product-compliance
Lightning Source LLC
Chambersburg PA
CBHW011744290426
44113CB00017BA/2644